ALEXANDER HAMILTON

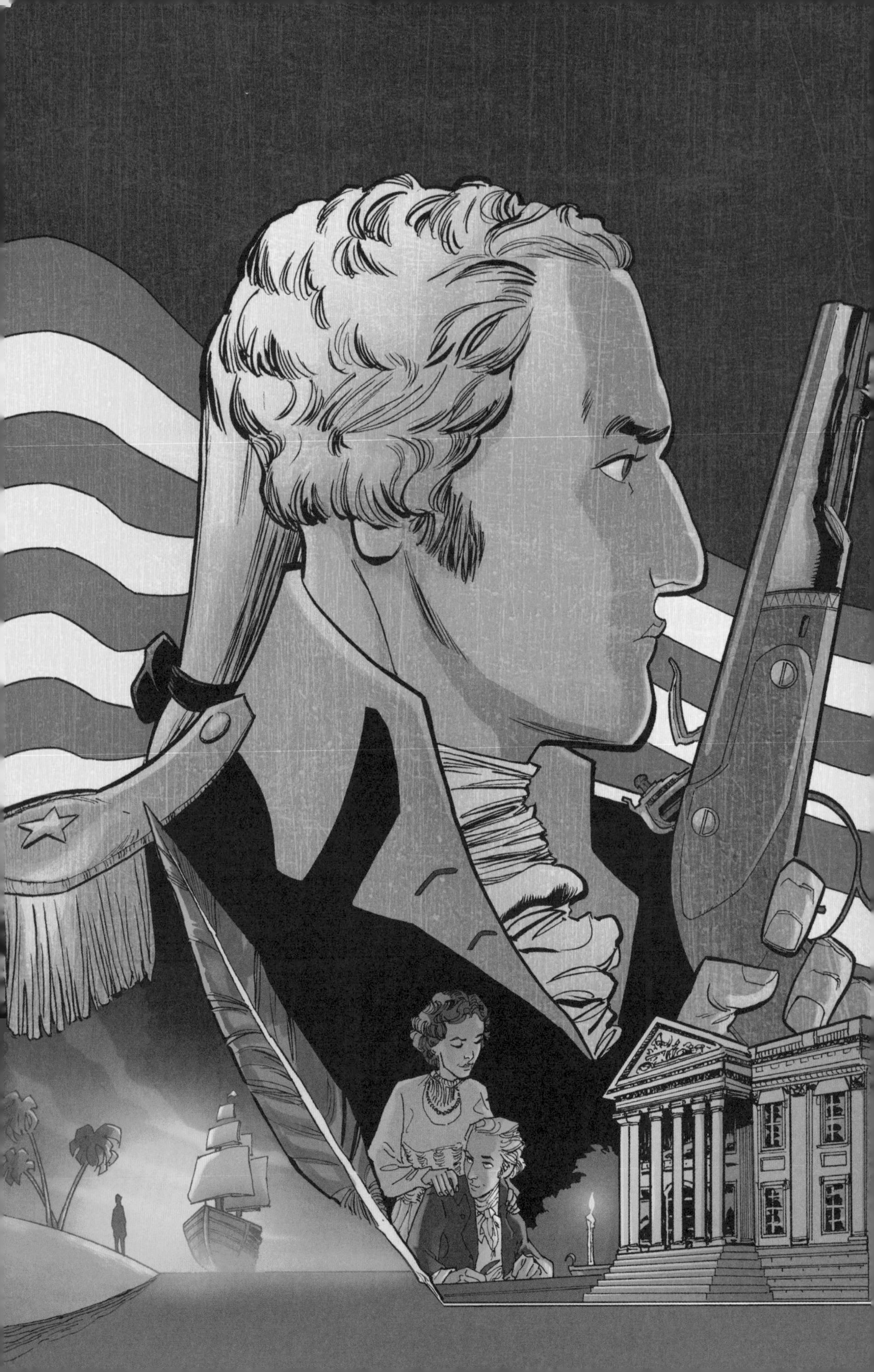

ALEXANDER
★HAMILTON★

THE GRAPHIC HISTORY OF AN AMERICAN FOUNDING FATHER

JONATHAN HENNESSEY
Art by **JUSTIN GREENWOOD**
Colors by **BRAD SIMPSON**
Inking/Background Assists by **MATT HARDING**
Lettering by **PATRICK BROSSEAU**

TEN SPEED PRESS
California | New York

"The desire of liberty...

"...was the cause of the fall of Adam.

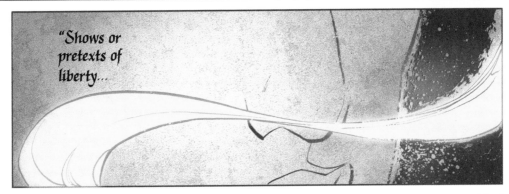

"Shows or pretexts of liberty...

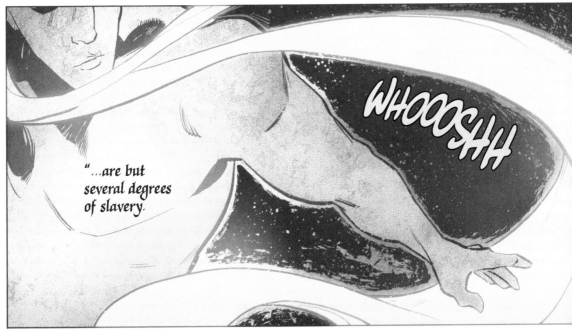

"...are but several degrees of slavery.

WHOOOSHH

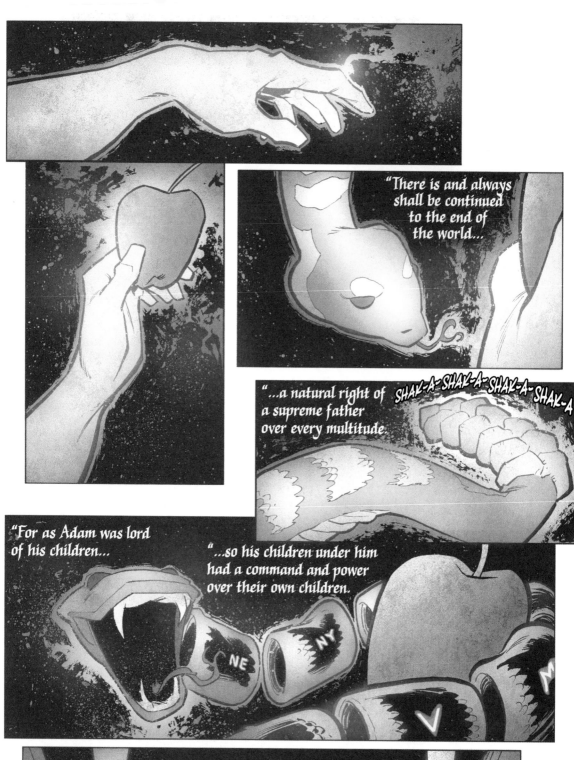

"There is and always shall be continued to the end of the world...

"...a natural right of a supreme father over every multitude.

SHAK-A-SHAK-A-SHAK-A-SHAK-A

"For as Adam was lord of his children...

"...so his children under him had a command and power over their own children.

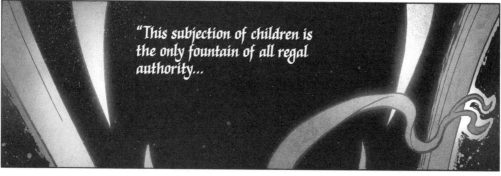

"This subjection of children is the only fountain of all regal authority...

"...by the ordination of God himself.

"For as kingly power is by the law of God...

"...so it hath no inferior law to limit it.

"When God gave the Israelites kings, he reestablished the ancient and prime right...

"...of lineal succession to paternal government.

"The greatest liberty in the world...

"...is for people to live under a monarch.

"And in no other form of government."

SIR ROBERT FILMER, PATRIARCHA, 1680.

SEPTEMBER 1775.

CAMBRIDGE, MASSACHUSETTS.

HURRY, MATTHIAS, WON'T YOU?!

YOU PROMISED ME A WAY OUT OF THIS INFERNAL CAMP! AND INTO ACTION!

MEANWHILE...

YOU ASK ME TO SERVE AS YOUR CHAPLAIN...

...FOR AN INVASION OF...CANADA?!

SUCH IS THE ONLY MEANS TO PREVENT THE KING'S TROOPS FROM INVADING OUR "REBEL PROVINCE" FROM THE NORTH.

AND CONSIDER: THE CANADIANS SUFFER THE SAME DESPOTISM WE DO FROM PARLIAMENT IN LONDON!

IF WE SMASH THE REDCOATS AT MONTREAL? SMASH THEM AT QUEBEC?

WE CAN DEPEND ON THE NORTHERNERS TO JOIN OUR STRUGGLE AGAINST GREAT BRITAIN!

BUT HOW TO MOVE SO MANY MEN? BY SEA? THE LOBSTERBACKS HOLD BOSTON HARBOR WITH THE GRASP OF A POPISH WIDOW TO HER BEADS!

AH! BUT NEWBURYPORT REMAINS WITH *US!*

FROM THERE WE FERRY TO THE MOUTH OF THE KENNEBEC. THEN ROW UPSTREAM IN BOATS, PORTAGING THEM WHERE WE MUST.

THUP!

≷GASP!≷ BUT THAT'S JUST A WILDERNESS OF SWAMPS AND THICKETS--FOR HUNDREDS OF MILES!

YET INDIANS, LIKE THE *ABENAKI*, HAVE PLIED THE ROUTE IN WARTIME. AND I TELL YOU, REVEREND...

...HIS EXCELLENCY, GENERAL WASHINGTON, HAS ENTRUSTED ME WITH MANY WHO FOUGHT AT BUNKER HILL!

BOYS WHOSE *HEARTS SO BURN WITH LOVE OF AMERICAN LIBERTY* THAT...

BEGGING YOUR INDULGENCES, COLONEL!

CAPTAIN?

BEHOLD. THE FRIEND I WAS MOST HEARTILY RECOMMENDING TO BE YOUR AIDE.

HMM. BIT OF A *WHELP*, I'D SAY...

SIR, THEY SAY THAT ALSO OF THE *FISHER CAT* NATIVE TO THIS LAND.

AS A COUSIN TO THE WEASEL, IT IS WANTING IN SIZE. YET ITS *FIGHTING SPIRIT* MAKES IT A TERROR TO LYNX AND WOLVERINE ALIKE.

I REQUIRE A MAN WHOSE *MIND* IS GOLDEN. NOT JUST HIS *TONGUE*.

I GRADUATED THE COLLEGE OF NEW JERSEY, SIR...

...AND WAS READING LAW BEFORE THE CALL OF PATRIOTISM NEGATED EVERY LESSER COMPACT TO WHICH MY LIFE AND EXERTIONS WOULD BE PARTY.

≡HEH HEH≡ MY BOYHOOD CHUM AND HIS *VILE MODESTY!*

COLONEL, BEFORE YOU STANDS A GRANDSON OF *JONATHAN EDWARDS*-- THE ESTEEMED MINISTER!

HE WHO BLESSED ME AND MY FOOT GUARDS WHEN WE DEPARTED NEW HAVEN!

WELL! AS YOU ARE TO BE MY AIDE, THEN, A PROPER INTRODUCTION IS OWING.

I AM *BENEDICT ARNOLD.*

AND MY NAME IS *AARON BURR.*

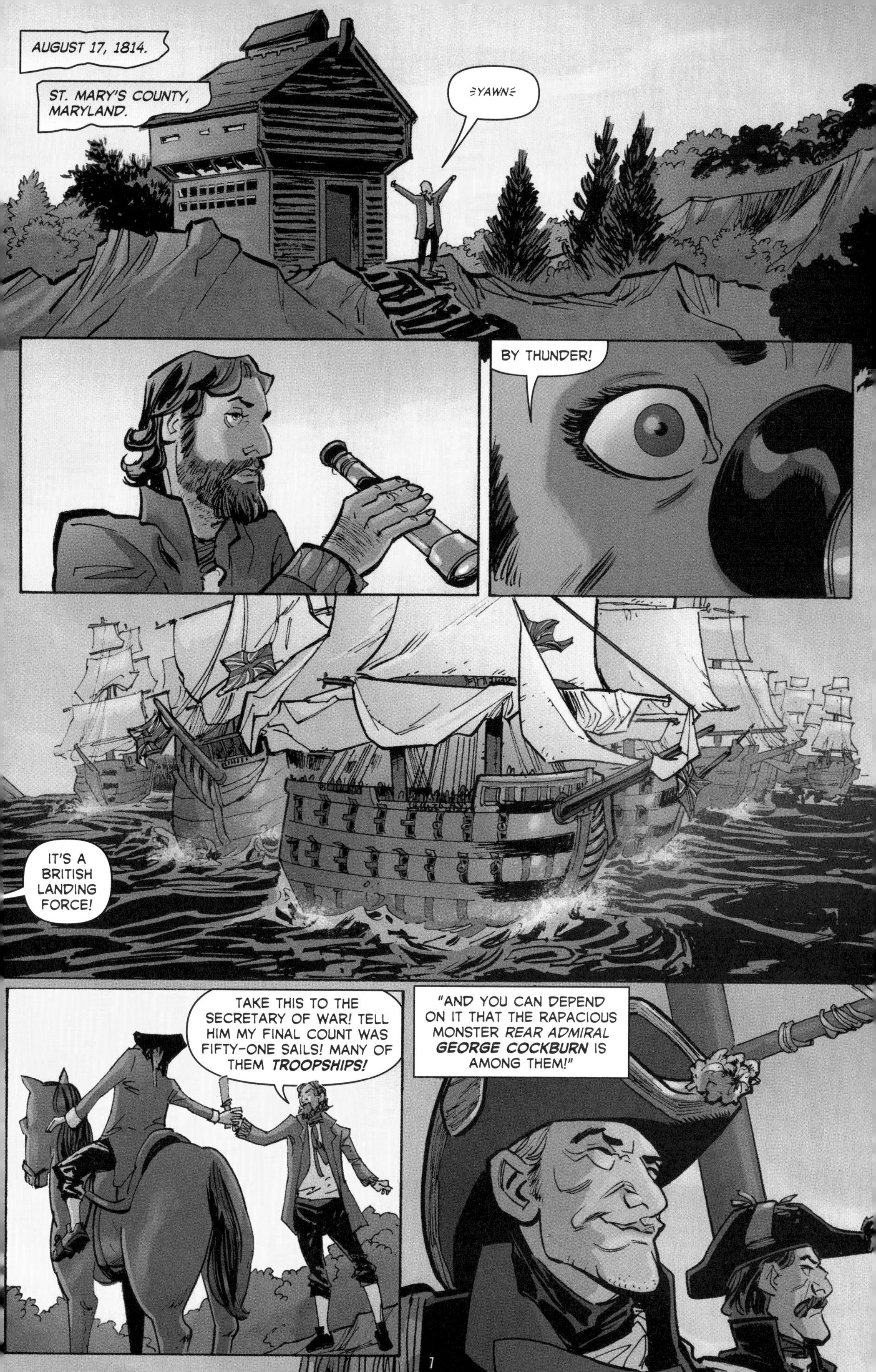
AUGUST 17, 1814.
ST. MARY'S COUNTY, MARYLAND.
YAWN
BY THUNDER!
IT'S A BRITISH LANDING FORCE!
TAKE THIS TO THE SECRETARY OF WAR! TELL HIM MY FINAL COUNT WAS FIFTY-ONE SAILS! MANY OF THEM *TROOPSHIPS!*
"AND YOU CAN DEPEND ON IT THAT THE RAPACIOUS MONSTER *REAR ADMIRAL* **GEORGE COCKBURN** IS AMONG THEM!"

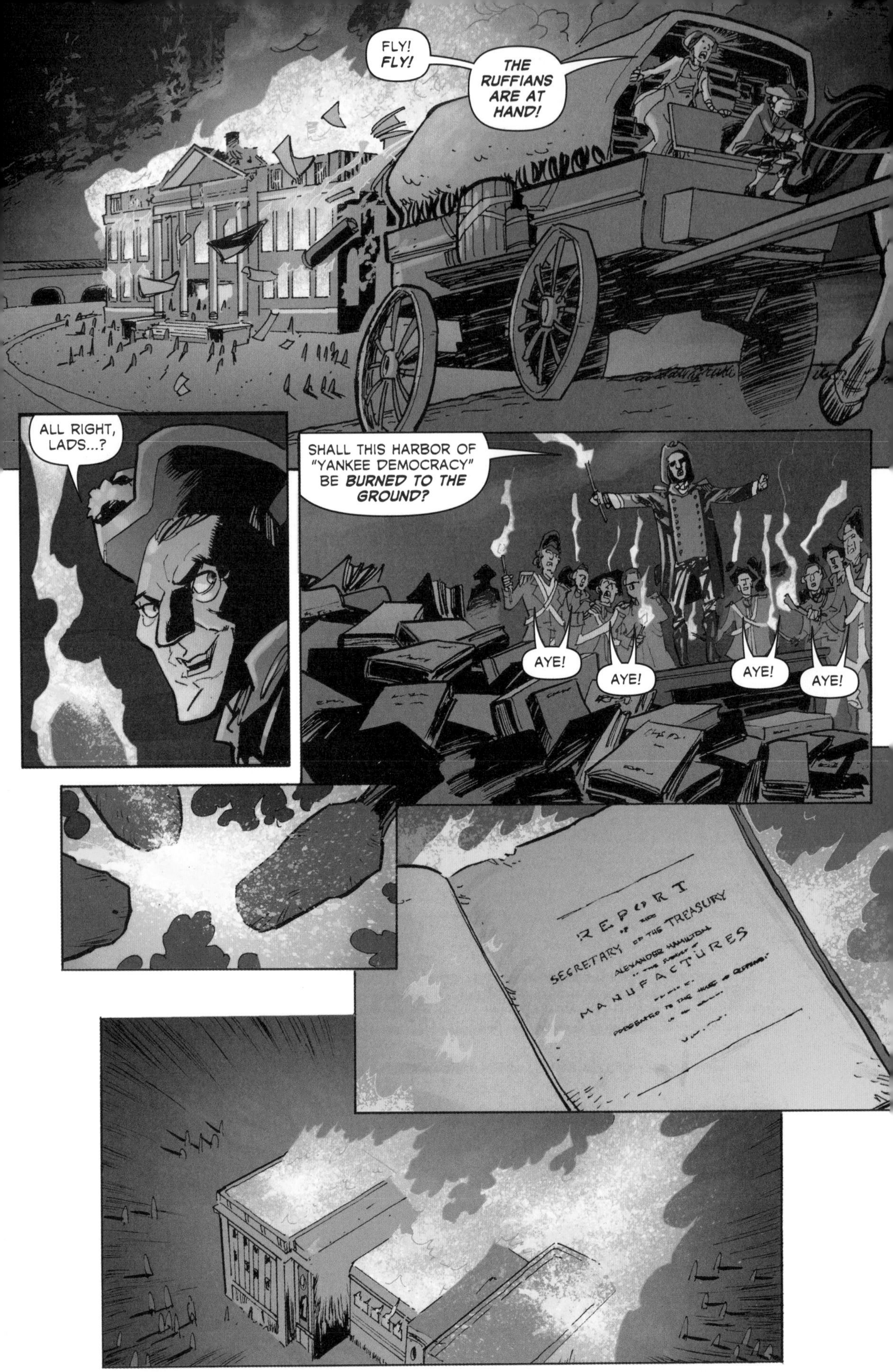
FLY! FLY!
THE RUFFIANS ARE AT HAND!
ALL RIGHT, LADS...?
SHALL THIS HARBOR OF "YANKEE DEMOCRACY" BE BURNED TO THE GROUND?
AYE!
AYE!
AYE!
AYE!
REPORT
SECRETARY OF THE TREASURY
ALEXANDER HAMILTON
MANUFACTURES

ALBEMARLE COUNTY, VIRGINIA.

NOVEMBER 1824.

LOOK! I SEE HIM!

THE HERO OF BRANDYWINE!

SAVIOR OF OUR COUNTRY!

WELCOME THE *CHEVALIER!*

MY DEAR MARQUIS DE LAFAYETTE!

MY DEAR PRESIDENT JEFFERSON!

JUCUNDI ACTI LABORES, OLD FRIEND. WHAT WE HAVE SEEN, DONE, AND BEEN THROUGH! NOW COME IN AND REST.

WAS THE LANDAU TO YOUR LIKING? I WILL HAVE YOU KNOW IT IS OF MY OWN PERSONAL DESIGN.

AND THESE HERE WERE PROCURED FROM...

AH!

JE N'EN CROIS PAS MES YEUX!

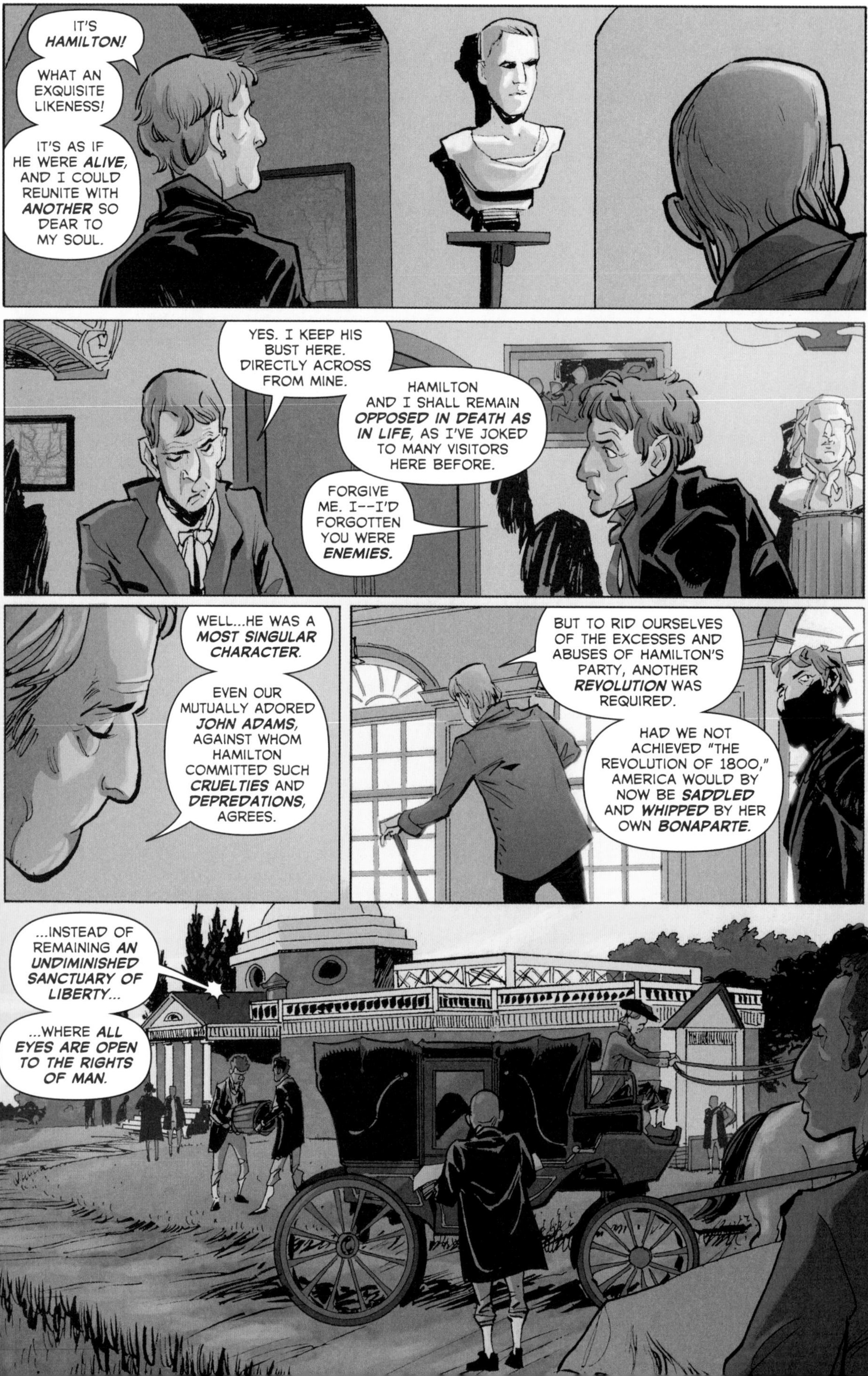
IT'S HAMILTON!
WHAT AN EXQUISITE LIKENESS!
IT'S AS IF HE WERE ALIVE, AND I COULD REUNITE WITH ANOTHER SO DEAR TO MY SOUL.
YES. I KEEP HIS BUST HERE. DIRECTLY ACROSS FROM MINE.
HAMILTON AND I SHALL REMAIN OPPOSED IN DEATH AS IN LIFE, AS I'VE JOKED TO MANY VISITORS HERE BEFORE.
FORGIVE ME. I--I'D FORGOTTEN YOU WERE ENEMIES.
WELL...HE WAS A MOST SINGULAR CHARACTER.
EVEN OUR MUTUALLY ADORED JOHN ADAMS, AGAINST WHOM HAMILTON COMMITTED SUCH CRUELTIES AND DEPREDATIONS, AGREES.
BUT TO RID OURSELVES OF THE EXCESSES AND ABUSES OF HAMILTON'S PARTY, ANOTHER REVOLUTION WAS REQUIRED.
HAD WE NOT ACHIEVED "THE REVOLUTION OF 1800," AMERICA WOULD BY NOW BE SADDLED AND WHIPPED BY HER OWN BONAPARTE.
...INSTEAD OF REMAINING AN UNDIMINISHED SANCTUARY OF LIBERTY...
...WHERE ALL EYES ARE OPEN TO THE RIGHTS OF MAN.

Let Candid Men Judge

ALEXANDER HAMILTON SET OUT IN LIFE WITH ALL THE BLESSINGS TRUE GENIUS CAN BESTOW.

YET HE WAS ALSO FORCED TO RECKON WITH SUCH AN AFFLICTION OF BURDENS AND HANDICAPS, IT WAS AT TIMES AS IF HE WERE SUFFERING A *CURSE.*

GRUELING POVERTY. MISERABLE MISFORTUNE. SHAMEFUL, STIGMATIZING SOCIAL STATUS.

NEAR TOTAL REMOVAL FROM ANY SEAT OF CULTURAL, EDUCATIONAL, OR POLITICAL INFLUENCE.

THESE WERE ALMOST-- **ALMOST**--SUFFICIENT TO CONDEMN THE NAME "ALEXANDER HAMILTON" TO THE MASS GRAVE WHERE THOSE BILLIONS FORGOTTEN BY HISTORY ARE BURIED.

BUT IN HAMILTON'S TEENAGE YEARS, A SINGLE, SMALL-YET-DEFINING POSSIBILITY FELL INTO HIS LAP.

THIS GRANTED HIM A PRICELESS ASSET HE NEVER BEFORE HAD KNOWN, AND THAT HE HAD NO RIGHT TO EXPECT...

...OPPORTUNITY.

TALENT, AS A MEASURE OF HUMAN POTENTIAL, HAD LONG BEEN AT BEST A SECONDARY CONSIDERATION. IN THE FEUDAL WORLD OF PEASANTS AND NOBLES, TALENT WOULD GENERALLY NOT GET YOU VERY FAR.

YET HAMILTON FOUND HIMSELF TRANSPLANTED TO A NEW LAND AT THE VERY MOMENT ITS PEOPLE FACED THE CHANCE TO **FLIP** THAT ORDER--TO MAKE **TALENT** ECLIPSE BLOOD IN A WAY IT SELDOM, IF EVER, HAD BEFORE.

ONCE THROWN UPON HIS TALENTS, HAMILTON **SOARED**.

HE SOARED FROM AGITATOR AND PAMPHLETEER TO MILITIA OFFICER.

WAR HERO.

LAWYER.

CONFEDERATION CONGRESSMAN.

DELEGATE TO THE U.S. CONSTITUTIONAL CONVENTION.

BANKER AND FINANCIER.

PUBLISHER.

SECRETARY OF THE UNITED STATES TREASURY.

FOUNDER OF THE U.S. COAST GUARD.

MAJOR GENERAL OF THE ARMY.

AS HE CAME OF AGE, HAMILTON IDEALIZED THE LAW-GIVERS AND NATION-BUILDERS FROM THOUSANDS OF YEARS PAST. FIGURES SO **IMMENSE IN THEIR ACHIEVEMENTS** THAT THEY HAD COME TO STRADDLE BOTH HISTORY **AND** MYTH.

HAMILTON WAS NOT MERELY AMBITIOUS. THE MERELY AMBITIOUS SEEK MAINLY TO RISE ABOVE THEIR CIRCUMSTANCES AND "MAKE SOMETHING OF THEMSELVES."

HE TRACKED AFTER AN EVEN MORE EXALTED DESTINY...

...TO BE IMMORTALIZED. TO BE A NEW **THESEUS**. A NEW **ROMULUS**.

AND HIS LIFE'S STORY BEGAN ON AN ISLAND.

The Terms on Which These Lands Were Really Dispensed

FOR GENERATIONS, ISLANDS HAVE CAPTIVATED THE GREAT MINDS OF BOTANY AND ZOOLOGY.

ISOLATED FROM THE VIGOROUS COMPETITION OF MAINLAND POPULATIONS, ISLAND SPECIES CAN EVOLVE AT A BREAKNECK CLIP--SEEMINGLY UNKNOWN TO THE REST OF NATURE.

BECAUSE OF THIS, FAR-FLUNG LAND MASSES OFTEN PRODUCE EXOTICS.

DRYOCOCELUS AUSTRALIS OR LORD HOWE ISLAND STICK INSECT

ISLANDS ARE THE SEEDBEDS OF DWARFS...

BROOKESIA MINIMA OR PYGMY LEAF CHAMELEON

...AND OF GIANTS.

VARANUS KOMODOENSIS OR KOMODO DRAGON

THE STAGE FOR ALEXANDER HAMILTON'S LIFE AND TIMES CAN BE SET THROUGH A THOUGHT EXPERIMENT INVOLVING ISLANDS...

...SEVERAL NOT USUALLY ASSOCIATED WITH HIM AT ALL.

ALEXANDER HAMILTON WAS BORN ON THE ISLAND OF NEVIS IN THE WEST INDIES.

IT MAY SEEM FAR-FETCHED FOR SO TINY AND REMOTE A PLACE TO BEAR CONNECTION TO THE GREAT MOVEMENTS OF HISTORY. BUT CLOSE INSPECTION PROVES OTHERWISE...

THE WEST INDIES OWE THEIR NAME TO COLUMBUS. THE SPICE-AND-SILK-SEEKING ITALIAN HAD BEEN SAILING FOR "THE INDIES"--THE VICINITY OF THE INDIAN SUBCONTINENT IN SOUTH ASIA.

THE ISLAND OF NEW GUINEA REMAINS ONE OF EARTH'S LEAST EXPLORED PLACES.

THIS SPOT CLEAR ON THE OPPOSITE SIDE OF THE GLOBE FROM NEVIS IS SIGNIFICANT BECAUSE...

...IT WAS HERE THAT THE SPECIES SACCHARUM OFFICINARUM WAS FIRST DOMESTICATED.

THIS RELATIVE OF BAMBOO IS KNOWN POPULARLY AS SUGARCANE.

FROM SOUTHEAST ASIA TO INDIA, THEN CHINA, THE MIDDLE EAST TO THE MEDITERRANEAN-- IT TOOK THOUSANDS OF YEARS FOR SUGAR TO REACH EUROPE.

THERE, IT WAS FIRST USED AS MEDICINE.

IN EUROPE, AS CENTURIES PASSED, SUGAR GRADUATED FROM RARE LUXURY TO MASS CONSUMER ITEM, ENDLESSLY IN DEMAND.

IT WAS SOUGHT AFTER IN ORDER TO SATISFY THE NEW EUROPEAN OBSESSION WITH COFFEE, TEA, AND CHOCOLATE.

BUT THE PLANT NEEDED A WARM, RAINY CLIMATE TO GROW RELIABLY.

AMBITIOUS EUROPEANS STEPPED UP THEIR CONQUEST OF TROPICAL TERRITORY, WITH EITHER THE SIMPLE PLANTING OF A FLAG OR THE USE OF FORCE.

ENGLAND GRABBED NEVIS IN 1626, WHILE SPAIN--WHICH CONTROLLED MOST OF THE CARIBBEAN-- WASN'T LOOKING.

NEVIS AND NEIGHBORING ISLANDS WERE VOLATILE PLACES-- PRONE TO DISEASES AND NATURAL DISASTERS LIKE HURRICANES, DROUGHTS, AND EARTHQUAKES.

BUT SOME WERE STILL WILLING TO RISK THEIR LIVES AND FORTUNES IN THE TROPICS BECAUSE SUGAR--"WHITE GOLD"-- COULD MAKE THEM INCREDIBLY RICH.

MUCH RICHER THAN TOBACCO, COD, WHALE OIL, ANIMAL PELTS, OR ANY EXPORT FROM THE EUROPEAN COLONIES THAT WERE ESTABLISHED FAR TO THE NORTH, IN WHAT WOULD BECOME THE UNITED STATES.

SUGAR MAY HAVE BEEN A PATH TO GREAT FORTUNE BUT IT WAS NOT AN EASY ONE. NOR A FOOLPROOF ONE.

PROPAGATING AND HARVESTING THE PLANT WAS EXCRUCIATINGLY LABOR INTENSIVE.

PRAY REMEMBER THE POOR DEBTORS HAVING NO ALLOWANCE

AND EUROPEANS COULDN'T PAY-- OR FORCE--OTHER EUROPEANS TO WORK HARD ENOUGH TO MAKE SUGAR PLANTATIONS PROFITABLE.

IN THE 1500s, THE PORTUGUESE HAD DISCOVERED SÃO TOMÉ, AN UNINHABITED ISLAND OFF CENTRAL AFRICA.

IT WAS IDEAL FOR SUGAR.

THE PORTUGESE METHOD TO MANAGE THE LABOR PROBLEM WAS TO ESTABLISH AFRICAN SLAVERY.

SLAVERY SPREAD WITH SUGAR WEST TO THE NEW WORLD.

MANY SLAVES BROUGHT TO NEVIS FROM MODERN NATIONS SUCH AS TOGO, BENIN, GHANA, AND NIGERIA, CAME THROUGH SÃO TOMÉ.

ALEXANDER HAMILTON, IN HIS FORMATIVE YEARS, WAS EYEWITNESS TO A PARTICULARLY GALLING VERSION OF SLAVERY.

CONDITIONS ON CARIBBEAN SUGAR PLANTATIONS WERE SO HARSH AND PESTILENT THAT MANY SLAVES LIVED ONLY A FEW YEARS AFTER ARRIVING.

THE INSTITUTION OF SLAVERY WOULD UNDERSCORE AND AFFECT EVERY FACET OF HAMILTON'S LIFE.

FOR SLAVERY WOULD HAVE AN ALMOST INESTIMABLE BEARING ON THE LAW, POLITICS, AND ECONOMY OF THE UNITED STATES.

ALSO INFLUENTIAL WOULD BE THE LEGACY OF ANOTHER ISLAND, OR **GROUP OF ISLANDS**: THE REPUBLIC OF VENICE.

EXISTING LONG BEFORE ITALY BECAME A UNIFIED NATION IN 1871, MANY TRACE THE ORIGINS OF MODERN CAPITALISM TO VENICE IN THE 1400s.

IT WAS ALSO THE ENTRY POINT FOR SUGAR FROM THE ARAB WORLD TO EUROPE.

HAMILTON WOULD BECOME A CHAMPION OF THE FINANCIAL MARKETS AND ECONOMIC INSTRUMENTS THAT VENETIANS PIONEERED.

THE INVENTION OF BANKS ON THE MODERN PRINCIPLE ORIGINATED IN VENICE.

DUTCH TRADERS PURCHASED MANHATTAN FROM NATIVE AMERICANS IN 1626-- IMMEDIATELY SENDING BACK A CARGO OF FURS THAT COMMANDED A FORTUNE OF 45,000 GUILDERS IN AMSTERDAM.

SOME 1,750 MILES FROM NEVIS LIES ANOTHER ISLAND APPROPRIATED BY EUROPEANS HUNGRY FOR TRADE IN NEW WORLD PRODUCTS.

INITIALLY A DUTCH SETTLEMENT, NEW YORK WAS TAKEN BY THE ENGLISH IN 1664 IN A BLOODLESS SHOW OF FORCE.

SUGARCANE CAME THERE IN GREAT QUANTITIES TO BE REFINED AND SOLD.

RHINELANDER'S SUGAR HOUSE WOULD BE USED AS A BRITISH PRISON FOR AMERICAN "TRAITORS" DURING THE REVOLUTIONARY WAR.

NEW YORK'S ECONOMY BENEFITED SIGNIFICANTLY FROM SUGAR AND-- BY EXTENSION--SLAVE LABOR.

BUT NOT AS MUCH AS THE SLAVE ECONOMIES OF THE WEST INDIES BENEFITED FROM MERCHANDISE SHIPPED OUT OF NEW YORK.

ENGLISH SETTLERS ON NEVIS, JAMAICA, BARBADOS, ANGUILLA, AND SO ON PLANTED SUGAR ALMOST TO THE EXCLUSION OF ALL ELSE.

LEFT IN NEED OF MEAT, FLOUR, CHEESE, SALT, SOAP, LUMBER, CANDLES, HORSES, AND HOGS, THE WEST INDIANS LOOKED TO THE NORTH AMERICANS FOR TRADE.

BUT DID THE RICH SUGAR BARONS IDENTIFY WITH, OR SPEND THEIR NEWFOUND FORTUNES IN VIRGINIA, NEW YORK, OR MASSACHUSETTS?

NO.

AS AN OBSERVER AT THE TIME PUT IT:

"NEITHER INTEREST NOR HONOUR HAS PREVAILED UPON [THE WEST INDIANS] TO THINK MORE REGARD WAS DUE TO THE AMERICANS...

...THAN IF THEY HAD BEEN THE NEGRO SLAVES THEY EMPLOY IN EVERLASTING DRUDGERY AND HOPELESS SERVITUDE, TO MAINTAIN THEM IN SPLENDOUR AND EXTRAVAGANCE."

WHAT MATTERED TO THEM WAS CASHING IN TO GAIN CLOUT, RESPECT, AND LEGITIMACY IN THE MOTHER COUNTRY...

...THE ISLAND NATION OF GREAT BRITAIN.

A "NEW MONEY" WEST INDIAN PLANTER CLASS PLUCKED UP HUGE ESTATES IN ENGLAND. AND ONE PERK OF EXTENSIVE LAND OWNERSHIP WAS...

EARNSHILL, A 1725 MANSION IN SOUTHWEST ENGLAND BUILT BY THE COMBE FAMILY, WHO OWNED A SLAVE PLANTATION ON NEVIS.

...THE ABILITY TO GET ELECTED TO BRITISH PARLIAMENT. A CONTEMPORARY COUNTED FORTY WEST INDIAN LEGISLATORS.

MEANWHILE, AMERICAN INTERESTS HELD NOT A SINGLE SEAT.

19

AND THERE WAS ONE THING THE WEST INDIANS COULD NOT TOLERATE...

AMERICANS BUYING LOWER-COST SUGAR FROM FOREIGN COMPETITORS.

SO SUGAR BOUGHT NOT JUST **ECONOMIC** POWER OVER POORER, UNFASHIONABLE COUSINS IN AMERICA, SUGAR BOUGHT **DIZZYING** POLITICAL SWAY AS WELL.

SO IN 1733, SPURRED BY WEST INDIAN INFLUENCE, PARLIAMENT PASSED A TAX MEASURE PUNISHING AMERICANS FOR BUYING SUGAR FROM THE FRENCH, SPANISH, DUTCH, OR DANISH.

WITH NO LEGISLATIVE SAY OF THEIR OWN, THIS WAS **TAXATION WITHOUT REPRESENTATION** FOR THE AMERICANS.

AND SO WERE SOUNDED THE FIRST EARLY RUMBLINGS...

...OF **WAR**.

There Are Strong Minds in Every Walk of Life That Will Rise Superior to the Disadvantages of Situation

ALEXANDER HAMILTON'S ENTRY ON THE WORLD STAGE WAS IN THE COURSE OF THAT WAR STARTED OVER TAXATION WITHOUT REPRESENTATION: **THE AMERICAN REVOLUTION.** HE RISKED HIS LIFE FIGHTING BRITAIN AND ITS ANCIENT SYSTEM OF HEREDITARY POWER.

BATTLE OF MONMOUTH COURTHOUSE, 1778.

DESPITE THIS, IN HIS LATER CAREER HE WAS **ENDLESSLY DENOUNCED** FOR SUPPOSEDLY CONSPIRING TO **RETURN THE FLEDGLING AMERICAN REPUBLIC TO MONARCHY.**

ABETTOR OF TORIES!

JAMES NICHOLSON, 1795.

[HAMILTON'S] FEELINGS ARE SO PERFECTLY BRITISH, AND MONARCHICAL, THAT IT SEEMS INCONCEIVABLE HOW HE EVER CAME TO FIGHT, AS HE DID, FOR THE AMERICAN REVOLUTION.

JAMES T. CALLENDER, 1797.

MY OBJECTION TO THE CONSTITUTION WAS THAT IT WANTED A BILL OF RIGHTS.

COLONEL HAMILTON'S WAS THAT IT WANTED A **KING** AND **HOUSE OF LORDS.**

THOMAS JEFFERSON, 1792.

HE NEVER FAILED, ON VERY OCCASION, TO ADVOCATE THE EXCELLENCE OF AND AVOW HIS ATTACHMENT TO MONARCHICAL GOVERNMENT.

GOUVERNEUR MORRIS, 1811.

FOR A REVOLUTIONARY, HAMILTON **DID** CLING TO AN ELITIST, EVEN TRADITIONAL VIEW OF SOCIETY. PURE, UNCHECKED DEMOCRACY HE HELD TO BE **MOB RULE.**

HE WAS A CREATURE OF A EUROPEAN CIVILIZATION **STEEPED** IN HIERARCHY. ITS FOLKWAYS HAD HELD THAT IF THE PEOPLE WERE TO RENOUNCE THE DIVINE ORDER OF MONARCHY, CHAOS AND DEATH-- **THE WRATH OF GOD**--WOULD FOLLOW.

AND THERE WAS MORE THAN SUPERSTITION TO FUEL SUCH WORRIES.

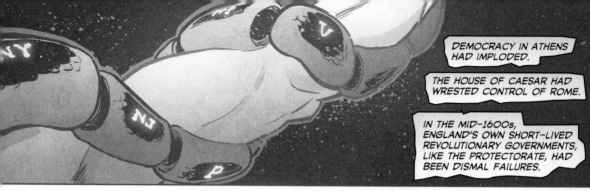

DEMOCRACY IN ATHENS HAD IMPLODED.

THE HOUSE OF CAESAR HAD WRESTED CONTROL OF ROME.

IN THE MID-1600s, ENGLAND'S OWN SHORT-LIVED REVOLUTIONARY GOVERNMENTS, LIKE THE PROTECTORATE, HAD BEEN DISMAL FAILURES.

HAMILTON COULD NOT TRUST POWER.

NOR COULD HE TRUST THE ABSENCE OF POWER.

THE EXPULSION OF A "SUPREME FATHER" OVER THE MULTITUDES WAS A HAUNTING ANXIETY FOR MOST EVERY THINKING PERSON IN THE REVOLUTIONARY GENERATION. THEY DREADED THAT THEIR HIGH-MINDED, EXPERIMENTAL REPUBLIC MIGHT END IN DICTATORSHIP.

FOR HAMILTON, THE FEARS OF ANARCHY AND DISORDER WERE INTENSE AND PERSONAL.

HIS NEED TO KEEP REVOLUTION FROM GOING TOO FAR WAS ALL-CONSUMING. IT WOUND UP COSTING HIM HIS LIFE.

THE TENDENCY TO SEE THE FOUNDING FATHERS AS INFALLIBLE STATESMEN AND SAGES WHO CAPABLY DELIVERED UP A NATION TO FLOURISH FOR HUNDREDS OF YEARS...

...OBSCURES THE FACT THAT, IN MANY VERY REAL WAYS, THEY WERE WHITE-KNUCKLING IT THROUGH COMPLETELY UNCHARTED WATERS.

THE GREAT MAJORITY WERE UNTESTED AS THE SOLDIERS, LEGISLATORS, AND DIPLOMATS REQUIRED TO WIN A WAR AND SET UP A COUNTRY.

THERE WAS NO SCRIPT TO FOLLOW ON HOW TO BE AN AMERICAN, OR AN EFFECTIVE AMERICAN LEADER.

I FEEL MYSELF UNEQUAL TO THE BURTHEN [SIC] ASSIGNED ME.

WE ARE IN SUCH A WRETCHED STATE OF PREPARATION.

AND THAT COULD INSPIRE PANICKY CRISES OF CONFIDENCE.

JOHN DICKINSON, 1776.

FOR MOST, HOWEVER, THERE WERE STILL SOME PRECEDENTS TO LOOK TO AT TIMES WHEN RESERVOIRS OF CONVICTION THREATENED TO DRY UP.

NEW ENGLANDERS AND QUAKERS COULD INVOKE THE EXAMPLES OF THEIR FRUGAL, PRACTICAL, *RELIGIOUS SEPARATIST* ANCESTORS--AND THEIR LIVES OF DILIGENT WORK.

Under this stone rest the ashes of WILLᵐ BRADFORD a zealous puritan & sincere christian Gov of Ply. Col. from April 1621 to 1657 the year he died aged 69 except 5 yrs which he declined

SOUTHERNERS OF DISTINCTION COULD HEW TO A LEGACY OF LAND-OWNING GENTILITY. HELD TO BE ABOVE PETTY LABOR, THEY WERE THEREFORE ENTITLED TO PURSUE HIGHER CALLINGS-- LIKE POLITICS.

HAMILTON COULD CLAIM NEITHER OF THESE PREPACKAGED AMERICAN IDENTITIES.

HIS WEST INDIAN BACKGROUND MADE HIM AN ANOMALY, A WILD CARD.

BECAUSE OF HIS OUTSIDER STATUS, DISPARAGING LABELS SOMETIMES STUCK EASILY TO HAMILTON.

CREOLIAN BOY!

BASTARD BRAT OF A SCOTCH PEDLAR!

JOHN ADAMS.

SOME MISUNDERSTANDINGS PERSIST TODAY. THE COMPLEXITY OF HIS FAMILY BACKGROUND, THE LACK OF DEFINITIVE RECORDS, AND HAMILTON'S OWN DETERMINATION TO **BURY HIS PAST** CONTRIBUTE TO THAT.

TAKE THE NOTION THAT HAMILTON'S MOTHER WAS A "CAMP-GIRL," OR PROSTITUTE.

NEVIS-BORN **RACHEL FAUCETTE** WOULD SPEND MUCH OF HER LIFE ON THE LARGER, MORE PROSPEROUS ISLAND OF ST. CROIX--THEN UNDER THE FLAG OF DENMARK AND NORWAY.

THE FAUCETTES HAD FRENCH ROOTS. BUT THEIR CONVERSION TO PROTESTANTISM LEFT THEM PERSECUTED BY FRANCE'S CATHOLIC KINGS. FUGITIVES, THE FAMILY MOVED TO THE CARIBBEAN.

RACHEL'S SISTER, ANN, HAD MARRIED INTO A PROMINENT ST. CROIX FAMILY. RACHEL HAD INHERITED A SMALL FORTUNE FROM HER FATHER, INCLUDING NINE SLAVES.

THIS QUALIFIED HER AS A YOUNG WOMAN OF RANK AND RESPECT--ESPECIALLY IN AN ISLAND SOCIETY COMPOSED CHIEFLY OF AFRICAN SLAVES AND LOW-CLASS WHITE INDENTURED SERVANTS.

RACHEL'S CONDITIONS WERE THE POLAR OPPOSITE OF THE POVERTY THAT DROVE AS MANY AS ONE IN FIVE YOUNG WOMEN IN EIGHTEENTH-CENTURY LONDON INTO THE SEX TRADE.

GIVEN HER SOCIAL CAPITAL AND THE PERIOD'S RIGID AND DEEP-SEATED IDEAS OF WOMANLY VIRTUE, IT'S ALMOST UNTHINKABLE RACHEL COULD HAVE BEEN A PROSTITUTE.

IN ALL LIKELIHOOD, IT WAS **JOHN MICHAEL LAVIEN** MOST RESPONSIBLE FOR BRANDING HER SO.

WHEN RACHEL WAS ABOUT SIXTEEN, HER MOTHER ARRANGED FOR HER TO WED LAVIEN: A SMALL-TIME CLOTHING MERCHANT, PROBABLY FROM GERMANY.

RACHEL AND JOHN PRODUCED ONE SON, PETER, IN 1746.

UNDER ENGLISH AND EUROPEAN LAW AT THE TIME, A HUSBAND WAS A WIFE'S "LORD" OR "BARON."

IN FACT, A WOMAN HAD **NO SEPARATE LEGAL EXISTENCE.** A MAN COULD NOT EVEN EFFECT A **CONTRACT** WITH HIS WIFE, SINCE THIS WOULD AMOUNT TO A LEGAL AGREEMENT WITH HIMSELF.

THEIR MARRIAGE LEGALLY CONVEYED ALL OF RACHEL'S PROPERTY TO LAVIEN.

LAVIEN WAS SPOILING TO BECOME A MONEYED PLANTER. BUT THE INEPT BUSINESSMAN SQUANDERED HIS WIFE'S CAPITAL.

RACHEL OBVIOUSLY **DETESTED** HER HUSBAND. SHE QUIT HIS HOUSEHOLD (AND HER SON)...

...AND TOOK TO HAVING RELATIONSHIPS WITH OTHER MEN.

LAVIEN ATTESTED THAT RACHEL WAS...

...WHORING WITH EVERYONE!

THEN AGAIN, DETERMINED AS HE WAS TO PERMANENTLY CONTROL HER WEALTH, IT **WAS IN HIS INTEREST** TO EXAGGERATE.

IF A WIFE COULD BE FOUND TO HAVE BEEN UNFAITHFUL MULTIPLE TIMES, UNDER DANISH LAW SHE COULD BE IMPRISONED.

LAVIEN HAD RACHEL LOCKED UP FOR SEVERAL MONTHS IN A DISMAL ST. CROIX DUNGEON USUALLY RESERVED FOR PUNISHING ERRANT SLAVES.

LAVIEN WANTED TO BREAK AND REFORM HIS WIFE. BUT SHE REFUSED TO BEND TO HIS WILL. SENTENCE SERVED, RACHEL CUT AND RAN BEYOND THE REACH OF ST. CROIX LAW.

PROBABLY ON ST. KITTS-- CLOSE NEIGHBOR TO NEVIS-- SHE TOOK UP WITH **JAMES HAMILTON**.

RECALL THE TRADITION THAT CLAIMED THAT THE RIGHT TO RULE DESCENDED FROM GOD TO THE BIBLICAL ADAM TO MODERN KINGS. THOSE SAME IDEAS HAD LED IN BRITAIN TO...

...THE LAW OF **PRIMOGENITURE**.

PRIMOGENITURE DESTINED A FATHER'S **ENTIRE ESTATE**--LAND AND WEALTH--TO HIS **FIRST LEGITIMATE SON**.

JAMES WAS SIRED BY A MINOR SCOTS NOBLEMAN. BUT HE HAD **THREE OLDER BROTHERS**. SO NO INHERITANCE WAS LIKELY COMING HIS WAY.

LOW-LEVEL INVOLVEMENT IN BUSINESS WOULD TYPICALLY HAVE BEEN HUMILIATING FOR SOMEONE OF JAMES'S CASTE. YET HE HAD COME TO THE CARIBBEAN TO WORK AS AN AGENT FOR ONE OF GLASGOW'S PREEMINENT TOBACCO MERCHANTS.

GEORGE WASHINGTON HAD AN OLDER HALF-BROTHER FROM HIS FATHER'S FIRST MARRIAGE. IF NOT FOR PRIMOGENITURE, HE MIGHT NEVER HAVE CHOSEN A MILITARY CAREER.

PRIMOGENITURE WAS, FURTHER, A LEADING REASON WHY MANY MEN CHOSE TO LEAVE THE OLD WORLD IN THE FIRST PLACE, AND TRY THEIR CHANCES IN TRANSATLANTIC COLONIES.

JAMES AND RACHEL'S ROMANTIC LINK PRODUCED TWO CHILDREN THAT SURVIVED INTO ADULTHOOD.

JAMES, JUNIOR

...AND ALEXANDER, SOMETIMES REFERRED TO AS "ELICKS."

CONTROVERSY EXISTS REGARDING HAMILTON'S BIRTH YEAR. LONG TAKEN TO BE 1757, NEW EVIDENCE HAS PERSUADED SOME SCHOLARS TO PREFER 1755.

RACHEL AND JAMES MOVED FROM ISLAND TO ISLAND-- JAMES IN SEARCH OF CHANCES TO RAISE UP FROM POVERTY, RACHEL TO BE FREE FROM THE DISGRACE OF BIGAMY.

THE TERMS OF THE DIVORCE LAVIEN EVENTUALLY WRANGLED CONTAINED A MISOGYNISTIC, PUNITIVE MEASURE FOR RACHEL: **SHE WAS NOT LEGALLY FREE TO REMARRY.**

IN THE EYES OF OFFICIALDOM, THIS MADE ALEXANDER AND JAMES ILLEGITIMATE.

IN ENGLAND, "BASTARDY" WAS EXPECTED OF THE POOR. THE RICH COULD PASS OFF SUCH OFFSPRING AS, SAY, DISTANT FAMILY COUSINS.

BUT TO ANYONE ELSE, THE LABEL WAS A STINGING BLACK MARK, AS IT SURELY WAS AMONG THE SMALL, STRATIFIED WHITES OF THE ISLANDS.

IN 1765, JAMES WAS INFORMED HE MUST GO TO ST. CROIX TO TAKE ON A LENGTHY LEGAL PROCESS TO COLLECT A DEBT OWED TO HIS EMPLOYER.

RACHEL AND THE BOYS, IT WAS DECIDED, WOULD FOLLOW.

THIS WOULD BE THE BEGINNING OF THE END FOR THE FAMILY.

ONE WONDERS IF RACHEL SAW IT COMING.

No Man Can Command the Winds

ONLY MONTHS LATER AND UNDER UNRECORDED CIRCUMSTANCES, RACHEL AND JAMES HAMILTON SPLIT UP.

THE NEXT YEAR, HE LEFT ST. CROIX, NEVER TO SEE ALEXANDER AGAIN.

RACHEL EVEN STOPPED USING THE LAST NAME HAMILTON.

WE CAN ONLY SPECULATE HOW ALEXANDER FELT ABOUT THE FAMILY RUPTURE.

MY FATHER... FROM A SERIES OF MISFORTUNES, WAS REDUCED TO GREAT DISTRESS.

MY HEART BLEEDS AT THE RECOLLECTION OF HIS MISFORTUNES AND EMBARRASSMENTS.

IN ADULT LETTERS, HE STRIKES AN ALMOST UNDERSTANDING TONE. IN 1795, HE EVEN REPORTED PRESSING HIS INDIGENT, AGED, AND INFIRM FATHER TO COME TO HIM--THOUGH HE NEVER DID.

JAMES MAY HAVE PERSUADED HIS YOUNGEST SON THAT IN DEPARTING, HE WAS SOMEHOW DOING THE **HONORABLE**--THE **MANLY**-- THING FOR THE FAMILY.

SUCH LESSONS IN HONOR AND MANHOOD FORMED AN **INDISPENSABLE** PART OF HAMILTON.

RESPECT FOR RACHEL--IN A TOWN WHERE EVERYONE KNEW HER SORDID PAST--MUST HAVE BEEN IN SHORT SUPPLY.

THE NOTIONS OF HONOR AND MANHOOD HE RECEIVED SEEM TO HAVE GIVEN HAMILTON A WAY TO *JUSTIFY* THAT HIS FATHER'S ACTIONS HAD BEEN WORTHY OF RESPECT.

DID THIS PUBLIC DISFAVOR RUB OFF ON HER SON? IN ALL HAMILTON'S WRITING, HE MAKES NO AFFECTIONATE MENTION OF HIS MOTHER.

RACHEL, TO GET BY, HIRED OUT THE SLAVES SHE OWNED. SHE ALSO KEPT A SMALL STORE.

THE STORE'S MODERATE SUCCESS MAY HAVE BEEN DUE TO HAMILTON.

SHARP AND BOOKISH, THE BOY HAD ALREADY PICKED UP SOMETHING OF A HEAD FOR BUSINESS. IN 1766, HE BEGAN CLERKING FOR A ST. CROIX MERCANTILE FIRM.

THEN THE FAMILY'S LUCK WITH AVOIDING DEADLY TROPICAL EPIDEMICS RAN OUT.

RACHEL TOOK GRAVELY ILL.

30

ALEXANDER CAME DOWN WITH THE SAME ILLNESS.

LIKELY IT WAS YELLOW FEVER OR MALARIA.

EIGHTEENTH-CENTURY MEDICINE *AT ITS BEST* COULD DO MORE HARM THAN GOOD.

RACHEL'S AFFLICTION WORSENED.

ON FEBRUARY 9, 1768, SHE DIED.

HAMILTON SLOWLY RECOVERED.

A VENGEFUL JOHN MICHAEL LAVIEN APPEARED IN COURT TO STOP WHAT THE RECORDS HAD CALLED RACHEL'S "OBSCENE" CHILDREN, BORN IN "WHOREDOM," FROM INHERITING HER POSSESSIONS.

EVERYTHING NOT CLAIMED BY BILL COLLECTORS WENT TO PETER LAVIEN--RACHEL'S FIRST SON, WHO BY THEN HAD IMMIGRATED TO SOUTH CAROLINA.

ALEXANDER AND JAMES JR. WERE LEFT ORPHANED AND DESTITUTE.

RACHEL'S SISTER HAD ALSO DIED. ANN'S AFFLUENT IN-LAWS, THE LYTTONS, WERE HAMILTON'S ONLY REMAINING FAMILY TIES.

THEY, HOWEVER, WERE MIRED IN BANKRUPTCIES AND LEGAL TROUBLES. THE BASTARD SONS OF A DECEASED, DERELICT WOMAN RELATED SOLELY BY MARRIAGE COULD ONLY BE A BURDEN.

DENMARK HAD PURCHASED WILD ST. CROIX JUST DECADES EARLIER. A REAL ESTATE BUBBLE FOR SUGAR PLANTATIONS WAS GOING ON, AND THE ISLAND HAD BEEN RUSHED INTO DEVELOPMENT.

A FLIMSY "GET RICH QUICK" MIND-SET PREVAILED. HAMILTON, DESPITE HIS CIRCUMSTANCES, LEARNED NOTHING BUT SCORN...

...FOR THE VULGAR, MONEYGRUBBING SPECULATION OF LOW-CLASS AND MIDDLING SORTS.

THE LYTTONS TOO HAD FALLEN VICTIM TO THE SHAKY AND UNSTABLE SUGAR-BASED ECONOMY.

HAMILTON'S COURT-APPOINTED CUSTODIAN-- COUSIN PETER LYTTON--COMMITTED SUICIDE A YEAR AND HALF AFTER RACHEL'S DEATH, LEAVING NOTHING IN HIS WILL TO ALEXANDER OR JAMES JR.

THE AUTHORITIES ASSIGNED JAMES JR. TO APPRENTICE WITH A CARPENTER IN THE "WATER GUT" SECTION OF THE ISLAND.

JAMES JR. WOULD NEVER LEAVE THE CARIBBEAN OR EMERGE FROM POVERTY.

HAMILTON COULD HARDLY HAVE NEEDED ANY FURTHER REASONS TO LOATHE THE CARIBBEAN-- AND HOW THINGS WORKED THERE.

IT SEEMS HAMILTON WAS NEXT TAKEN UNDER THE ROOF OF MERCHANT THOMAS STEVENS.

STEVENS'S SECOND SON, EDWARD, HAD BECOME HIS FRIEND.

THE FIXATION ON SUGAR MEANT THE ISLANDS INVESTED IN ALMOST NOTHING ELSE. CERTAINLY NOT COLLEGES.

PLANS TO BE A DOCTOR LEFT "NEDDY" WITH NO CHOICE BUT TO STUDY ABROAD. HE SAILED FOR NEW YORK IN 1769.

HAMILTON WAS ALSO INTERESTED IN MEDICINE. FOLLOWING IN HIS FRIEND'S FOOTSTEPS WOULD PROBABLY HAVE BEEN A FANTASY COME TRUE.

CONTAINING

I. M... INSTI... gieine
P... emietice,
II. A... ious Sy...
II... , Operations
...ied in SURGERY,
MATERIA MEDICA,
well ...mical 23 Galenical.
VI... TORY, c...aining ... reat Variety of the mof
...ous Prescrip...

BUT THE COSTS INVOLVED--TUITION, PASSAGE ON A SHIP--WERE INSURMOUNTABLE FOR A WRETCHED ORPHAN.

THAT FALL, HAMILTON WROTE TO THE MORE FORTUNATE EDWARD STEVENS. HE BARED HIS TURBULENT, TEENAGE SOUL...

...CONFESSING DISGUST WITH HIMSELF, HIS LIFE, AND THE GRIM FUTURE IN WHICH HE COULD ONLY GO TO WASTE.

TO CONFESS MY WEAKNESS, NED, MY AMBITION IS PREVALENT...

"...SO THAT I CONTEMN THE GROVELLING CONDITION OF A CLERK OR THE LIKE, TO WHICH MY FORTUNE, ETC., CONDEMNS ME."

I WOULD WILLINGLY RISK MY LIFE, THOUGH NOT MY CHARACTER, TO EXALT MY STATION.

MY FOLLY MAKES ME ASHAMED, AND I BEG YOU'LL CONCEAL IT.

I SHALL CONCLUDE SAYING...

...I WISH THERE WAS A WAR.

MEN DISSATISFIED WITH THEIR SOCIAL STATUS COULD SEIZE BATTLEFIELD GLORY DURING WAR--AND USE THIS AS LEVERAGE FOR FUTURE POWER, WEALTH, AND POSITION.

YET HAMILTON AT THE TIME MAY HAVE FELT CHEATED OF EVEN THIS CHANCE. AFTER ALL, THERE HAD MORE OR LESS JUST BEEN A MAJOR WAR ON BOTH SIDES OF THE ATLANTIC.

IN THE FRENCH AND INDIAN WAR (1754-1763), AMERICAN COLONISTS AND BRITISH REGULARS HAD FOUGHT SIDE BY SIDE TO FULLY EJECT FRANCE, BRITAIN'S DIRE ENEMY, FROM AMERICA.

WAR COULD NOT ONLY HELP MEN ADVANCE. IT COULD DO THE SAME FOR CITIES.

DURING THE CONFLICT, KING GEORGE II MADE NEW YORK THE "GENERAL MAGAZINE OF ARMS AND MILITARY STORES" FOR THE BRITISH FORCES.

THE FRENCH AND INDIAN WAR HAD HELPED MINT GEORGE WASHINGTON AS A COURAGEOUS AND RESPECTED LEADER.

THIS SO ENRICHED NEW YORK THAT IT PUT THE CITY ON COURSE TO ECLIPSE RIVALS BOSTON AND PHILADELPHIA.

NEW YORK IS GROWING IMMENSELY RICH, BY MONEY BROUGHT INTO IT FROM ALL QUARTERS FOR THE PAY AND SUBSISTANCE [SIC] OF THE TROOPS.

BENJAMIN FRANKLIN, 1756.

WITH ONE OF THE BEST NATURAL HARBORS IN THE WORLD, THE BRITISH WOULD LATER RECALL WHAT A PERFECT BASE FOR MILITARY OPERATIONS NEW YORK MADE...

...MUCH TO HAMILTON AND WASHINGTON'S CHAGRIN.

FURTHER SEEDING HAMILTON WITH VISIONS OF FAR-OFF NEW YORK WERE THE MERCHANTS FOR WHOM HE WORKED. ALL HAD STRONG FAMILY OR BUSINESS TIES THERE.

NICHOLAS CRUGER

DAVID BEEKMAN

CORNELIUS KORTRIGHT

HAMILTON'S CLERKSHIP WAS A CRASH COURSE IN CAPITALISM. HAVING DEALT WITH FOREIGN EXCHANGE, CUSTOMS LAW, FLUCTUATING MARKETS, SMUGGLERS, AND BUREAUCRATS, HE WOULD RECALL THE TIME AS...

...THE MOST USEFUL OF MY EDUCATION.

HAMILTON NEXT CAME UNDER THE WING OF A TRUE INTELLECTUAL AND SPIRITUAL MENTOR:

THE REVEREND HUGH KNOX.

AS A PRESBYTERIAN OF SCOTS-IRISH DESCENT, KNOX CAME FROM A TRADITION THAT HAD PROUDLY OPPOSED-- EVEN MILITARILY--THE BRITISH MONARCHY.

KNOX HAD BEEN EDUCATED IN NEW JERSEY (AND ORDAINED BY THE FATHER OF AARON BURR) BEFORE COMING TO THE CARIBBEAN TO PREACH.

POPULAR CHRISTIAN DOCTRINE THEN PROFESSED THAT GOD WOULD SEND MOST PEOPLE TO HELL--REGARDLESS OF THEIR ACTIONS IN LIFE.

YET KNOX SUBSCRIBED TO FREE WILL. HE PROCLAIMED THAT HUMANS HAD OPEN, UNWRITTEN DESTINIES.

NOT ONLY DID KNOX BELIEVE HAMILTON COULD BETTER HIMSELF, BUT ALSO THAT HE HAD AMBITIONS TO EDUCATE SLAVES.

WHEN TIME ALLOWED, KNOX TUTORED HAMILTON. THE YOUTH, WHO HAD NO PRIOR FORMAL SCHOOLING, TACKLED SUBJECTS FROM CHEMISTRY TO THEOLOGY.

THIS LIFE IS SUPPORTED AND NOURISHED NOT BY MEAT AND DRINK AND SLEEP, AS THE ANIMAL LIFE IS...

...BUT BY REFLECTION, CONSIDERATION, MEDITATION, SELF-DENIAL, AND SELF-GOVERNMENT.

REPUTED FOR EXCELLENT CRAFTING OF ARGUMENTS AND ELEGANT TURNS OF PHRASE, KNOX HELPED MAKE A **WRITER** OF HAMILTON.

SOME BOYISH ROMANTIC AND EROTIC POEMS HAVE BEEN ATTRIBUTED TO HAMILTON, BUT UNDER KNOX'S TUTELAGE HIS WRITING MATURED INTO A **PROVIDENTIAL MINI-MASTERPIECE OF SPIRITUAL AGITATION.**

THE HURRICANE LETTER.

ON AUGUST 31, 1772, A MASSIVE STORM HIT ST. CROIX. THIRTY PEOPLE ON THE ISLAND WOULD DIE BECAUSE OF IT.

BUT ONE WOULD BE BLOWN CLEAR INTO A NEW LIFE.

The roaring of the sea and wind...

...the prodigious glare of almost perpetual lightning...

...the crash of the falling houses, and the earpiercing shrieks of the distressed...

...were sufficient to strike astonishment into angels.

That which, in a calm unruffled temper, we call a natural cause, seemed then like the correction of the deity.

HAMILTON PENNED THESE LINES TO HIS FATHER, THEN LIVING ON THE ISLAND OF TOBAGO.

KNOX READ THE LETTER FIRST.

THE MINISTER WAS TAKEN BOTH WITH HAMILTON'S POETIC DESCRIPTION OF THE HURRICANE...

...AND WITH HIS TESTIMONIAL OF A HEARTFELT FEAR OF GOD.

HAMILTON PROBABLY HAD NOT PREVIOUSLY BEEN, AND CERTAINLY WOULD NOT ALWAYS REMAIN, SO PIOUS.

IT WOULD BE NO SURPRISE IF THE ARDENT RELIGIOUS FEELING EXPRESSED IN THE LETTER SIGNALED A PERSONALITY STILL NOT FULLY FORMED; THE "UNDER CONSTRUCTION" MIND OF A BRIGHT-YET-IMPRESSIONABLE TEENAGER LOOKING TO RESPECTED ELDERS FOR WAYS TO MAKE SENSE OF THE WORLD.

PERHAPS, FOR THE MOMENT, HAMILTON HAD LATCHED JUST AS FIRMLY ONTO KNOX'S IDEAS ABOUT FAITH AS HE HAD ONTO THE CONCEPTIONS OF WHAT IT IS TO BE A *GENTLEMAN*.

THE YOUTHFUL HAMILTON INDISPUTABLY ASPIRED TO AN HONORABLE, MASCULINE WAY OF *DOING THINGS RIGHT*. THE SAME LETTER ALSO PRAISES ST. CROIX'S GOVERNOR AS "THE MAN" FOR RESPONDING TO THE HURRICANE WITH LEADERSHIP THAT WAS UP TO HAMILTON'S HIGH STANDARDS.

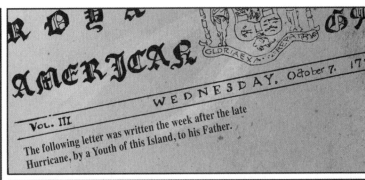

ROYAL AMERICAN G...
GLORIA EXAL... REGI ATRIA...
WEDNESDAY, October 7. 17...

VOL. III

The following letter was written the week after the late Hurricane, by a Youth of this Island, to his Father.

EVIDENTLY, IT TOOK A FEW WEEKS FOR KNOX TO PERSUADE HAMILTON TO LET HIM ANONYMOUSLY PUBLISH THE LETTER IN A ST. CROIX NEWSPAPER.

READ THIS! AND TELL ME IF IT DOES NOT MEET WITH YOUR SATISFACTION.

TZZ TZZZTZZZ

IF IT HAD NEVER BEFORE OCCURRED TO HAMILTON'S MENTORS AND BENEFACTORS THAT HIS TALENTS WERE **WASTED** IN A CLERKSHIP ON AN ISLAND WITHOUT EVEN THE EQUIVALENT OF A HIGH SCHOOL, THE HURRICANE LETTER PRESENTED AN OPEN-AND-SHUT CASE.

WITNESSING A YOUNG MAN STRIVING TO BE SO **GOOD**, AND REMAINING SO DEVOTED TO AN INDOLENT, VAGABOND FATHER, MUST ALSO HAVE MOVEDMANY HEARTS.

IN THE MONTHS THAT FOLLOWED, IT SEEMS ST. CROIX'S HEADMOST CITIZENS BANDED TOGETHER TO RAISE A FUND FOR HAMILTON'S BENEFIT.

THAT WHICH HAD ONCE BEEN HOPELESSLY OUT OF REACH WAS NOW PRESSED INTO HAMILTON'S GRASP.

HE WAS TO BE SENT TO AMERICA. HE WAS TO BE ADMITTED TO THE SMALL, PRIVILEGED CLASS OF THE WELL-EDUCATED.

THE CITIZENS OF THE ISLAND MAY HAVE PLANNED FOR HIM TO BECOME A DOCTOR AND RETURN TO PRACTICE MEDICINE AMONG THEM. THAT WAS THE PATH STEVENS'S LIFE TOOK.

IT'S HARD NOT TO THINK OF HIS DEPARTURE AS AN **ESCAPE**. WHETHER OR NOT HE AT ANY POINT CONSIDERED THE MOVE TEMPORARY, HAMILTON NEVER WENT BACK--**AND APPARENTLY NEVER EVEN ENTERTAINED THE IDEA OF GOING BACK**--TO THE CARIBBEAN.

BY THIS POINT IN ANY BIOGRAPHY OF THE MAN, IT CAN BE SAID THAT THE READER KNOWS MORE ABOUT THE INTIMATE DETAILS OF HAMILTON'S EARLY LIFE THAN EVEN MOST OF HIS CLOSEST FRIENDS, PERHAPS EVEN HIS FAMILY, WOULD HAVE.

MANY OF THE DOCUMENTS THAT HISTORIANS WOULD LATER USE TO PIECE TOGETHER THE PAST THAT HAMILTON HAD METICULOUSLY KEPT SECRET SAT IN DANISH ARCHIVES UNTIL WELL INTO THE TWENTIETH CENTURY.

A Friend to America

HAMILTON ARRIVED IN NEW YORK SOMETIME IN 1773.

REVOLUTION WAS IN THE VERY NEAR FUTURE. STILL, NEW YORK WAS **QUIET.** A GREAT MAJORITY REMAINED UNFLINCHINGLY LOYAL TO THEIR "MOST GRACIOUS SOVEREIGN," THE KING.

AND NOW A SPLENDID ENTERTAINMENT IN HONOR OF HIS MAJESTY'S BIRTHDAY!

CLAP CLAP CLAP CLAP

ROYAL GOVERNOR WILLIAM TRYON, JUNE 4, 1773.

THE FRENCH AND INDIAN WAR HAD BEEN A MASSIVE EXPENSE FOR GREAT BRITAIN. IT LEFT THE COUNTRY WITH A PAINFUL BUDGET CRISIS.

OUR MINISTERS HAVE LEFT NEAR TEN MILLIONS IN OUTSTANDING DEBT, WHICH, TILL FUNDED, WILL INFALLIBLY DEPRESS ALL THE OTHER STOCKS!

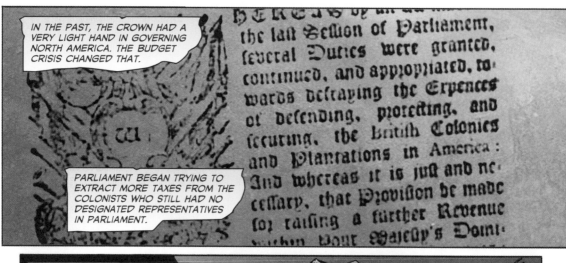

IN THE PAST, THE CROWN HAD A VERY LIGHT HAND IN GOVERNING NORTH AMERICA. THE BUDGET CRISIS CHANGED THAT.

PARLIAMENT BEGAN TRYING TO EXTRACT MORE TAXES FROM THE COLONISTS WHO STILL HAD NO DESIGNATED REPRESENTATIVES IN PARLIAMENT.

ENGLISHMEN, EVEN AS THEY LIVED UNDER A KING, HAD DEEP PRIDE IN THEIR RIGHTS AND LIBERTIES...

...GAINED THROUGH A LONG AND ANCIENT HISTORY OF RESTRAINING ROYAL POWER THROUGH CHARTERS LIKE THE **MAGNA CARTA** AND THE **PETITION OF RIGHT**.

WHEN THE SUPREME POWER IS LODGED IN A SOLE MONARCH, OR IN A SET OF NOBLES, IT OFTEN DEVIATES INTO TYRANNY.

LORD **CHARLES NOEL SOMERSET**, 1738.

AMERICANS DID NOT ACCEPT THAT CROSSING THE OCEAN HAD EXEMPTED THEM OF THEIR BIRTHRIGHT.

EVERY BRITISH SUBJECT BORN ON THE CONTINENT OF AMERICA IS ENTITLED TO ALL THE NATURAL, ESSENTIAL, INHERENT, AND INSEPARABLE RIGHTS OF OUR FELLOW SUBJECTS IN GREAT BRITAIN.

SO THE COLONISTS PUSHED BACK.

NEW YORK PATRIOTS BURN STAMP ACT PAPER, 1765.

TENSIONS AND SHARPNESS OF RHETORIC ROSE ON BOTH SIDES.

BOSTON LAWYER **JAMES OTIS**, 1764.

WE HAVE BEEN SPURNED, WITH CONTEMPT, FROM THE FOOT OF THE THRONE! IF WE WISH TO BE FREE...

...WE MUST FIGHT!

VIRGINIAN **PATRICK HENRY**, 1765.

BUT THIS WASN'T HAMILTON'S FIGHT. HE HAD COME TO BE A STUDENT, NOT A REBEL.

LAWRENCE KORTRIGHT, BROTHER OF HAMILTON'S OLD EMPLOYER, WAS IN CHARGE OF HAMILTON'S COLLEGE FUND.

A JUNIOR PARTNER IN THE FIRM SET UP THE NEW ARRIVAL AS A HOUSE GUEST OF HIS BROTHER...

...HERCULES MULLIGAN, A MEN'S CLOTHIER ABOUT FIFTEEN YEARS OLDER THAN HAMILTON.

HERCULES WAS SAID TO HAVE BEEN AMONG THE "LIBERTY BOYS" WHO FOR YEARS HAD TAUNTED BRITISH SOLDIERS WITH "LIBERTY POLES" REERECTED WHENEVER REDCOATS CUT THEM DOWN.

IN JANUARY 1770, THIS SNIPING AND BAITING ERUPTED INTO A STREET BRAWL. SOME CREDIT THIS AS THE FIRST BLOOD SPILLED IN THE REVOLUTION.

SOLDIERS, DRAW YOUR BAYONETS AND CUT YOUR WAY THROUGH THEM!

HAMILTON DIDN'T YET QUALIFY TO EVEN ATTEND COLLEGE. FLUENCY IN LATIN AND ANCIENT GREEK WAS A PREREQUISITE.

TO CATCH UP, IT WAS ARRANGED FOR HIM TO LIVE IN NEARBY ELIZABETHTOWN*, NEW JERSEY, AND ATTEND ITS PRESBYTERIAN ACADEMY.

*NOW ELIZABETH.

IT'S QUITE POSSIBLE THAT HERE HAMILTON FIRST LAID EYES ON A YOUNG MAN NAMED **AARON BURR.**

BURR HAD GRADUATED FROM THE SAME ACADEMY. HE HAD NUMEROUS LOCAL FRIENDS AND SOCIAL TIES.

DRIVER! I AM BESIEGED BY THE OBNOXIOUS URCHINS OF THIS VILLAGE!

RETURN ME AT ONCE TO PRINCETON!

HAMILTON MAY TOO HAVE CROSSED PATHS WITH A YOUNG GIRL FROM A GRAND ESTATE FAR UP WHAT WAS THEN CALLED THE NORTH RIVER.

REVEREND KNOX HAD ASKED VILLAGE ELDER **WILLIAM LIVINGSTON** TO KEEP TABS ON HAMILTON.

ELIZABETH SCHUYLER WAS HIS NIECE.

FOR HAMILTON, CRAMMING FOR HIS FUTURE, SURROUNDED BY BOOKS, IDEAS, AND FRIENDS, MUST HAVE BEEN AN INTOXICATING DEPARTURE FROM HIS OLD LIFE.

THIRD PERSON PLURAL, "TO TAKE COUNSEL."

HAMILTON'S WORK ETHIC WAS SO **INDEFATIGABLE** THAT HE WAS DEEMED READY FOR COLLEGE IN **LESS THAN A YEAR.**

...TENSIONS BETWEEN AMERICA AND GREAT BRITAIN...

YET BY THEN...

...HAD ONCE AGAIN BEEN BROUGHT TO BOIL.

EVEN HAMILTON'S CHOICE OF SCHOOLS WAS **POLITICIZED**.

THE COLLEGE OF NEW JERSEY* WAS A BEDROCK OF PRESBYTERIANISM AND, BY EXTENSION, RESISTANCE TO ROYAL PREROGATIVE.

*FOUNDED BY AARON BURR SR., AND LATER KNOWN AS PRINCETON UNIVERSITY.

IT WAS ALSO THE ALMA MATER OF HUGH KNOX-- WHO HAD MOLDED HAMILTON INTO SUCH A ZEALOUS PRESBYTERIAN.

WERE HAMILTON TO DECLINE TO STUDY THERE, MANY WOULD BE DISAPPOINTED.

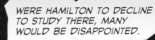

MEANWHILE, THE APPROPRIATELY NAMED KING'S COLLEGE*--BACK IN NEW YORK-- WAS ANGLICAN...

...AND THUS AN INSTRUMENT OF MONARCHICAL RULE.

*LATER KNOWN AS COLUMBIA UNIVERSITY.

SEPARATION OF CHURCH AND STATE WAS A WIDELY UNWELCOME CONCEPT IN THE EUROPEAN WORLD AT THE TIME.

IN GREAT BRITAIN, THE CHURCH OF ENGLAND (OR ANGLICAN DENOMINATION) WAS THE OFFICIAL OR "ESTABLISHED" RELIGION. EVEN NONBELIEVERS, BY LAW, HAD TO PAY TAXES TO FUND IT.

THE KING WAS THE CHURCH'S SUPREME GOVERNOR. LOYALTY AND OBEDIENCE TO GOD AND GOVERNMENT WERE MEANT TO BE ONE AND THE SAME.

ANGLICANISM'S SPREAD PUT MANY AMERICANS ON HIGH ALERT. THE RELIGIOUS OPPRESSION THAT HAD AILED THEIR ANCESTORS MIGHT BE UNLEASHED IN THE VERY LANDS TO WHICH THOSE OLD WORLD BRETHREN HAD FLED.

[ANGLICAN OPERATIVES] HAVE LONG HAD A FORMAL DESIGN TO DISSOLVE AND ROOT OUT ALL OUR NEW-ENGLAND CHURCHES.

THE PEOPLE OF NEW-ENGLAND [MUST] STAND FAST IN THE LIBERTY WHEREWITH CHRIST HATH MADE THEM FREE; AND NOT RETURN UNDER THAT YOKE OF EPISCOPAL BONDAGE, WHICH SO MISERABLY GALLED THE NECKS OF OUR FOREFATHERS!

BOSTON MINISTER JONATHAN MAYHEW, 1763

NEVERTHELESS, HAMILTON PICKED KING'S.

IN A RUSH TO GRADUATE, HE INSISTED ON AN INDEPENDENT, ACCELERATED COURSE. KING'S PRESIDENT INDULGED THE WISH. THE COLLEGE OF NEW JERSEY HAD NOT.

AS A BONUS, KING'S PUT HIM CLOSE TO THE EXCITEMENT OF THE CITY. AND HIS OLD FRIEND EDWARD STEVENS WAS AMONG THE TWENTY-FOUR OTHER STUDENTS IN THE SINGLE-BUILDING "CAMPUS."

HAMILTON'S DECISION SUGGESTS THAT AMERICA'S GRIEVANCES WITH THE MOTHER COUNTRY HAD NOT YET SWAYED HIM.

HE WAS TOO CONSERVATIVE IN NATURE TO THROW IN WITH POLITICAL RADICALS LIKE THE SONS OF LIBERTY.

RASCALS!

TOP LOCAL RABBLE-ROUSER **ISAAC SEARS** WAS A ROUGH, COMMANDING, CAPE COD-BORN SEA CAPTAIN AND FRENCH AND INDIAN WAR PRIVATEER.

HE WAS A LONG-STANDING THORN IN THE SIDE OF THE BRITISH.

PARLIAMENT, SINCE 1767, HAD BEEN STRUGGLING TO ENFORCE **A TAX ON TEA** IN THE COLONIES.

OFTEN ACCOMPANIED BY WEST INDIAN SUGAR, TEA WAS A CRUCIAL, NEARLY **SACRED** PART OF EVERYDAY SOCIAL CEREMONIES.

SYMPATHIZERS ON THE SIDE OF AMERICAN LIBERTY HAD FOR YEARS BEEN PROTESTING THE TAX BY **BOYCOTTING** BRITISH TEA.

THE HEAD OF KING'S COLLEGE, REVEREND DOCTOR **MILES COOPER**, WAS A "TORY": A LOYALIST TO THE CROWN. SERVING DUTY-PAID ENGLISH TEA WOULD FOR HIM HAVE BEEN A **BADGE OF PRIDE.**

THE BRITISH TEA BOYCOTT WAS A **WINDFALL** FOR MEN LIKE ISAAC SEARS--WHO WERE **MAKING A KILLING** PROCURING CHEAP, UNTAXED TEA FROM THE DUTCH.

IN AUTUMN 1773, AS HAMILTON SHRUGGED OFF ANY POLITICAL SENSITIVITIES OVER HIS CHOICE OF COLLEGE, DISQUIETING NEWS REACHED AMERICA...

...OF THE TEA ACT.

PARLIAMENT HAD GRANTED A BRITISH CORPORATION--THE EAST INDIA COMPANY--A MONOPOLY ON SELLING TEA. TAX BREAKS WOULD ENSURE THEIR PRICES **WOULD UNDERCUT EVEN THE DUTCH CONTRABAND.**

THE RANKS OF ANTI-BRITISH AGITATORS SWELLED WITH FOILED SMUGGLERS-- AND THE RUFFIANS WHO LOOKED UP TO THEM.

BUT MEN OF REPUTATION-- LIKE DOCTORS AND LAWYERS-- ALSO SAW A **POISON PILL** CUNNINGLY SNUCK INTO THE BREW.

YOU HAVE HEARD OF THE MACHINATIONS OF THE ENEMIES OF OUR COUNTRY, TO **ENSLAVE US** BY MEANS OF THE EAST INDIA COMPANY.

SHOULD [THE TEA] BE LANDED...THEN FAREWELL AMERICAN LIBERTY! WE ARE UNDONE FOREVER!

PHILADELPHIA DOCTOR, WRITER, AND EDUCATOR BENJAMIN RUSH, 1763.

THE POISON PILL WAS MORE **TAXATION WITHOUT REPRESENTATION**. NOT THE **SIZE** OF THE TAX, BUT INSTEAD THE INJUSTICE OF BEING TAXED AT ALL WITHOUT A VOICE IN PARLIAMENT. THIS WAS AN OUTRAGE TO THE CHERISHED RIGHTS OF ENGLISHMEN.

BY VAGARIES OF WIND AND WEATHER, THE "ACCURSED" TEA REACHED BOSTON FIRST.

LEADERS OF THE RESISTANCE MOVEMENT TRIED TO SEND THE SHIPS BACK. ROYAL CUSTOMS OFFICIALS ORDERED THEM TO STAY.

FINALLY, ON DECEMBER 16, 1773, PROTESTERS MADE THEMSELVES ANONYMOUS BY DONNING MOHAWK INDIAN COSTUMES. NO PARTICIPANT, IF ARRESTED, COULD IDENTIFY OR TESTIFY AGAINST ANOTHER.

AN ENORMOUS CROWD WATCHED THEM BOARD THE SHIPS AND DUMP **92,000 POUNDS OF TEA** INTO THE WATERS OFF GRIFFIN'S WHARF. BOSTON HARBOR STANK FOR DAYS.

TO DEMONSTRATE THAT THESE WERE **POLITICAL ACTIONS**, NOT THE **MARAUDING OF AN OUTLAW MOB**, THE SHIPS WERE NOT DAMAGED. LOCKSMITHS HAD EVEN BEEN BROUGHT ALONG TO REPAIR DAMAGED TEA CHESTS.

THE GREAT CARE TAKEN BY THE "MOHAWKS" DID NOT, HOWEVER, PROVE SO COMPELLING ACROSS THE ATLANTIC.

PARLIAMENT RESPONDED WITH SHOCKING FORCE.

IT **CLOSED** BOSTON HARBOR--SEVERING THE CITY'S ECONOMIC LIFELINE. LOCAL LEADERS WERE STRIPPED OF POWER. TO BRING NEW ENGLANDERS TO HEEL, MORE BRITISH TROOPS WERE DEPLOYED.

"THE PEOPLE AT BOSTON BEGAN MANY YEARS AGO TO ENDEAVOR TO THROW OFF ALL OBEDIENCE TO THIS COUNTRY.

"WE ARE NOW IN EARNEST AND WILL PROCEED WITH FIRMNESS AND VIGOR."

"THE TOWN OF BOSTON OUGHT TO BE KNOCKED ABOUT THEIR EARS, AND DESTROYED."

YOU WILL NEVER MEET WITH THAT PROPER OBEDIENCE UNTIL YOU HAVE DESTROYED THAT NEST OF LOCUSTS!

PRIME MINISTER LORD NORTH AND AN UNIDENTIFIED MEMBER OF THE HOUSE OF COMMONS, 1774.

ROBERT TROUP, HAMILTON'S LIFELONG FRIEND FROM COLLEGE, MANY YEARS LATER OFFERED AN ACCOUNT OF HOW THE YOUNG MAN FROM ST. CROIX RESPONDED.

[HAMILTON] TOOK A JOURNEY TO BOSTON, SOON AFTER THE DESTRUCTION OF THE TEA, WHEN THE PUBLIC MIND WAS IN A STATE OF VIOLENT FERMENTATION.

WHILST AT BOSTON HIS NOBLE AND GENEROUS HEART, AGITATED BY WHAT HE SAW AND HEARD, LISTED HIM ON THE SIDE OF AMERICA.

FROM BOSTON HE RETURNED TO NEW YORK A WARM REPUBLICAN, AND QUITE AN ENTHUSIAST FOR RESISTING THE CLAIMS OF THE BRITISH PARLIAMENT.

NO OTHER EVIDENCE OF SUCH A TRIP, HOWEVER, HAS EVER EMERGED.

A PAT CONVERSION NARRATIVE LIKE TROUP'S WOULD HAVE BEEN USEFUL TO SHORE UP THE LEGACY OF A MAN BOMBARDED BY MONARCHIST ALLEGATIONS.

NEVERTHELESS, CLEARLY IT WAS THE EVENTS IN BOSTON THAT SWEPT HAMILTON'S HEART ACROSS THE THRESHOLD FROM APATHY TO CONVICTION.

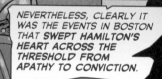

THAT AMERICANS ARE ENTITLED TO FREEDOM, IS INCONTESTIBLE UPON EVERY RATIONAL PRINCIPLE.

WE CAN HAVE NO RESOURCE BUT IN A RESTRICTION OF OUR TRADE, OR IN A RESISTANCE *VI & ARMIS* [BY FORCE AND ARMS].

HAMILTON BEGAN STUDYING POLITICAL PAMPHLETS PROVIDED BY SONS OF LIBERTY ACTIVIST **ALEXANDER MCDOUGALL**.

ACCORDING TO LEGEND, HAMILTON DRAMATICALLY AND PUBLICLY CAME OUT AS A PATRIOT AT A MASS MEETING AT THE LIBERTY POLE ON JULY 6, 1774, JUST STEPS FROM A REDCOATS BARRACKS.

IT IS A COLLEGIAN!

WHETHER OR NOT THIS REPORT HAS ANY BASIS IN FACT, HAMILTON BEGAN TO ACCRUE A REPUTATION. **A PUBLIC PERSONA.**

ANY WORDS HE THEORETICALLY SPOKE THAT DAY ARE A **DROP IN THE BUCKET.** AN **ASTRONOMICAL** AMOUNT OF PRO-REVOLUTIONARY RHETORIC IS LOST TO HISTORY BECAUSE IT WAS **DELIVERED OUT LOUD AND NEVER WRITTEN DOWN.**

THE SPOKEN WORD WAS AN INCISIVE AND DEMOCRATIC POLITICAL TOOL. LIKE THE OPEN-AIR RELIGIOUS REVIVALS OF THE GREAT AWAKENING, THEY WERE OPTIMAL FOR REACHING THE MASSES WHEN MANY, ESPECIALLY OUTSIDE NEW ENGLAND, WERE ILLITERATE.

THE PRINTED WORD WAS, ON THE OTHER HAND, MORE THE DOMAIN OF ELITES...

?!

FREE THOUGHTS,
ON
The PROCEEDINGS of
THE
CONTINENTAL CONGRESS
Held at Philadelphia Sept 5, 1774

...A DOMAIN HAMILTON WAS COMFORTABLE TREADING INTO HIMSELF.

HE BECAME A FIREBRAND WITH HIS **LETTERS**, DRAWING UPON THE SAME WIZARDRY WITH WORDS AND IDEAS THAT HAD EARNED HIM HIS EXODUS FROM ST. CROIX.

THE COLONIES-- WHO HAD NEVER HAD AS CLOSE AND AFFECTIONATE TIES TO EACH OTHER AS THEY HAD TO THE MOTHER COUNTRY-- ORGANIZED.

IN SEPTEMBER 1774, THEIR BEST AND BRIGHTEST--INCLUDING VIRGINIA'S GEORGE WASHINGTON, NEW YORK'S **JOHN JAY**, AND MASSACHUSETTS'S JOHN ADAMS-- GATHERED AS DIPLOMATS IN PHILADELPHIA.

THE **FIRST CONTINENTAL CONGRESS** WAS TO DETERMINE A WAY FORWARD.

"RESOLVED, THAT THIS ASSEMBLY DEEPLY FEELS THE SUFFERINGS OF THEIR COUNTRYMEN IN THE MASSACHUSETTS BAY, UNDER THE OPERATION OF THE LATE UNJUST, CRUEL, AND OPPRESSIVE ACTS OF THE BRITISH PARLIAMENT."

THEY PROPOSED THAT THE COLONIES REFUSE TO BUY BRITISH GOODS--THUS DEALING A RETALIATORY BLOW TO THE ROYAL ECONOMY.

RICHARD HENRY LEE.

IN RESPONSE, A WRITER IDENTIFYING HIMSELF AS A NEW YORK FARMER PUBLISHED A SCREED BELLYACHING THAT THIS WOULD HURT THE HUMBLE, HARDWORKING MEN OF THE AMERICAN BACKCOUNTRY.

TELL ME NOT OF DELEGATES, CONGRESSES, COMMITTEES, RIOTS, MOBS, INSURRECTIONS, ASSOCIATIONS-- A PLAGUE ON THEM ALL!

THE "FARMER" WAS A CHARADE. **ONE HAMILTON SAW RIGHT THROUGH.**

SURELY THE FARMER'S MANIFESTO WAS THE WORK OF A TORY ARISTOCRAT IN DISGUISE--ONE **CYNICALLY** AND **TRANSPARENTLY** PITTING CITY MERCHANT AGAINST COUNTRY HOMESTEADER TO "DIVIDE AND CONQUER" AMERICANS.

A RILED-UP HAMILTON DECLARED A **WAR OF WORDS.** HE REPLIED WITH HIS **OWN** PAMPHLETS TO INTELLECTUALLY AND PERSONALLY EXCORIATE THE AUTHOR. HE SIGNED THEM, ANONYMOUSLY, "FRIEND TO AMERICA."

HAMILTON'S RESPONSES CAN BE A BIT OVERBLOWN. BUT IN THEM HE WIELDS PHILOSOPHY, HISTORY, POLITICAL THEORY, AND LAW LIKE SOMEONE WHO HAD STUDIED FOR DECADES INSTEAD OF JUST A FEW YEARS.

THE "FARMER" WAS, INDEED, NO TILLER OF THE SOIL. HE WAS AN UPSTATE ANGLICAN MINISTER, **SAMUEL SEABURY**...

ARTIFICE, SOPHISTRY, MISREPRESENTATION, AND ABUSE!

...WHO TOOK **UMBRAGE** AT BEING TANGLED INTO A PUBLIC FEUD AT THE HANDS OF AN UPSTART YOUTH...

...IMPUDENT ENOUGH TO DELIVER A CUTTING POINT-BY-POINT TAKEDOWN OF HIS PROPAGANDA.

MEANWHILE, PROPAGANDA WAS BEING EVER MORE OFTEN UPSTAGED BY ACTS OF VIGILANTE VIOLENCE.

⹀SOB⹀ GOD ⹀SOB⹀ **BLESS** KING GEORGE...!

OOOHHHH...!

SAY IT! SAY, "GOD **DAMN** KING GEORGE!"

53

THEN, BEFORE DAWN ON APRIL 19, 1775, THE BRITISH--DETERMINED TO PREEMPTIVELY CRIPPLE THE COLONISTS' ABILITY TO WAGE WAR--DEPLOYED A CLOAK AND DAGGER MISSION OUTSIDE BOSTON.

PROCEED WITH THE UTMOST EXPEDITION AND SECRECY TO CONCORD...

...WHERE YOU WILL SEIZE ALL THE ARTILLERY, AMMUNITION, PROVISIONS, TENTS, SMALL ARMS, AND ALL MILITARY STORES WHATSOEVER.

BRITISH GENERAL **THOMAS GAGE.**

BUT AMERICAN MILITIAMEN WERE TIPPED OFF IN ADVANCE. IN THE VILLAGE OF LEXINGTON, THEY POSITIONED TO FACE THE BRITISH DOWN.

FIRE, BY GOD! FIRE!

P-T-TFF!

P-T-TFF!

P-T-TFF!

HUZZAH!!

THE STANDOFF WAS SO COMBUSTIBLE THAT THE TINIEST SPARK COULD-- AND DID--IGNITE AN **INFERNO.**

AGK!

ULTIMATELY, THE REDCOATS RETREATED. BUT BY THEN, **HUNDREDS ON BOTH SIDES WERE DEAD.** AND THE BRITISH OCCUPIERS WERE LEFT HEMMED INTO BOSTON PROPER--SURROUNDED BY 15,000 ARMED COLONISTS WHO HAD RACED IN FROM ALL POINTS.

NOT EVERY APOSTLE OF LIBERTY WAS PREPARED TO OFFER UP THE BLOOD OF THEIR VEINS AS READILY AS THE INK OF THEIR PENS, BUT HAMILTON SEEMED UTTERLY DEVOID OF HAMLET-LIKE SOUL WRANGLINGS OVER HIS MORTALITY.

HERE FOR A SECOND TIME, WHAT HAMILTON DEARLY WANTED, BUT HAD NO RIGHT TO EVER EXPECT, DROPPED IN HIS LAP.

AND AS SINGULAR AS HIS JOURNEY TO SOLDIERHOOD MAY HAVE BEEN, IN THIS DESIRE HE WAS **ONE OF MANY.**

...I WISH THERE WAS A WAR.

...I WISH THERE WAS A WAR.

...I WISH THERE WAS A WAR.

...I WISH THERE WAS A WAR.

PERHAPS IT WAS HIS INTIMACY WITH SUFFERING AND BRUTALITY--SURELY MORE THAN THE AVERAGE FARM BOY OR CARPENTER'S SON--THAT RENDERED HIM SO PHYSICALLY BRAVE.

...I WISH THERE WAS A WAR.

...I WISH THERE WAS A WAR.

WAR HAD BEGUN.

YET LOYALTY TO KING GEORGE III REMAINED INGRAINED IN AMERICANS. MOST BLAMED **PARLIAMENT** FOR THE HOSTILITIES-- EVEN REFERRING TO THE AMASSING, OPPRESSIVE BRITISH SOLDIERS AS "MINISTERIAL TROOPS."

AMERICA AS A SEPARATE POLITICAL ENTITY STILL SEEMED **UNTHINKABLE** TO MOST. YET THE PACE OF YOUNG MEN FLOCKING TO VOLUNTEER MILITARY COMPANIES TO DEFEND THE COLONIES LEAPED INTO HIGH GEAR.

HAMILTON AND TROUP JOINED A BAND CALLED **THE CORSAIRS** (LATER RENAMED **HEARTS OF OAK**).

JOIN YOUR RIGHT HAND TO YOUR FIRELOCK!

RECOVER YOUR...**ARMS!**

THEIR RESPECTED LEADER, CAPTAIN **EDWARD FLEMING**, HAD BEEN A SOLDIER OF REPUTE IN THE FRENCH AND INDIAN WAR.

IN TAKING **SWANTIE DE PEYSTER** AS A WIFE, FLEMING HAD "MARRIED UP" INTO A PEDIGREED, OLD DUTCH FAMILY--ONE OF PRINCELY POWER AND INFLUENCE.

FLEMING WAS AN OBJECT LESSON IN **UPWARD SOCIAL MOBILITY THROUGH WAR AND MARRIAGE.** THIS COULD NOT HAVE ESCAPED YOUNG HAMILTON'S NOTICE.

THESE WERE HEADY AND UNCERTAIN TIMES, WITH NO CENTER OF GRAVITY.

NEW YORK WAS NOT QUITE AT WAR, NOT QUITE AT PEACE. IT WAS NOT DECISIVELY RULED BY ROYAL AUTHORITY, NOR WAS IT SOVEREIGN AND INDEPENDENT. AND ANYONE MIGHT HAVE QUESTIONED...

COME NOW! JOIN US!

THE MOMENT OF RECKONING HAS ARRIVED FOR THE COWARDLY CRIMINAL MILES COOPER!

...WHETHER THE INDEPENDENCE MOVEMENT WAS TO BE GOVERNED BY THE MOB...

?

...OR BY MEN OF QUALITY.

I AM ALWAYS MORE OR LESS ALARMED AT EVERY THING WHICH IS DONE OF MERE WILL AND PLEASURE, WITHOUT ANY PROPER AUTHORITY.

AGITATORS SPOOKED THE TORY PRESIDENT OF KING'S COLLEGE TO FLEE FOR ENGLAND, AND HAMILTON'S EDUCATION PETERED OUT ACCORDINGLY.

ON JUNE 25, 1775, GEORGE WASHINGTON PASSED THROUGH EN ROUTE TO BOSTON.

THERE HE WAS TO TAKE COMMAND OF THE AMERICAN FORCES SQUARING OFF WITH THE BRITISH OCCUPIERS.

WHILE CAMPAIGNING AGAINST THE FRENCH IN THE 1750s, THE HAUGHTINESS OF THE BRITISH OFFICERS COMMANDING WASHINGTON HAD REVOLTED HIM.

[THE INDIAN] SAVAGES MAY, INDEED, BE A FORMIDABLE ENEMY TO YOUR RAW AMERICAN MILITIA; BUT UPON THE KING'S REGULAR AND DISCIPLINED TROOPS, SIR, IT IS IMPOSSIBLE THEY SHOULD MAKE ANY IMPRESSION.

GENERAL EDWARD BRADDOCK, 1755.

THOSE SAME MEN HAD CLUNG TO CUMBERSOME EUROPEAN-STYLE WARFARE THAT, IN THE UNTAMED WILDS OF AMERICA, LED ONLY TO THEIR SLAUGHTER.

WASHINGTON HAD SEEN FIRSTHAND THAT *THE WORLD'S MIGHTIEST EMPIRE WAS NOT INVINCIBLE.*

HNUNGH!

YI-YI-YI-YI-YI!!

BATTLE OF MONONGAHELA, 1755.

ALLOW ME TO PRESENT A YOUNG MAN OF LETTERS WHO SUPPORTS OUR CASE: MR. ALEXANDER HAMILTON, LATELY OF THE WEST INDIES.

I ONCE ACCOMPANIED MY LATE BROTHER TO TAKE THE CONSUMPTION CURES AT BARBADOS. DO YOU KNOW THE PLACE?

NOT AS SUCH, YOUR EXCELLENCY. BUT *ALL* THE ISLANDS SHARE CERTAIN--

AND I BELIEVE YOU KNOW COLONEL JOHN LASHER...

THAT I DO, SIR. GOOD EVENING.

AS TO MILITARY SERVICE, HAMILTON HAD FAR MORE GLORIOUS DESIGNS THAN TO BE A COMMON SOLDIER.

THE Compleat Canonier:
OR,
The Gunners Guide,

wherein are fet forth Exactly the chief Grounds and Principals of the whole Art, in a very brief and Compendions, never by any fet forth in the Like Nature before,

With divers Excellent Conclutions, both A Medical and Generations belonging the As alfo fundry ferviceable Exre-wo both For Sea and Land fever

A study delightful and very ufefel fm and imbred by grateful Pin

FIRTUS GLORIUM PARE
thers of veras Rim

BENT ON BECOMING AN ARTILLERY OFFICER, YET WITH NO ONE TO TEACH WHAT HE NEEDED TO KNOW, HAMILTON TURNED TO BOOKS.

AFTER MONTHS OF STUDY AND PULLING STRINGS WITH IMPORTANT MEN, IN MARCH 1776, HE BROUGHT HIS GOAL TO FRUITION.

ORDERED: THAT THE SAID ALEXANDER HAMILTON BE, AND HE IS HEREBY, APPOINTED CAPTAIN OF THE PROVINCIAL COMPANY OF ARTILLERY OF THIS COLONY.

NEW YORK PROVINCIAL CONGRESSMAN PHILIP VAN CORTLANDT.

ARTILLERY WOULD MAKE HIM VITAL TO THE CAUSE.

AFTER ALL, THAT SAME MONTH, AN INSPIRED MANEUVER TRANSPORTING CANNONS FROM HUNDREDS OF MILES AWAY...

...ALLOWED WASHINGTON TO FORCE THE THE BRITISH TO EVACUATE BOSTON.

HUZZAH!!

THE GOOD NEWS WAS, HOWEVER, TEMPERED BY WORRYING SETBACKS.

AFTER AN ARDUOUS WILDERNESS MARCH THAT HAD DECIMATED THEIR FORCES...

CRACK!

CRACK! CRACK!

...AARON BURR AND THE OTHER VOLUNTEERS IN BENEDICT ARNOLD'S DARING INVASION OF CANADA MET A SHATTERING DEFEAT ON DECEMBER 31, 1775.

AND THE ENEMY ARMADA THAT HAD WITHDRAWN FROM BOSTON HAD **DISAPPEARED.**

WASHINGTON KNEW IT COULD POP UP AT ANY MOMENT, UNANNOUNCED, TO ATTACK ANY STRETCH OF COAST WITHIN THE REBEL COLONIES.

RECALL WHAT THE BRITISH LEARNED FROM THE PREVIOUS WAR: NEW YORK'S CROSSROADS OF BAYS AND RIVERS MADE IT A **PERFECT MILITARY BASE.**

WASHINGTON RETURNED TO NEW YORK IN APRIL 1776 TO PROTECT THE CITY.

IF HE COULD.

CORRESPONDING WITH A NEW YORK FRIEND, AN ENGLISHMAN WROTE...

"I FEEL FOR YOU...FOR I EXPECT YOUR CITY WILL BE LAID TO ASHES."

HAMILTON WAS PLACED IN CHARGE OF A PORTION OF THE CITY'S FORTIFICATIONS--JUST OUTSIDE THE NOW ANCIENT DUTCH FORT BUILT A CENTURY AND A HALF EARLIER.

IT WAS A POSITION THAT OFFERED A WIDE AND UNOBSTRUCTED VIEW...

B-BOOM!

B-BOOM!

THAT'S THE SIGNAL!

THE ARMADA IS HERE!

...OF THE BRITISH LANDING FORCE THAT SAILED, PRACTICALLY UNCHALLENGED, INTO NEW YORK HARBOR ON JULY 2, 1776.

IT WAS THE FORCE COMMANDED BY SIR **WILLIAM HOWE**, WHOM WASHINGTON HAD DRIVEN FROM BOSTON.

AND IT WAS ONLY AN **ADVANCE TEAM**. ON AUGUST 12, 400 SHIPS WITH MORE THAN 10,000 SAILORS ARRIVED TO REINFORCE THE BUILDUP.

FOR MONTHS, RUMORS HAD FLOWN THAT **FOREIGN MERCENARIES** WOULD ALSO COME TO SUBDUE AMERICANS.

IT WAS TRUE. GEORGE III USED FAMILY CONNECTIONS TO BEEF UP HIS INVASION WITH **"HESSIANS"**-- AUXILIARIES FROM THE GERMAN STATES OF HESSE-KASSEL, HESSE-HANAU, BRUNSWICK, AND OTHERS.

AS AN IMMIGRANT PROPAGANDIST REQUIRING JUST A FEW YEARS TO IDENTIFY AS AN AMERICAN, HAMILTON WAS NOT ALONE.

THOMAS PAINE, A POOR CORSET MAKER FROM ENGLAND, IN 1776 PUBLISHED THE PAMPHLET COMMON SENSE.

THE GAME-CHANGING BEST SELLER BLASTED ALL THE EVILS OF MONARCHY, CLAIMING KINGS WERE A "HEATHEN" IDEA FORCED ON ENGLISHMEN AT THE POINT OF A SWORD BY...

MON SENSE,

ADDRESSED TO THE

INHABITANTS

OF

AMERICA,

On the following interesting

SUBJECTS.

I. Of the Origin and Design of G with concise Remarks on the Eng

II. Of Monarchy and Hereditary Succ

Thoughts on the present State

the pre

"...A FRENCH BASTARD [WILLIAM THE CONQUEROR IN 1066] LANDING WITH AN ARMED BANDITTI."

PAINE'S POWERS OF PERSUASION TIPPED THE SCALES. A CRITICAL MASS OF AMERICANS ABANDONED THEIR DELUSIONS ABOUT GEORGE III AND EMBRACED PAINE.

NOTHING CAN SETTLE OUR AFFAIRS SO EXPEDITIOUSLY AS AN OPEN AND DETERMINED DECLARATION FOR INDEPENDENCE.

THE CONTINENTAL CONGRESS DRAFTED AND DELIVERED EXACTLY THAT.

THERE WAS NO BETTER PROOF OF GEORGE III'S BRUTAL INTENTIONS THAN THE 8,000 HIGHLY TRAINED HESSIANS WHO, WHEN FIGHTING BEGAN ON AUGUST 26...

JULY 4, 1776, WAS A POINT OF NO RETURN.

...VICIOUSLY BAYONETED AMERICANS WHO TRIED TO SURRENDER ON A BROOKLYN BATTLEFIELD WELL OUT OF HAMILTON'S SIGHT.

WASHINGTON BETRAYED HOW LITTLE HIS PREVIOUS SERVICE PREPARED HIM FOR WARFARE OF THIS SCALE.

AS THE PATRIOTS' DEFENSES COLLAPSED AND THE ENEMY ENCROACHED ON LOWER MANHATTAN, HAMILTON LIKELY SAW THE FIRST ACTION OF HIS COMMAND...

...COVERING AN AMERICAN RETREAT.

BOOM!

MAKE READY...!

...GIVE FIRE!!

GOOD GOD, WHAT BRAVE FELLOWS I MUST THIS DAY LOSE.

ULTIMATELY HE AND HIS MEN HAD TO ABANDON THEIR GUNS AND RUN FOR THEIR LIVES TEN MILES NORTH.

CAPTAIN! YOUR BAGGAGE!

CAN'T BE HELPED! LEAVE IT!

AARON BURR, RETURNED IN ONE PIECE FROM THE CANADIAN DISASTER, HAD BEEN MADE AN AIDE TO GENERAL ISRAEL PUTNAM.

UP THE BLOOMINGDALE ROAD, SIR. ≷COUGH≷ THERE'S NO BETTER WAY.

BURR WAS INSTRUMENTAL IN LEADING THOUSANDS OF MEN SAFELY OUT OF THE BESIEGED CITY.

SATISFIED BY SEIZING NEW YORK CITY, THE REDCOATS BLUNDERED BY NOT PRESSING ONWARD.

WASHINGTON'S FORCES CONSOLIDATED IN HARLEM FOR SEVERAL WEEKS.

IN THE FACE OF SUCH PUNISHING UPSETS, HAMILTON'S HIGHER-UPS WERE IMPRESSED THAT HE MAINTAINED SUCH ORDER AND DISCIPLINE IN HIS RANKS.

WORTHY SOLDIERS ARE WELL REWARDED IN COMMANDS LIKE MINE, YOU KNOW.

GENERAL GREENE, YOU MAKE ME A FLATTERING COMPLIMENT. BUT I AM COMMITTED TO THE ARTILLERY.

AT THE NEXT MAJOR BRITISH MOVE, WASHINGTON RETREATED EVEN FARTHER-- OFF MANHATTAN ISLAND AND INTO THE INTERIOR.

AT THE VILLAGE OF WHITE PLAINS, HAMILTON, UNDER FIRE, REPEATEDLY CONFOUNDED HESSIAN ATTACKS.

AGAIN, AMERICANS HAD TO GO ON THE RUN.

WASHINGTON'S RETREAT ENDED ONLY AFTER MONTHS OF LOSING TERRITORY. IN DECEMBER 1776, HIS ARMY CROSSED THE DELAWARE RIVER INTO BUCKS COUNTY, PENNSYLVANIA.

BY THE THOUSANDS, THEIR NUMBERS HAD DWINDLED FROM CASUALTIES, DESERTIONS, AND THE LAPSING OF SHORT-TERM ENLISTMENTS.

HAMILTON, WITH THE PRESSURE OFF FOR THE MOMENT, GREW GRAVELY ILL.

THE CONFIDENT BRITISH PULLED BACK. THEY WOULD PASS THE WINTER IN MANHATTAN-- AND CAVORT WITH ITS MANY SATISFIED LOYALISTS.

NEW YORK CITY WOULD BELONG TO THEM FOR THE NEXT SEVEN YEARS.

A TOAST TO THE LORD ADMIRAL'S HEALTH!

AND MAY THE NEW YEAR FIND THIS GOOD LAND FREE OF THE TRIFLING MISCHIEFS OF REBELS!

HUZZAH!

THE KING'S FORCE LEFT BEHIND OUTPOSTS TO GUARD ALL THEIR CONQUERED TERRITORY.

ONE SUCH OUTPOST, AT TRENTON, NEW JERSEY, HELD ABOUT 1,500 OF THE FEARED HESSIANS.

A DESPERATE-FOR-VICTORY WASHINGTON CORRECTLY PREDICTED THE HESSIANS WOULD BE HUNGOVER AND OFF THEIR GUARD IN THE EARLY MORNING HOURS AFTER CHRISTMAS DAY 1776.

ORDERS WERE HANDED DOWN. HAMILTON ROSE FROM HIS SICKBED...

...AND SOON FOUND HIMSELF CROSSING THE RIVER AND ON A TOUGH NIGHTTIME MARCH THROUGH A BLIZZARD.

IN TRENTON, HAMILTON AND HIS MEN LET LOOSE ON AN ENEMY AS UNPREPARED AS WASHINGTON COULD HAVE HOPED.

BOOOM!

THE AMERICANS, WITH NEARLY NO LOSSES ON THEIR SIDE, CAPTURED ALMOST 900 OF THE DREADED FOREIGN AUXILIARIES.

ALTHOUGH NOT OF GREAT MILITARY CONSEQUENCE, THE BATTLE OF TRENTON IMMENSELY BOOSTED REVOLUTIONARY MORALE.

WASHINGTON KEPT HIS ARMY ON THE OFFENSIVE. JUST OVER A WEEK LATER, WHILE ELUDING REVENGEFUL, FAST-MOVING REDCOATS, HIS ARMY ATTACKED ANOTHER OUTPOST--THIS ONE AT PRINCETON, NEW JERSEY. THIS AFFORDED HAMILTON THE STRANGE AND RARE OPPORTUNITY OF POURING CANNON FIRE AT THE ENEMY-OCCUPIED BUILDINGS OF...

...THE COLLEGE THAT HAD REBUFFED HIS WISH FOR ACCELERATED STUDY.

LOAD THE SHOT!

RAM THE SHOT!

By Virtue of Powers from His Excellency General Washington

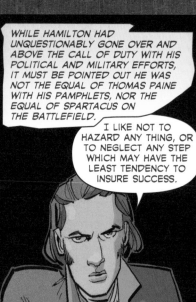

WHILE HAMILTON HAD UNQUESTIONABLY GONE OVER AND ABOVE THE CALL OF DUTY WITH HIS POLITICAL AND MILITARY EFFORTS, IT MUST BE POINTED OUT HE WAS NOT THE EQUAL OF THOMAS PAINE WITH HIS PAMPHLETS, NOR THE EQUAL OF SPARTACUS ON THE BATTLEFIELD.

I LIKE NOT TO HAZARD ANY THING, OR TO NEGLECT ANY STEP WHICH MAY HAVE THE LEAST TENDENCY TO INSURE SUCCESS.

BUT HIS EXCEPTIONAL TALENT TO MAKE AN IMPRESSION ON SUPERIORS PERHAPS INEVITABLY MATCHED UP WITH ONE PARTICULAR SUPERIOR'S EXCEPTIONAL ABILITY FOR NOTICING TALENT.

NAMELY, GEORGE WASHINGTON'S.

OVER THE REVOLUTIONARY WAR, THE COMMANDER IN CHIEF HAD A TOTAL OF THIRTY-ONE AIDES ON HIS STAFF TO DELIVER ORDERS, PROCESS AVALANCHES OF LETTERS, AND CARRY OUT SENSITIVE MISSIONS.

| TENCH TILGHMAN | WILLIAM GRAYSON | EDMUND RANDOLPH | JOSEPH REED |

HAMILTON HAD LITTLE APPETITE FOR SUCH A POSITION, BUT IN EARLY 1777, HIS ARTILLERY UNIT HAD RUN ITS COURSE.

DEATHS AND DESERTIONS REDUCES IT AT PRESENT TO THE SMALL NUMBER OF TWENTY-FIVE MEN.

HIS BEST PROSPECT WAS TO ACCEPT THE INVITATION THAT CAME TO WORK FOR WASHINGTON. THIS WOULD GIVE HIM THE HONORARY RANK OF LIEUTENANT COLONEL.

HIS EXCELLENCY HAS BEEN PLEASED TO APPOINT ME ONE OF HIS AID DU CAMPS [SIC].

AS A TIRELESS WORKER WHO WAS FEARLESS IN THE FIELD, HAMILTON HAD MUCH TO RECOMMEND HIM.

IT WOULD NOT TAKE LONG FOR HIM TO BECOME THE MOST EFFECTIVE AND VALUABLE OF WASHINGTON'S "FAMILY."

COMING TO AMERICA FROM ABROAD GAVE HAMILTON THE GIFT OF SEEING IT AS A WHOLE, RATHER THAN--LIKE OTHERS-- BEING TAINTED WITH REGIONAL PREJUDICES.

DAMNED YANKEE!

SAY THAT ONCE MORE ABOUT CAROLINA MEN AND YOU'LL BE CUFFED!

WASHINGTON HAD LIKEWISE WORKED TO ADOPT A "CONTINENTALIST" POINT OF VIEW, PRIORITIZING NATIONAL OVER STATE AFFAIRS.

A CHOICE ASPECT OF HAMILTON'S RESUME WAS THAT HE KNEW FRENCH...

"JE NE SAIS PAS LE NOMBRE, MAIS IL Y EN A ASSEZ POUR TRANSPORTER NOTRE ARMÉ A TRAVERS DU DELAWARE..."

...AN IMPORTANT SKILL FOR SEVERAL REASONS.

ENGLAND AND FRANCE HAD BEEN BELLIGERENTS FOR CENTURIES. AND UNLIKE AMERICA, FRANCE HAD MONEY, A NAVY, AND INTERNATIONAL RESPECT.

ENGLAND VERSUS FRANCE AT THE BATTLE OF BARFLEUR, 1692.

IT WAS CRUCIAL TO THE UNITED STATES TO RECEIVE RECOGNITION AND AID FROM FRANCE. BUT THAT COUNTRY DID NOT WANT TO RISK BLOOD, TREASURE, OR PRESTIGE FOR WHAT MIGHT BE A HOPELESS CAUSE.

BENJAMIN FRANKLIN

SILAS DEANE

CHARLES GRAVIER, COUNT OF VERGENNES, FOREIGN MINISTER TO KING LOUIS XVI

MEANWHILE, SOME FRENCHMEN SAW THE OPPORTUNITY FOR SOCIAL CLIMBING--AND WANTED IN TO THE CONFLICT.

...I WISH THERE WAS A WAR.

...I WISH THERE WAS A WAR.

...I WISH THERE WAS A WAR.

...I WISH THERE WAS A WAR.

...I WISH THERE WAS A WAR.

BUT FOR OTHERS, THE AMERICAN REVOLUTION WAS MORE THAN A CHANCE TO RISE THROUGH THE RANKS.

IN EUROPE, THERE WAS A PERVASIVE FEELING THAT THEIR SOCIETIES HAD GROWN DECADENT AND THEIR GOVERNMENTS CORRUPT AND UNJUST--THAT SOMETHING **NOBLE** AND **PURE** ABOUT HUMANITY WAS OUT OF REACH.

ROMANTIC, LIBERAL IDEAS WERE TAKING HOLD EVEN AMONG YOUNG NOBLEMEN, LIKE...

...MARIE-JOSEPH PAUL YVES ROCH GILBERT DU MOTIER, THE MARQUIS DE LAFAYETTE.

A MERE CAPTAIN IN THE RESERVES, SPEAKING BARELY A WORD OF ENGLISH, AND WITH NEXT TO NO MILITARY EXPERIENCE...

THE WELFARE OF AMERICA IS INTIMATELY CONNECTED WITH THE HAPPINESS OF ALL MANKIND.

...LAFAYETTE CROSSED THE ATLANTIC AND WOULD SOON BECOME ANOTHER MEMBER OF WASHINGTON'S "FAMILY."

CONGRESS AND ITS WHIMSICAL FAVOURITISM IN THEIR PROMOTIONS!

ABSURD TO SO QUICKLY MAKE A *MAJOR GENERAL* OF A *FOREIGN PRETENDER!*

HAMILTON MAY HAVE FELT COMPETITIVE WITH LAFAYETTE AT FIRST BLUSH. BUT THE FRENCHMAN'S CHARMS WON HIM OVER.

WHEN POOR, I SPEND LAVISHLY. BUT WHEN FORTUNE POURS HER FAVORS INTO MY PURSE, I AM A MISERLY WRETCH.

I WILL BRAVE THE UTMOST HARDSHIPS, BUT HANG MYSELF IF THE WIND IS FROM THE EAST.

WHO AM I?

...AN ENGLISHMAN!

HA! HA! HA! HA!

AND AS A HEALTHY YOUNG MAN, HAMILTON WAS NOT INTERESTED IN BROTHERLY LOVE ALONE.

WHEN THE REDCOATS OCCUPIED ELIZABETHTOWN, SOME PRETTY YOUNG LADIES HE HAD ONCE KNOWN WERE DISPLACED BACK INTO HIS LIFE.

I AM CONFIDENT, MY DEAR MR. HAMILTON, THAT OUR KITTY IS *MOST DESIROUS* OF HEARING FROM YOU.

HAMILTON MOUNTED A CAMPAIGN TO WIN THE HEART OF *CATHARINE LIVINGSTON,* DAUGHTER OF A PROMINENT NEW JERSEY POLITICIAN.

IF YOU WOULD CHOOSE TO BE A GODDESS, AND TO BE WORSHIPPED AS SUCH...

...YOU SHALL BE ONE OF THE GRACES, OR DIANA, OR VENUS, OR SOMETHING SURPASSING THEM ALL.

IN THIS ENDEAVOR, HOWEVER, HE WAS DESTINED TO MIRROR THE, AT BEST, *MIXED SUCCESS* OF WASHINGTON'S ARMY IN THESE OPEN YEARS OF THE REVOLUTIONARY WAR.

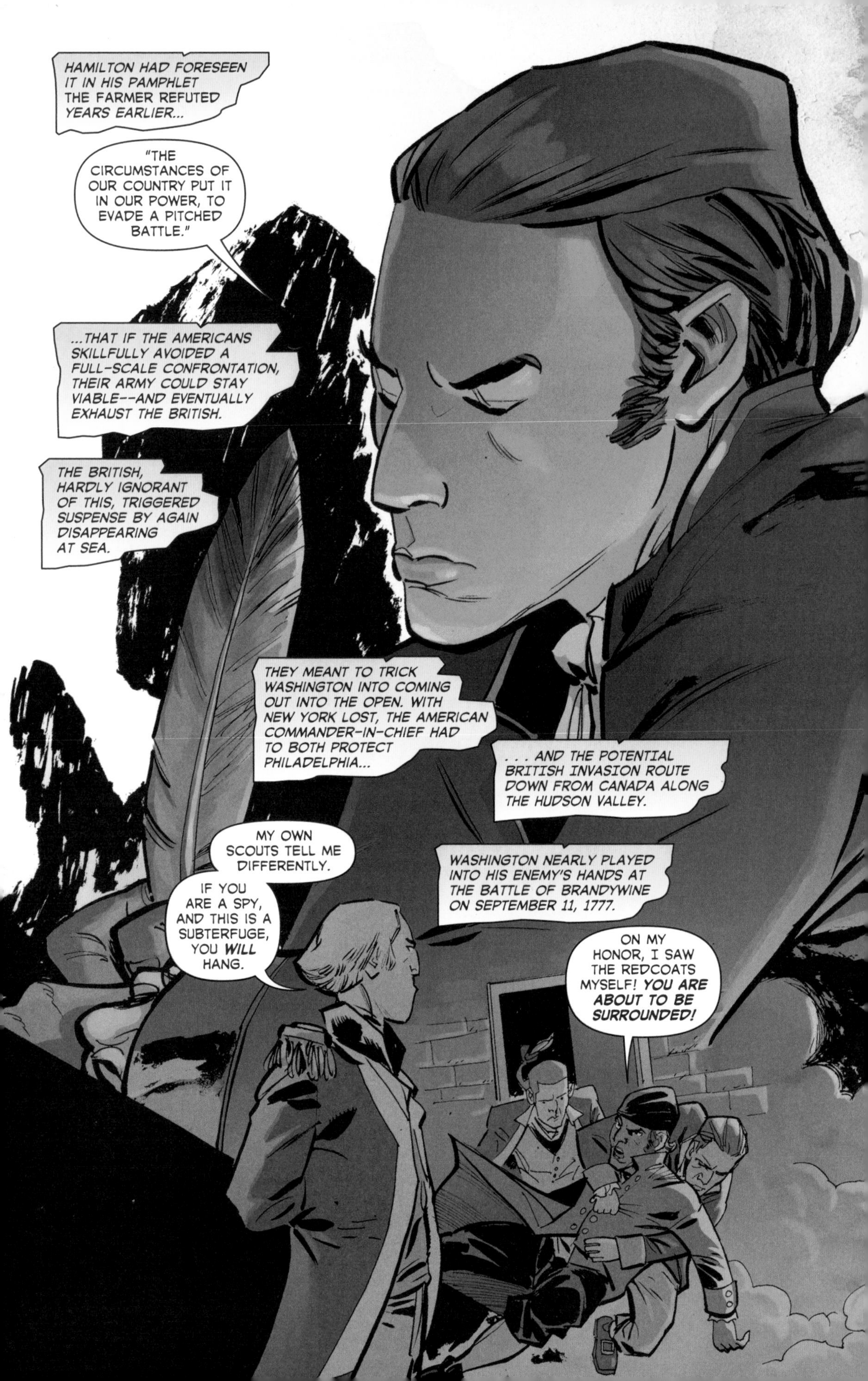
HAMILTON HAD FORESEEN IT IN HIS PAMPHLET THE FARMER REFUTED YEARS EARLIER...
"THE CIRCUMSTANCES OF OUR COUNTRY PUT IT IN OUR POWER, TO EVADE A PITCHED BATTLE."
...THAT IF THE AMERICANS SKILLFULLY AVOIDED A FULL-SCALE CONFRONTATION, THEIR ARMY COULD STAY VIABLE--AND EVENTUALLY EXHAUST THE BRITISH.
THE BRITISH, HARDLY IGNORANT OF THIS, TRIGGERED SUSPENSE BY AGAIN DISAPPEARING AT SEA.
THEY MEANT TO TRICK WASHINGTON INTO COMING OUT INTO THE OPEN. WITH NEW YORK LOST, THE AMERICAN COMMANDER-IN-CHIEF HAD TO BOTH PROTECT PHILADELPHIA...
. . . AND THE POTENTIAL BRITISH INVASION ROUTE DOWN FROM CANADA ALONG THE HUDSON VALLEY.
MY OWN SCOUTS TELL ME DIFFERENTLY.
IF YOU ARE A SPY, AND THIS IS A SUBTERFUGE, YOU **WILL** HANG.
WASHINGTON NEARLY PLAYED INTO HIS ENEMY'S HANDS AT THE BATTLE OF BRANDYWINE ON SEPTEMBER 11, 1777.
ON MY HONOR, I SAW THE REDCOATS MYSELF! **YOU ARE ABOUT TO BE SURROUNDED!**

WASHINGTON'S ARMY WAS ABLE TO RETREAT, BUT THEY HAD HAD ANOTHER CLOSE BRUSH WITH ANNIHILATION--AND WASHINGTON'S REPUTATION TOOK ANOTHER HIT.

SENT TO BURN A FLOUR MILL THE ENEMY MIGHT SEIZE, HAMILTON WAS NEARLY SHOT BY MARAUDING REDCOATS A STONE'S THROW FROM PHILADELPHIA.

HE SENT AN URGENT MESSAGE FOR CONGRESS TO FLEE THE CITY--WHICH IT DID IN FEAR, CONFUSION, AND SHAME.

THE BRITISH TOOK PHILADELPHIA ON SEPTEMBER 24, 1777.

A WEEK AND A HALF LATER, AT THE BATTLE OF GERMANTOWN, WASHINGTON TRIED TO REPEAT A TRENTON-STYLE GAMBIT.

BURNING FIELDS OF BUCKWHEAT MADE THE BATTLEFIELD SMOKY AND ETHEREAL.

WASHINGTON AND HAMILTON WERE POWERLESS TO RALLY THEIR OWN TROOPS WHEN THEY RAN OUT OF GUNPOWDER AND FLED.

BUT THEN ON OCTOBER 17, WASHINGTON'S RIVAL GENERAL HORATIO GATES--AIDED BY NEW YORK MILITIAMEN AND THE COURAGE OF BENEDICT ARNOLD--THWARTED A MAJOR BRITISH ADVANCE DOWN FROM CANADA.

GATES, IN BLOCKING A POTENTIALLY CHECKMATE MOVE BY THE ENEMY, FORCED A TURNING POINT IN THE WAR. SOME HAVE CALLED THE BATTLE OF SARATOGA THE GETTYSBURG OF THE AMERICAN REVOLUTION.

GENERAL **HORATIO GATES**

The Line of Conduct Proscribed to Us

GENERALS JEALOUS AND SKEPTICAL OF WASHINGTON FLOCKED TO GATES, EXPOSING RANCOROUS DIVISIONS WITHIN THE ARMY.

GENERAL THOMAS CONWAY

GENERAL CHARLES LEE

THE BITTER POLITICS ENTANGLED WASHINGTON AIDES LIKE HAMILTON AND STRAPPING SOUTH CAROLINIAN **JOHN LAURENS,** A NEW MEMBER OF THE "FAMILY."

WASHINGTON'S POSITION AFFECTED THEIR OWN. SO, WHAT TO DO? DOUBLE DOWN ON LOYALTY TO THEIR COMMANDER OR DISTANCE THEMSELVES?

MONTHS OF PRIVATION IN THE ARMY'S WINTER QUARTERS AT VALLEY FORGE LEFT WASHINGTON MOODY. HE PLEADED TO THE REFUGEE CONTINENTAL CONGRESS:

NOVEMBER 8, 1777: "THE MILITARY CHEST IS AGAIN EMPTY AND THE ARMY IS UNPAID FOR THE MONTHS OF SEPTEMBER AND OCTOBER."

NOVEMBER 17, 1777: LACK OF CLOTHING IS SO GREAT THAT IT IS A "WONDER" THAT SOLDIERS "KEEP THE FIELD AT ALL, IN TENTS, AT THIS SEASON OF THE YEAR."

DECEMBER 23, 1777: "I AM NOW CONVINCED BEYOND A DOUBT, THAT UNLESS SOME GREAT AND CAPITAL CHANGE SUDDENLY TAKES PLACE, THIS ARMY MUST INEVITABLY BE REDUCED TO ONE OR OTHER OF THESE THREE THINGS: STARVE, DISSOLVE, OR DISPERSE."

IT WAS NOT JUST FEVER MAKING HAMILTON ILL THAT SEASON. IT WAS THE STATES' **GUTTING THE WAR EFFORT** BY FAVORING THEIR OWN AFFAIRS ABOVE ALL ELSE.

[CONGRESS'S] CONDUCT WITH RESPECT TO THE ARMY IS **FEEBLE, INDECISIVE, AND IMPROVIDENT.** WE ARE REDUCED TO A MORE TERRIBLE SITUATION THAN YOU CAN CONCEIVE.

THE STATES HAD CLAIMED THEIR SEVERANCE FROM BRITAIN AND THEIR SOVEREIGNTY, BUT THE DECLARATION OF INDEPENDENCE PROVIDED NO FRAMEWORK FOR THEM TO ACT AS ONE OR COORDINATE THEIR AFFAIRS.

...AL UNION between the states of New York, New Jerfey, Pennfylvania, Delaware, Maryland, Virginia, North Carolina, South Carolina, and Georgia.

ARTICLE I. THE ftyle of this confederacy fhall be " The UNITED STATES of AMERICA.

ART. II. Each ftate retains its fovereignty, freedom, and independence, and every power, jurifdiction and right, which is not by this confederation exprefly delegated to the United States, in Congrefs affembled.

ART. III. The faid ftates hand...

YEARS OF DEBATE AND COMPROMISE FINALLY YIELDED A PLAN FOR A WEAK AND DECENTRALIZED "FEDERAL" GOVERNMENT.

YORK, PENNSYLVANIA--WHERE THE CONTINENTAL CONGRESS HAD FLED IN LATE 1777.

THE ARTICLES OF CONFEDERATION...

ESTABLISHED NO PRESIDENT OR SUPREME COURT. THEY DELEGATED CONGRESS NO AUTHORITY TO IMPOSE TAXES, REGULATE TRADE, OR EVEN ENFORCE ITS OWN MEASURES.

THE STATES--EQUAL PARTNERS REGARDLESS OF POPULATION OR RELATIVE WEALTH--COULD SIMPLY IGNORE ANY "LAWS" OR "POLICIES" CONGRESS RECOMMENDED.

...HAS, IN ITS PROGRESS, BEEN ATTENDED WITH UNCOMMON EMBARRASSMENTS AND DELAY.

TO FORM A PERMANENT UNION, ACCOMMODATED TO THE OPINION AND WISHES OF THE DELEGATES OF SO MANY STATES, DIFFERING IN HABITS...

THE NEGLECT OF THE MILITARY THAT HAMILTON SO DISDAINED WAS UNSURPRISING COMING FROM A PEOPLE SO FEARFUL OF CENTRALIZED POWER. MOST FAVORED STATE MILITIAS OVER "STANDING" ARMIES, WHICH THEY DESCRIBED AS:

"ODIOUS AND DANGEROUS."

"EVER DANGEROUS TO LIBERTY."

GEORGE MASON.

BENJAMIN FRANKLIN.

BUT IF THE STATES WERE REMISS IN AIDING THE CONTINENTAL ARMY...

≥PANT≤ ≥PANT≤ ≥PANT≤

...THE OUTCOME OF *THE BATTLE OF SARATOGA* WAS ENOUGH TO CONVINCE FRANCE TO RECOGNIZE THE UNITED STATES AND JOIN THE WAR.

FRANCE OPENED NEW BATTLEFRONTS IN THE EAST AND WEST INDIES. THE BRITISH, NOW FOILED IN THEIR PLAN TO DEAL THE REBELS A DEFT DEATH BLOW, RUSHED TO RESHUFFLE HOW AND WHERE THEIR MILITARY WAS DEPLOYED.

IN MAY 1778, THE REDCOATS ABANDONED PHILADELPHIA AND RETURNED TO NEW YORK.

WASHINGTON, HANKERING TO SILENCE CRITICS THROUGH A VICTORY, THOUGHT THE ON-THE-MARCH ENEMY MIGHT BE VULNERABLE.

HAMILTON, TOO, WAS PENT UP FOR A FIGHT.

WE FEEL OUR PERSONAL HONOR AS WELL AS THE HONOR OF THE ARMY...

...AND ARE HEARTILY DESIROUS TO ATTEMPT WHATEVER THE DISPOSITION OF OUR MEN WILL SECOND AND PRUDENCE AUTHORIZE!

WASHINGTON'S RIVAL, GENERAL CHARLES LEE, WISHY-WASHILY ACCEPTED, THEN REJECTED, THEN ACCEPTED AGAIN CHARGE OF THE OFFENSIVE.

BUT WHEN FACE-TO-FACE WITH THE BRITISH ON THE BLAZING HOT DAY OF JUNE 27, HE ORDERED A RETREAT.

WASHINGTON WAS IRATE. HE RUSHED TO FORM BATTLE LINES AGAIN AND ATTACK.

THE BATTLE OF MONMOUTH SAW HAMILTON RIDING ALL OVER THE LINES IN AN ALMOST RECKLESS FRENZY.

I WILL STAY HERE WITH YOU, MY DEAR GENERAL, AND DIE WITH YOU!

LET US ALL DIE RATHER THAN RETREAT!!!

SHEER EXHAUSTION AND SEARING TEMPERATURES SOON DRAINED HAMILTON OF STAMINA.

ELSEWHERE ON THE BATTLEFIELD, LIEUTENANT COLONEL AARON BURR SUCCUMBED TO SUNSTROKE AND WAS SERIOUSLY ILL FOR WEEKS.

RALLY, MEN! RALLY TO YOUR--

SHLUNK!

CHARLES LEE WAS SWIFTLY DISCIPLINED FOR HIS RETREAT.

FUTURE PRESIDENT JAMES MONROE SERVED AS AIDE TO THE GENERAL IN CHARGE OF THE COURT-MARTIAL PROCEEDINGS.

LEE'S CONDUCT WITH RESPECT TO THE *COMMAND* OF THIS CORPS WAS *TRULY CHILDISH*.

THIS MAN IS EITHER A DRIVELER IN THE BUSINESS OF SOLDIERSHIP OR SOMETHING MUCH WORSE!

LEE TOOK HIS DEFENSE TO THE PUBLIC. HE LEVELED PUNCTURING CRITICISM AT WASHINGTON.

HAD A *PROPER* KNOWLEDGE OF THE THEATRE OF ACTION BEEN OBTAINED, AND A GENERAL PLAN OF ACTION *WISELY* CONCERTED...

...PERHAPS A DECISIVE BLOW MIGHT HAVE BEEN STRUCK!

75

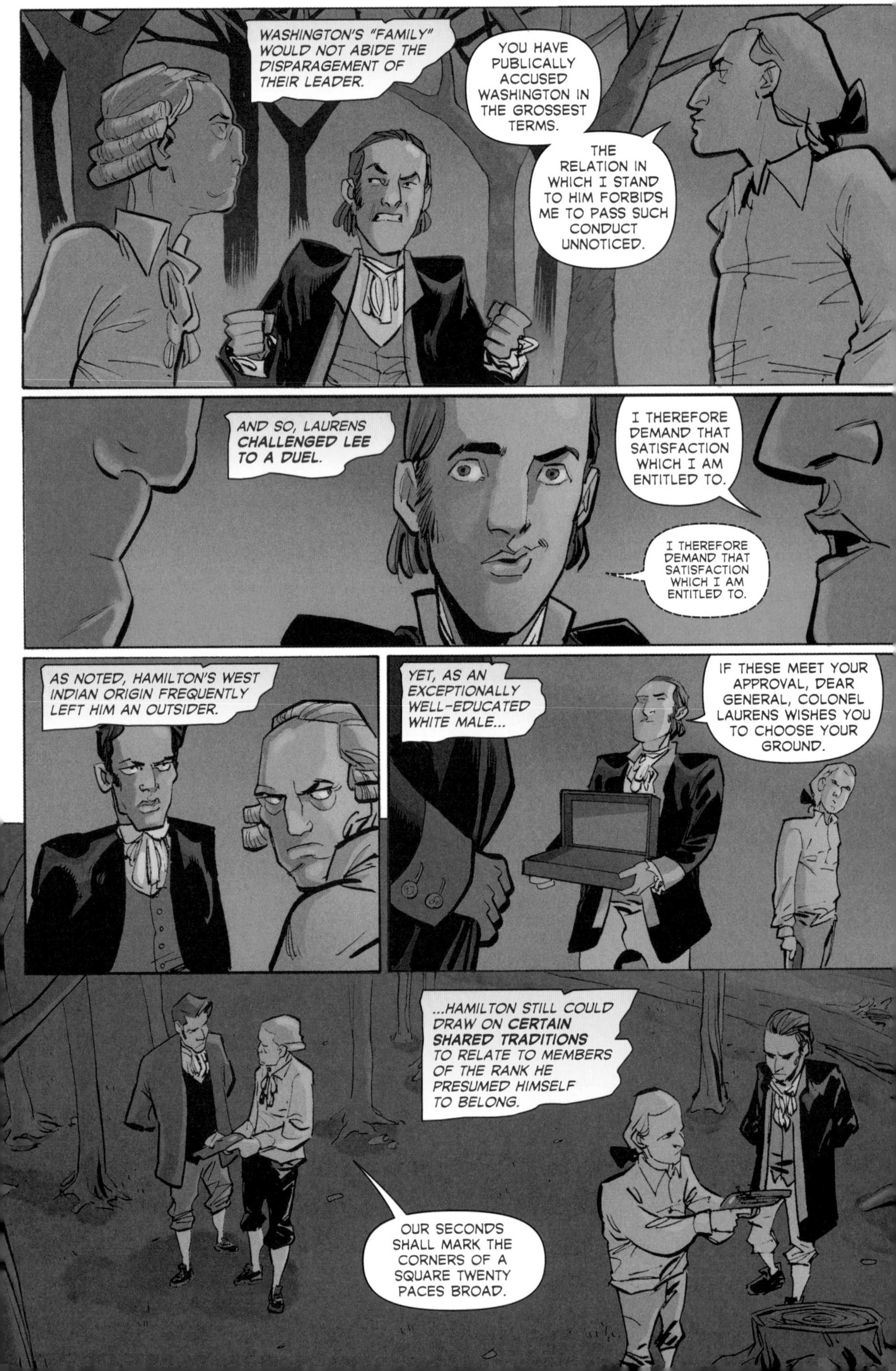
WASHINGTON'S "FAMILY" WOULD NOT ABIDE THE DISPARAGEMENT OF THEIR LEADER.
YOU HAVE PUBLICALLY ACCUSED WASHINGTON IN THE GROSSEST TERMS.
THE RELATION IN WHICH I STAND TO HIM FORBIDS ME TO PASS SUCH CONDUCT UNNOTICED.
AND SO, LAURENS CHALLENGED LEE TO A DUEL.
I THEREFORE DEMAND THAT SATISFACTION WHICH I AM ENTITLED TO.
I THEREFORE DEMAND THAT SATISFACTION WHICH I AM ENTITLED TO.
AS NOTED, HAMILTON'S WEST INDIAN ORIGIN FREQUENTLY LEFT HIM AN OUTSIDER.
YET, AS AN EXCEPTIONALLY WELL-EDUCATED WHITE MALE...
IF THESE MEET YOUR APPROVAL, DEAR GENERAL, COLONEL LAURENS WISHES YOU TO CHOOSE YOUR GROUND.
...HAMILTON STILL COULD DRAW ON CERTAIN SHARED TRADITIONS TO RELATE TO MEMBERS OF THE RANK HE PRESUMED HIMSELF TO BELONG.
OUR SECONDS SHALL MARK THE CORNERS OF A SQUARE TWENTY PACES BROAD.

EVEN THOUGH HAMILTON WAS BEREFT OF THE DEEP AMERICAN ROOTS OF AN ADAMS, JEFFERSON, OR WASHINGTON, AND EVEN THOUGH HE COULD SHARE IN NEITHER THE DISTINCTIVE IDENTITIES OF THE SOUTH NOR THE NORTH, HE COULD "SPEAK THE LANGUAGE" OF THE AMERICAN RULING ELITE BY INVOKING...

...CLASSICAL GREEK AND ROMAN HISTORY AND MYTH.

PHOCION

PUBLIUS

CINCINNATUS

PHILOSOPHY AND LITERATURE.

POPE

VON PUFENDO...

HUME

CHIVALRIC ROMANCE...

...AS SEEN IN HAMILTON'S POETRY AND LOVE LETTERS.

AND PERHAPS MOST IMPORTANT...

...NOTIONS OF GENTLEMANSHIP.

EVEN AS REVOLUTIONARY IDEAS WERE TAKING AIM AT THE PILLARS OF MONARCHY AND INHERITED STATUS...

AND I FURTHER PROPOSE, SIR...

...THAT WE ADVANCE UPON ONE ANOTHER AND FIRE AT THE TIME AND DISTANCE YOU THINK PROPER.

...THE MOVEMENT'S LEADERS KEPT UP THE OLD-WORLD BIFURCATION OF SOCIETY INTO "COMMON" AND "GENTLEMEN" CLASSES.

GENERAL LEE? YOU ARE, I TRUST, ACQUAINTED WITH THE MOTIVES THAT BROUGHT US HERE.

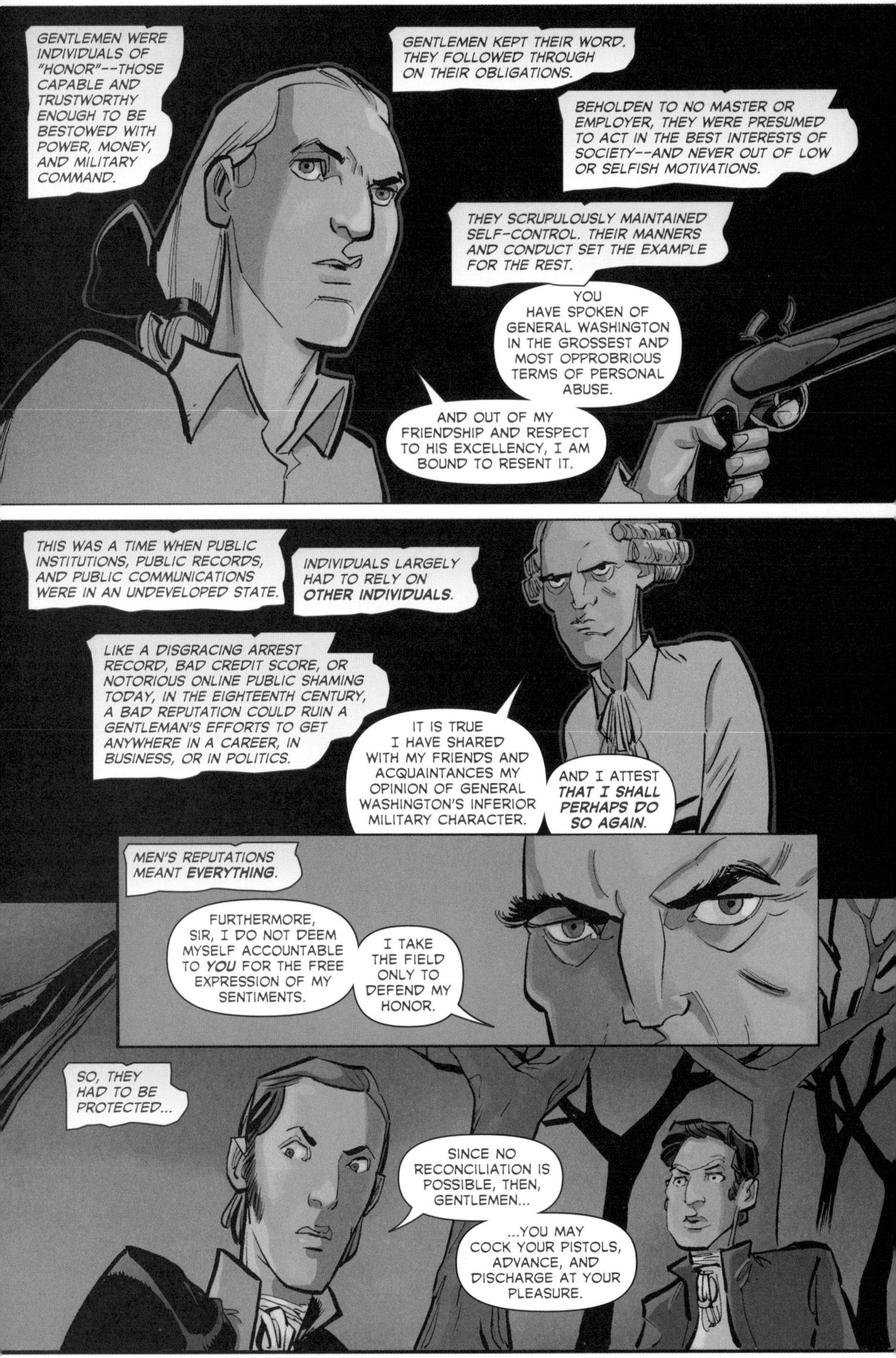
GENTLEMEN WERE INDIVIDUALS OF "HONOR"--THOSE CAPABLE AND TRUSTWORTHY ENOUGH TO BE BESTOWED WITH POWER, MONEY, AND MILITARY COMMAND.
GENTLEMEN KEPT THEIR WORD. THEY FOLLOWED THROUGH ON THEIR OBLIGATIONS.
BEHOLDEN TO NO MASTER OR EMPLOYER, THEY WERE PRESUMED TO ACT IN THE BEST INTERESTS OF SOCIETY--AND NEVER OUT OF LOW OR SELFISH MOTIVATIONS.
THEY SCRUPULOUSLY MAINTAINED SELF-CONTROL. THEIR MANNERS AND CONDUCT SET THE EXAMPLE FOR THE REST.
YOU HAVE SPOKEN OF GENERAL WASHINGTON IN THE GROSSEST AND MOST OPPROBRIOUS TERMS OF PERSONAL ABUSE.
AND OUT OF MY FRIENDSHIP AND RESPECT TO HIS EXCELLENCY, I AM BOUND TO RESENT IT.
THIS WAS A TIME WHEN PUBLIC INSTITUTIONS, PUBLIC RECORDS, AND PUBLIC COMMUNICATIONS WERE IN AN UNDEVELOPED STATE.
INDIVIDUALS LARGELY HAD TO RELY ON **OTHER INDIVIDUALS**.
LIKE A DISGRACING ARREST RECORD, BAD CREDIT SCORE, OR NOTORIOUS ONLINE PUBLIC SHAMING TODAY, IN THE EIGHTEENTH CENTURY, A BAD REPUTATION COULD RUIN A GENTLEMAN'S EFFORTS TO GET ANYWHERE IN A CAREER, IN BUSINESS, OR IN POLITICS.
IT IS TRUE I HAVE SHARED WITH MY FRIENDS AND ACQUAINTANCES MY OPINION OF GENERAL WASHINGTON'S INFERIOR MILITARY CHARACTER.
AND I ATTEST ***THAT I SHALL PERHAPS DO SO AGAIN.***
MEN'S REPUTATIONS MEANT **EVERYTHING**.
FURTHERMORE, SIR, I DO NOT DEEM MYSELF ACCOUNTABLE TO ***YOU*** FOR THE FREE EXPRESSION OF MY SENTIMENTS.
I TAKE THE FIELD ONLY TO DEFEND MY HONOR.
SO, THEY HAD TO BE PROTECTED...
SINCE NO RECONCILIATION IS POSSIBLE, THEN, GENTLEMEN...
...YOU MAY COCK YOUR PISTOLS, ADVANCE, AND DISCHARGE AT YOUR PLEASURE.

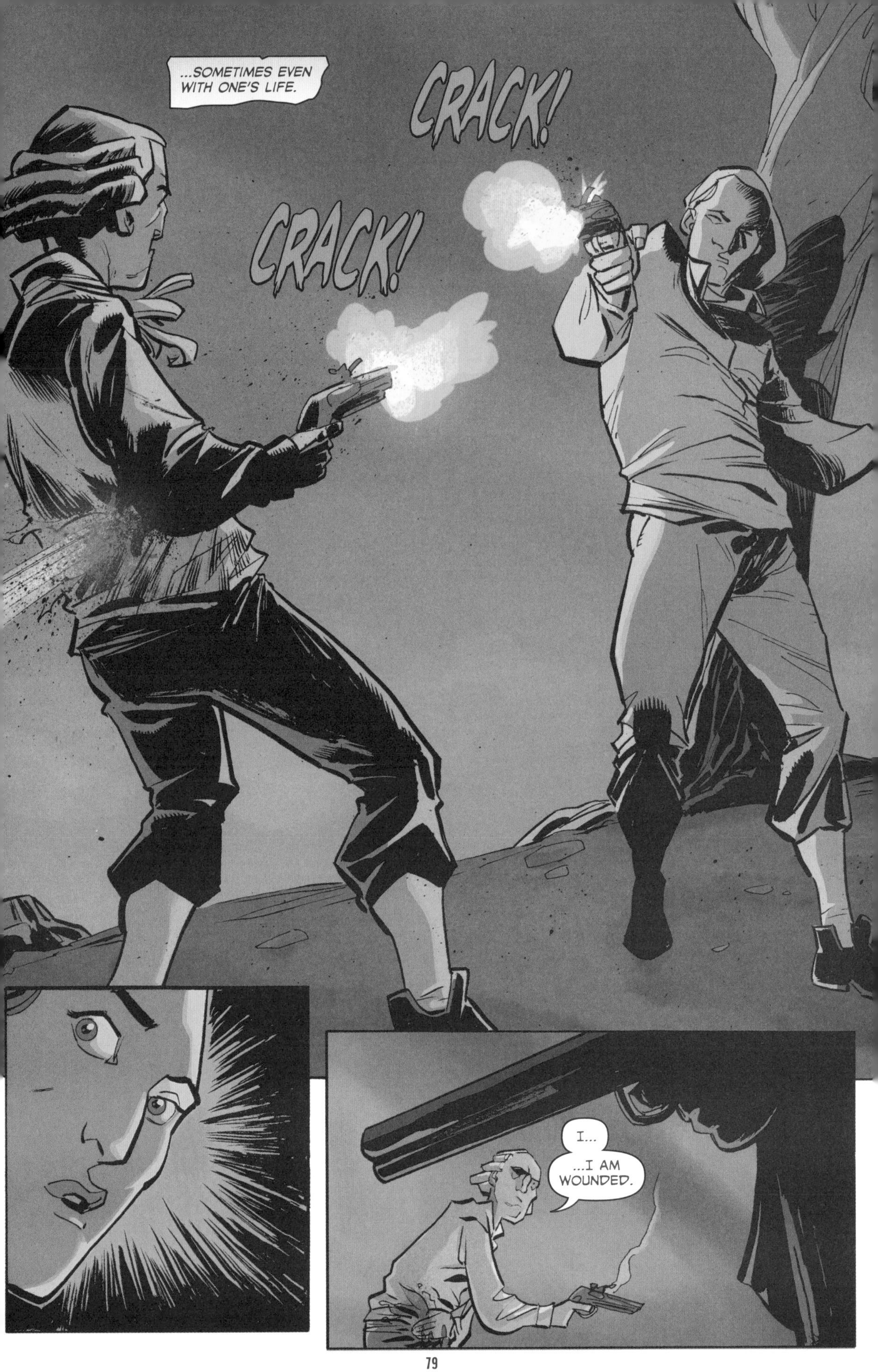
...SOMETIMES EVEN WITH ONE'S LIFE.
CRACK!
CRACK!
I...
...I AM WOUNDED.

ONE'S STANDING AS A GENTLEMAN WAS ALMOST LIKE A **TANGIBLE PIECE OF PROPERTY**--SOMETHING ONE OWNED AND DEPENDED ON TO MAKE A LIVING.

DAMAGED OR DIMINISHED, A HARMFUL LOSS WOULD ENSUE FOR THE OWNER OF THE REPUTATION.

YET YOU COULD NOT BUY INSURANCE TO SAFEGUARD SUCH A VALUABLE ASSET, AND NO COURT EXISTED TO SUE SOMEONE OVER SUCH A THING.

SO, DUELING EXISTED AS A HIGHLY FORMAL, **CHOREOGRAPHED, QUASI-LEGAL RITUAL** WHERE REPUTATIONS COULD, IN A WAY, BE PUT ON TRIAL.

≷GASP!≸ GENERAL--!

NEVER MIND.

THE INJURY IS INCONSIDERABLE. LESS ≷COUGH≸ THAN I IMAGINED AT THE FIRST STROKE OF THE BALL.

IT WAS A CONTEST FOR **GENTLEMEN** ONLY. YEOMEN AND KNAVES WERE NOT WELCOME TO PARTICIPATE-- OR SERVE, LIKE HAMILTON, AS ONE PARTY'S "SECOND."

HISTORIAN DR. JOANNE B. FREEMAN PUT IT IN THE FOLLOWING TERMS:

"DUELS WERE DEMONSTRATIONS OF MANNER, *NOT* MARKSMANSHIP.

"THEY WERE INTRICATE GAMES OF DARE AND COUNTERDARE, RITUALIZED DISPLAYS OF BRAVERY, MILITARY PROWESS, AND--ABOVE ALL-- WILLINGNESS TO SACRIFICE ONE'S LIFE FOR ONE'S HONOR."

DUELISTS SELDOM DIED. IN FACT, IT WOULD MOST OFTEN BE A **SCANDAL** IF ONE WERE TO BE KILLED BY THE OTHER.

DOES THE GENERAL HARBOR PERSONAL ENMITY TOWARD MY MAN? IS *THAT* WHY HE WISHES TO CONTINUE?

NO, NO. WE MUST AT ALL HAZARDS CONVINCE THEM TO END THIS.

I WISH TO PROCEED WITH A SECOND EXCHANGE OF FIRE.

DOES THE COLONEL CONCUR?

BUT IF BOTH MEN IN AN "AFFAIR OF HONOR" SHOWED UP AND PLAYED THEIR ROLES SATISFACTORILY...

WELL? DOES THE COLONEL WISH TO RENEW THE COMBAT?

I DO!

PLEASE, GENTLEMEN. LET US DISCUSS ALTERNATIVES.

...BOTH CHALLENGER AND CHALLENGED EMERGED WITH THEIR REPUTATIONS INTACT.

SO, DO YOU CONSENT, SIR, TO TERMINATING THE TRANSACTION AS IT STANDS?

I AM WILLING TO COMPLY.

SO BE IT. IT CONCLUDES.

THERE COULD EVEN BE A REWARD IN ENDURING A DUEL, FOR ALL INVOLVED WOULD HAVE BOTH REAFFIRMED AND RENEWED THEIR CREDENTIALS AS GENTLEMEN...

...UNLESS, THAT IS, SOME FLAW IN THE DUEL INVALIDATED ITS AUTHENTICITY.

WHEN AARON BURR HEARD OF THE LEE–LAURENS AFFAIR, HE DISMISSED IT AS IDIOCY THAT "ABUSED COMMON SENSE."

HAD LEE EVER ATTACKED LAURENS'S HONOR? NO. SO LAURENS HAD NO STANDING FOR A CHALLENGE.

≷SNICKER≷

THIS WAS HOTHEADED SOLDIER BOYS PLAYING AT GENTILITY AND POLISH.

NOT THE CONDUCT OF THE TRULY WELL-BRED. LIKE AARON BURR.

Amidst My Amorous Transports

BY NOW, WASHINGTON'S ARMY WAS FIGHTING THE ENEMY AS EQUALS, MORE THAN EVER BEFORE...

...SO THE BRITISH SHIFTED STRATEGY TO THE SOUTH.

THERE THEY COULD *FREE THE SLAVES* AND *TURN THEM AGAINST* THEIR "MASTERS."

GENERAL SIR HENRY CLINTON, 1779.

I DO PROMISE TO EVERY NEGRO WHO SHALL DESERT THE REBEL STANDARD, FULL SECURITY TO FOLLOW WITHIN THESE LINES ANY OCCUPATION WHICH HE SHALL THINK PROPER.

OUTLIERS FOR THEIR DAY, HAMILTON AND LAURENS NOT ONLY OPPOSED SLAVERY, BUT ALSO HAD ATTITUDES HARKENING TOWARD RACIAL EQUALITY.

[SLAVERY IS] FATAL TO RELIGION AND MORALITY. IT RELAXES THE SINEWS OF INDUSTRY, CLIPS THE WINGS OF COMMERCE, AND INTRODUCES MISERY AND INDIGENCE.

NEGROES' NATURAL FACULTIES ARE PROBABLY AS GOOD AS OURS.

JOHN LAURENS RETURNED HOME TO CONVINCE SOUTH CAROLINA TO LET BLACKS JOIN THE ARMY IN EXCHANGE FOR FREEDOM.

BUT THE GOVERNOR LITERALLY PREFERRED SURRENDER TO ARMING SLAVES.

HAMILTON TRIED TO JOIN THE MAN HE HAD LEARNED TO LOVE. WASHINGTON DENIED HIM PERMISSION.

LONELINESS, HOWEVER, WOULD NOT LAST FOR LONG.

"IN SHORT LAURENS, I AM DISGUSTED WITH EVERY THING IN THIS WORLD BUT YOURSELF AND VERY FEW MORE HONEST FELLOWS."

THAT WINTER WAS ONE OF THE COLDEST OF THE CENTURY. FOR WASHINGTON'S ARMY, IT WAS ANOTHER VALLEY FORGE--IF NOT WORSE.

YET THEIR QUARTERS IN MORRISTOWN, NEW JERSEY, WERE LIVENED UP WITH "DANCING ASSEMBLIES"...

...WHICH GAVE OFFICERS AND LADIES A CHANCE TO SOCIALIZE.

ELIZABETH SCHUYLER--WHOM HAMILTON MAY HAVE REMEMBERED FROM YEARS BEFORE--VISITED CAMP IN EARLY FEBRUARY 1780.

HAMILTON, RENOWNED IN WASHINGTON'S "FAMILY" FOR ATTRACTING (AND BEING ATTRACTED TO) YOUNG WOMEN WHEREVER THE ARMY TRAVELED...

...HAD LATELY BEEN MUSING ABOUT LANDING A WIFE.

ELIZABETH WAS A YOUNG WOMAN OF MODESTY, OBEDIENCE, AND FAITH--ESPECIALLY COMPARED TO SEVERAL OF HER SIBLINGS WHO HAD ALL ELOPED AGAINST THEIR PARENTS' WISHES.

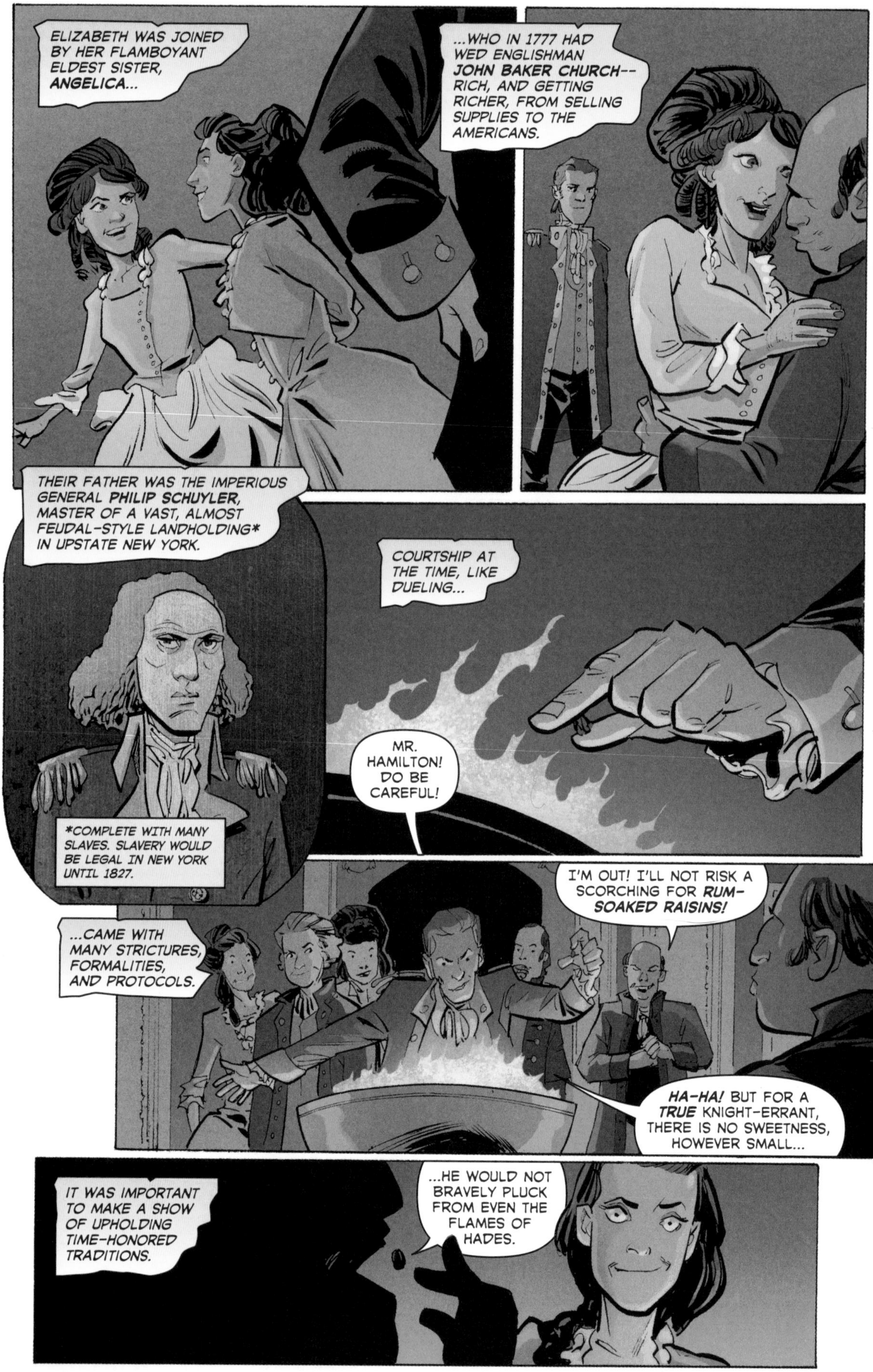
ELIZABETH WAS JOINED BY HER FLAMBOYANT ELDEST SISTER, ANGELICA...
...WHO IN 1777 HAD WED ENGLISHMAN JOHN BAKER CHURCH--RICH, AND GETTING RICHER, FROM SELLING SUPPLIES TO THE AMERICANS.
THEIR FATHER WAS THE IMPERIOUS GENERAL PHILIP SCHUYLER, MASTER OF A VAST, ALMOST FEUDAL-STYLE LANDHOLDING* IN UPSTATE NEW YORK.
*COMPLETE WITH MANY SLAVES. SLAVERY WOULD BE LEGAL IN NEW YORK UNTIL 1827.
COURTSHIP AT THE TIME, LIKE DUELING...
MR. HAMILTON! DO BE CAREFUL!
...CAME WITH MANY STRICTURES, FORMALITIES, AND PROTOCOLS.
I'M OUT! I'LL NOT RISK A SCORCHING FOR RUM-SOAKED RAISINS!
HA-HA! BUT FOR A TRUE KNIGHT-ERRANT, THERE IS NO SWEETNESS, HOWEVER SMALL...
IT WAS IMPORTANT TO MAKE A SHOW OF UPHOLDING TIME-HONORED TRADITIONS.
...HE WOULD NOT BRAVELY PLUCK FROM EVEN THE FLAMES OF HADES.

IT IS CLEAR ELIZABETH STRUCK HAMILTON...

...AS AN EXCELLENT ROMANTIC PROSPECT FOR SUPERFICIAL AS WELL AS HEARTFELT REASONS.

THOUGH MANY COUPLES HOPED TO FIND LOVE...

...MARRIAGE STILL LARGELY RETAINED ITS ANCIENT AFFILIATION WITH WEALTH, SOCIAL POSITION, AND POLITICAL ADVANTAGE.

HAMILTON COULD ONLY HAVE BEEN QUEASY ABOUT HIS BACKGROUND AND IMPOVERISHED STATE. YET ELIZABETH'S FAMILY WAS--AND WOULD STAY--TAKEN BY HIM.

HAMILTON PROPOSED TO ELIZABETH SCHUYLER WITHIN SEVEN WEEKS OF THEIR MEETING. BUT NUPTIALS WOULD HAVE TO WORK AROUND THE WAR'S SCHEDULE.

LOVE OFFERED WHAT CONSOLATION IT COULD WHEN OMENS OF RUIN AND DISASTER CAST A PALL ON ALL ELSE.

YOUR EXCELLENCY--?

CHARLESTON.

THAT DAMNED CORNWALLIS HAS TAKEN CHARLESTON.

Those Solid Arrangements of Finance, on Which Our Safety Depends

HAMILTON, TOO, WAS NEARLY AT THE END OF HIS EMOTIONAL ROPE.

I HATE THE ARMY. I HATE THE WORLD. I HATE MYSELF. THE WHOLE IS A MASS OF FOOLS AND KNAVES.

WASHINGTON--COPING WITH DISEASE, DEFEATS, BACK-STABBING RIVALS, AND UNFULFILLED PROMISES OF POLITICIANS--HAD STILL CREATED A LOYAL ARMY THAT COULD FIGHT.

YET NOW HE COULD ONLY STAND IN AWE OF THE ROBUSTNESS OF HIS OPPONENT.

IN LARGE PART IT CAME DOWN TO WHAT AMERICA WAS STRAPPED FOR, BUT THE MOTHER COUNTRY HAD IN SPADES--MONEY...

...AND THE MEANS TO GET *MORE* VIA TAXES AND HIGH FINANCE.

"IN MODERN WARS THE LONGEST PURSE MUST CHIEFLY DETERMINE THE EVENT.

"[GREAT BRITAIN'S] SYSTEM OF PUBLIC CREDIT IS SUCH, THAT IT IS CAPABLE OF GREATER EXERTIONS THAN THAT OF ANY OTHER NATION."

THE GOVERNMENT'S FINANCIAL IMPOTENCE AND INCOMPETENCE WERE ALSO SCARRING HAMILTON MORE DEEPLY BY THE DAY.

[THIS] IS NOW A *MOB*, RATHER THAN AN ARMY, WITHOUT *CLOTHING*, WITHOUT *PAY*, WITHOUT *PROVISION*, WITHOUT *MORALS*, WITHOUT *DISCIPLINE*.

WE BEGIN TO HATE THE COUNTRY FOR ITS NEGLECT OF US.

THE FUNDAMENTAL DEFECT IS A WANT OF POWER IN CONGRESS.

THESE TEN WORDS ARE ESSENTIALLY THE BATTLE CRY HAMILTON WOULD BE ECHOING FOR THE REST OF HIS LIFE.

EVEN AT LOW POINTS, WHEN **MUTINY** AND **DISUNION** SEEMED THREATENING, HE TURNED NOT TO SPASMS OF IMPULSIVE ACTION, BUT TO STUDY, DEBATE, DEEP THOUGHT, AND CORRESPONDENCE.

THOUGH HE LONGED FOR PERSONAL MILITARY GLORY...

...HE WAS SAVVY AND FORESIGHTED ENOUGH TO SEE THAT ONLY FEATS OF ECONOMICS AND ADMINISTRATIVE ORGANIZATION COULD SECURE AMERICA'S CAUSE.

THE UNIVERSAL DICTIONARY OF TRADE and COMMERCE

Monfieur SAVARY, INSPECTOR-GENERAL in the MANUFACTURE

NAVIGATION

HAMILTON'S FIRST GLIMPSES OF THE ADULT WORLD HAD BEEN THROUGH THE WINDOW OF INTERNATIONAL COMMERCE.

AND THIS MERE MILITARY AIDE HAD THE AUDACITY TO THINK THAT IF **HE** DIDN'T EXPAND ON WHAT HE KNEW AND TAKE ACTION, MAYBE NO ONE WOULD.

WE MUST CREATE ARTIFICIAL REVENUES, OR BORROW. [FRANCE] CAN ASSIST US, EITHER BY LENDING US HERSELF OR BY INFLUENCING SPAIN.

TO ERECT A BANK ON THE JOINT CREDIT OF THE PUBLIC AND OF INDIVIDUALS IS OF SO MUCH IMPORTANCE THAT THE EXPERIMENT OUGHT TO BE FULLY TRIED.

JAMES DUANE, CONGRESSMAN FROM NEW YORK AND FUTURE NEW YORK CITY MAYOR.

87

A Scene of Blackest Treason

HAMILTON WAS JUST ONE AMONG LEGIONS WHO HOPED WAR WOULD OVERCOME HUMBLE CIRCUMSTANCES AND CATAPULT THEM TO WITHIN REACH OF GREATNESS.

BUT NOT ALL WOULD SO DOGGEDLY PURSUE HAMILTON'S HIGH-MINDED STATECRAFT, AS THE WORLD WAS ABOUT TO SEE.

THE ROUT OF HIS DARING BID TO LIBERATE CANADA WAS NOT THE ONLY DISAPPOINTMENT BENEDICT ARNOLD SUSTAINED IN THE WAR.

ARNOLD AT THE BATTLE OF RIDGEFIELD, 1777.

DESPITE LEGENDARY BRAVERY AT SARATOGA AND OTHER ENGAGEMENTS, THIS MAN OF STRATOSPHERIC ASPIRATIONS HAD BEEN REPEATEDLY PASSED OVER FOR PROMOTION TO MAJOR GENERAL.

RAVENOUS FOR SOCIAL AS WELL AS MILITARY DISTINCTION, HE HAD MARRIED MARGARET "PEGGY" SHIPPEN--A FAMOUS BEAUTY OF WEALTHY PHILADELPHIA TORY STOCK.

ALREADY WITH A PASSION FOR LUXURIES, HIS MARRIAGE LEFT ARNOLD GOUGED WITH DEBT.

IN SEPTEMBER 1780, WASHINGTON WAS HEADING TO INSPECT WEST POINT--A FORT BEING ERECTED ON THE HUDSON RIVER UNDER ARNOLD'S SUPERVISION.

HAMILTON AND THE OTHER AIDES WERE HOTLY ANTICIPATING THE COMPANY OF THE RAVISHING PEGGY.

WHAT HAMILTON'S PARTY DIDN'T KNOW WAS THAT *THE ARNOLDS HAD SECRETLY SWITCHED SIDES.*

IN EXCHANGE FOR A FORTUNE IN SILVER, THE COUPLE CONSPIRED TO *SURRENDER WEST POINT TO THE BRITISH*--AND, POSSIBLY, HELP THEM KIDNAP GEORGE WASHINGTON.

LUCKILY, JUST BEFORE HAMILTON ARRIVED AT THE FORT, A BRITISH GO-BETWEEN HAD BEEN CAPTURED.

THE PLOT BEGAN TO UNRAVEL.

AND WHAT HAVE WE HERE?

WHEN THE RATTLING NEWS REACHED THEM, HAMILTON WAS DISPATCHED ON A DESPERATE RACE TO CAPTURE ARNOLD.

BUT HAMILTON WAS TOO LATE. THE TRAITOR HAD FLED TO THE WELCOMING ARMS OF BRITISH-OCCUPIED NEW YORK CITY.

ARNOLD HAS BETRAYED US!

WHOM CAN WE TRUST NOW?!

PEGGY BEGUILED HAMILTON BY RAVING LIKE A MADWOMAN, LEVERAGING THE TIME'S OVERSENTIMENTALIZED VIEW OF FEMININITY TO HER ADVANTAGE.

?!??!

THE SPIRITS HAVE TAKEN MY HUSBAND!

THEY HAVE PUT HOT IRONS IN HIS HEAD!

PEGGY'S THEATRICS BOUGHT HER THE RELIEF OF BEING SENT HOME TO HER FATHER.

EN ROUTE, SHE STOPPED AT *THE HERMITAGE*-- THE NEW JERSEY MANSION OF A BRITISH OFFICER'S WIFE AND SOCIALITE STRADDLING BOTH SIDES OF THE WAR.

ACCORDING TO SOME ACCOUNTS, PEGGY DROPPED HER CHARADE AND CONFESSED ALL TO WHOM SHE THOUGHT WAS ANOTHER LOYALIST--WOMAN OF THE HOUSE *THEODOSIA PREVOST.*

THEODOSIA HAD FOR SOME TIME BEEN CONDUCTING A DALLIANCE WITH AARON BURR.

IN LESS THAN TWO YEARS, HER ENGLISH HUSBAND WAS DEAD. SHE MARRIED BURR. IN 1783 THEY HAD A DAUGHTER, ALSO NAMED THEODOSIA.

BURR LEFT THE MILITARY BEFORE WAR'S END AND BEGAN WORKING AS A LAWYER IN ALBANY, NEW YORK.

THIS WOULD TRACK QUITE CLOSELY WITH THE CAREER PATH HAMILTON WOULD TAKE AFTER MARRYING ELIZABETH SCHUYLER ON DECEMBER 14, 1780.

A BLISSFUL RESPITE OF SEVERAL WEEKS AT THE SCHUYLER MANSION NEAR ALBANY THAT WINTER BROUGHT HAMILTON INTO THE COZY FOLD OF DOMESTIC LIFE HE HAD PROBABLY NEVER KNOWN.

BUT THE WAR WAS NOT OVER YET FOR HIM OR FOR AMERICA .

AND IF THERE WAS JOY IN BEING MADE A PART OF ONE FAMILY, THERE WAS A DISCORDANT BLOWUP IN LEAVING ANOTHER.

In the Enthusiasm of Heroic Valor

COLONEL HAMILTON! YOU HAVE KEPT ME WAITING AT THE HEAD OF THE STAIRS THESE TEN MINUTES!

ON FEBRUARY 6, 1781, GEORGE WASHINGTON AGAIN LET LOOSE THE FIERY TEMPER HE USUALLY HID FROM THE PUBLIC.

THE GENERAL'S BURNED-OUT AIDE HAD HAD ENOUGH. HE TOLD WASHINGTON HE WOULD QUIT.

I MUST TELL YOU, SIR! YOU TREAT ME WITH DISRESPECT!

I AM NOT CONSCIOUS OF *EVER* FAVORING YOU IN SUCH A MANNER, SIR.

BUT SINCE YOU HAVE THOUGHT IT NECESSARY TO ACCUSE ME, I MUST NOW PART FROM YOUR SERVICE.

VERY WELL, SIR!

SWOOSH

HAMILTON BEGRUDGINGLY KEPT UP HIS OFFICIAL DUTIES FOR A TIME AFTER THIS BLOWOUT.

BECAUSE THE FOCUS OF THE WAR REMAINED FAR TO THE SOUTH, AND FRENCH MILITARY AID WAS SO *ERRATIC*, THOSE MONTHS WERE AN AGGRAVATING GRIND.

HAMILTON DID FINALLY MAKE GOOD ON HIS THREAT TO RESIGN. BUT EVENTUALLY HE BEGAN WRITING HIS OLD BOSS FROM ALBANY, PESTERING THE GENERAL TO ASSIGN HIM A FIELD COMMAND.

"IT IS BECOME NECESSARY TO ME TO APPLY TO YOUR EXCELLENCY TO KNOW IN WHAT MANNER YOU FORESEE YOU WILL BE ABLE TO EMPLOY ME.

"UNCONNECTED AS I AM WITH ANY REGIMENT, I CAN HAVE NO OTHER COMMAND THAN IN A LIGHT CORPS."

WITH WHAT WOULD HAVE CHILLING CONSEQUENCES FOR THEM, THE BRITISH BEGAN TO HEAVILY INVEST ITS FORCES IN AMERICA'S RICHEST AND MOST POPULOUS STATE, VIRGINIA.

GENERAL *CHARLES CORNWALLIS*

FIRST, BENEDICT ARNOLD, LEADING LOYALISTS, BRITISH, AND HESSIANS, CONDUCTED A PUNISHING RAID.

HE TAUNTED THEN-GOVERNOR THOMAS JEFFERSON AND BURNED THE CAPITAL, RICHMOND, TO CINDERS.

AFTER A SUBSEQUENT RAMPAGE THROUGH THE STATE...

...CORNWALLIS DECIDED TO REST HIS TROOPS ON A PENINSULA ON THE SEABOARD. BY STICKING CLOSE TO WATERWAYS, THE GENERAL'S AIM WAS TO KEEP IN CLOSE TOUCH WITH NEW YORK CITY.

BUT HE HAD INADVERTENTLY **WALKED RIGHT INTO A TRAP.**

WASHINGTON HEARD OF CORNWALLIS'S BLUNDER FROM LAFAYETTE--NOW A GENERAL SENT TO DEFEND THE SOUTH.

SCURRYING TO TAKE ADVANTAGE, WASHINGTON HELPED COORDINATE A COLOSSAL MILITARY MANEUVER. AMERICAN TROOPS HAD TO QUICKLY AND DISCREETLY REPOSITION HUNDREDS OF MILES SOUTH TO YORKTOWN, VIRGINIA, AND RENDEZVOUS WITH A FRENCH FLEET SAILING UP FROM THE CARIBBEAN.

HAMILTON WAS FINALLY ASSIGNED A COMMAND HE COULD SETTLE FOR-- **A BATTALION OF HIS OWN.** HE JOINED THE RUSH DOWN THE COAST.

"A PART OF THE ARMY MY DEAR GIRL IS GOING TO VIRGINIA, AND I MUST OF NECESSITY BE SEPARATED AT A MUCH GREATER DISTANCE FROM MY BELOVED WIFE."

HAMILTON'S MISSIVES TO ELIZABETH BECAME PARTICULARLY GENTLE AND ATTENTIVE.

AFTER ALL, SHE WAS PREGNANT.

"REMEMBER THAT NOT ONLY YOUR OWN HEALTH, BUT PERHAPS THE EXISTENCE OF OUR BABE DEPENDS UPON THE TRANQUILITY OF YOUR MIND.

"ANY ACCIDENT WOULD AFFLICT ME MORE THAN I CAN TELL YOU."

BY LATE SEPTEMBER, GROUND FORCES HAD SUCCESSFULLY CUT CORNWALLIS OFF FROM THE INTERIOR--AND SHIPS HAD SEVERED HIS ACCESS TO THE SEA.

CORNWALLIS, WITH NO ESCAPE, HAD BEGUN TO DIG IN AND FORTIFY.

THE AMERICANS HAD DONE BEST ADAPTING THE INDIAN-STYLE GUERRILLA WARFARE WASHINGTON HAD SEEN IN THE 1750s. BUT THIS WOULD BE A CLASSIC SIEGE OPERATION...

...WHICH CALLED FOR EUROPEAN EXPERTISE.

LEAVE THIS TO US, MON CHER GÉNÉRAL.

SAPPERS AND ENGINEERS DUG TRENCHES CALLED PARALLELS EVER CLOSER TO THE ENEMY, ALLOWING ARTILLERY AND TROOPS TO CREEP WITHIN RANGE.

SH-FOOM!

BOOOM!

SSSSS

BUT BEFORE THE MAIN FORT COULD BE ATTACKED, TWO OUTLYING GUARDHOUSES, OR **REDOUBTS**, WOULD HAVE TO BE STORMED.

LAFAYETTE HAD COMMAND OF THE MISSION. HE PLANNED TO PLACE HIS OWN FORMER AIDE AT THE HEAD OF THE CHARGE.

HAMILTON WAS INCENSED. HIS LAST CHANCE FOR THE KIND OF LEGITIMATE BATTLEFIELD VALOR THAT WOULD PAY DIVIDENDS FOR DECADES WAS GOING UP IN SMOKE.

BUT HAMILTON, YOU HAVE NEVER LED INFANTRY! GIMAT IS THE MAN FOR THIS!

I SHALL APPEAL TO HEADQUARTERS!

DESPITE THEIR ROCKY PARTING OF WAYS, HAMILTON'S RECORD OF SERVING WASHINGTON HAD BEEN SPOTLESS.

THE COMMANDER IN CHIEF ULTIMATELY HONORED THE REQUEST.

WE HAVE IT! WE HAVE IT!

SO, ON THE NIGHT OF OCTOBER 14, 1781...

MAKE READY UPON THE SIGNAL.

AND REMEMBER: **NO SOUND.** WE SHALL NOT PROVOKE A FULL CONFRONTATION WITHOUT CAUSE. BAYONETS AND HAND WEAPONS ONLY!

...HAMILTON PERSONALLY LED THE MEN ON A GO-FOR-BROKE, QUARTER-MILE DASH INTO THE FACE OF THE ENEMY.

THIS WAS VICIOUS, INTIMATE, HAND-TO-HAND FIGHTING.

BUT IN TEN MINUTES, IT WAS OVER.

WAP!

K-TFFF!

HYEAH!!!

UNGHH!!

HRARRRHH!

AAAGGGHH!!

GASP!

HAMILTON HAD MADE IT HAPPEN.

MILITARY TRADITION, HOWEVER, RESERVED THE LION'S SHARE OF OFFICIAL CREDIT FOR SUCH OPERATIONS TO THEIR COMMANDING OFFICERS-- IN THIS CASE, LAFAYETTE.

≋PANT≋ ≋PANT≋ ≋PANT≋

THE REDOUBTS SECURED, THE PARALLELS WERE DUG EVEN CLOSER. FRENCH AND AMERICAN CANNONS PUMMELED AWAY.

CORNWALLIS WAS LIKE A MAN WITH A SWORD TO HIS NECK. HIS PLEAS TO TALK SURRENDER BEGAN LESS THAN FORTY-EIGHT HOURS LATER.

THE KING VOWED TO PRESS ON AFTER BRITAIN'S AGONIZING LOSS AT YORKTOWN, BUT NEITHER PARLIAMENT NOR THE PEOPLE WOULD PUT UP WITH FURTHER SQUANDERING OF LIVES AND MONEY.

OH, GOD! IT'S ALL OVER!

THE EXPENSE OF [THIS WAR] HAS BEEN ENORMOUS. FAR BEYOND ANY FORMER EXPERIENCE.

AND YET WHAT HAS THE BRITISH NATION RECEIVED IN RETURN? NOTHING BUT A SERIES OF *INEFFECTIVE VICTORIES* OR *SEVERE DEFEATS!*

PRIME MINISTER LORD NORTH.

WILLIAM PITT (THE YOUNGER).

HAMILTON SAVORED THE MOMENT, BUT NOT FOR LONG. HE WALKED AWAY FROM HIS BATTALION JUST DAYS LATER.

KLACK!

HE BID GOOD-BYE TO LAFAYETTE.

LAFAYETTE WOULD SAIL HOME TO WORK THE ONGOING DIPLOMATIC FRONT WITH JOHN ADAMS AND THOMAS JEFFERSON.

THE WAR BOTH WAS AND WASN'T OVER. CLASHES--LAST-DITCH EFFORTS BY THE BELLIGERENTS TO STRENGTHEN THEIR SIDES AT PEACE TALKS--CONTINUED, ESPECIALLY IN THE SOUTH.

HAMILTON'S DEAR FRIEND JOHN LAURENS WOULD DIE IN ONE OF THESE CLASHES IN AUGUST 1782.

P-T-T-TFF!

LAURENS'S FATHER SHARED HIS SON'S ABOLITIONIST LEANINGS.

NEVERTHELESS, AS A SOUTH CAROLINA ENVOY TO NEGOTIATE A TREATY WITH BRITAIN, HENRY LAURENS WAS TASKED WITH INSISTING THAT THE BRITISH *LEAVE BEHIND THE REST OF THE SLAVES* THEY HAD FREED.

THE SOUTH FURTHER DEMANDED FINANCIAL RESTITUTION FOR ALL SUCH "PROPERTY" LOST IN THE WAR.

WASHINGTON WOULD SOON LEARN THAT THE WAR HAD TEMPTED FOUR OF HIS OWN SLAVES TO FREEDOM.

The Universal Reluctance of These States to Do What Is Right

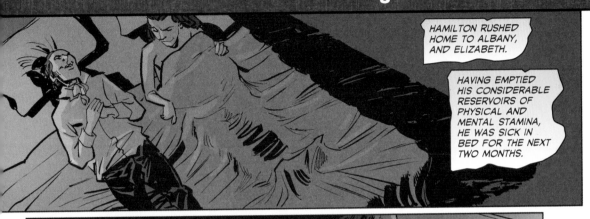

HAMILTON RUSHED HOME TO ALBANY, AND ELIZABETH.

HAVING EMPTIED HIS CONSIDERABLE RESERVOIRS OF PHYSICAL AND MENTAL STAMINA, HE WAS SICK IN BED FOR THE NEXT TWO MONTHS.

THE ARRIVAL OF A SON—PHILIP—IN JANUARY 1782, MUST HAVE REMINDED HIM THAT, FOR ALL HIS PRETENSIONS TO BE ABOVE GRUBBING AFTER MONEY, HAMILTON COULD NOT RELY FOREVER ON THE INDULGENCES OF HIS FATHER-IN-LAW.

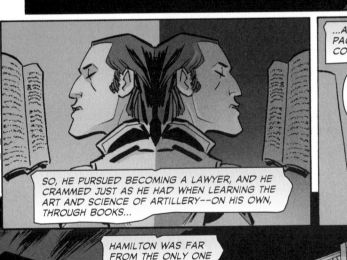

SO, HE PURSUED BECOMING A LAWYER, AND HE CRAMMED JUST AS HE HAD WHEN LEARNING THE ART AND SCIENCE OF ARTILLERY—ON HIS OWN, THROUGH BOOKS...

...AND AT A SPRINTER'S PACE NO MERE MORTAL COULD RIVAL.

I HAVE BEEN EMPLOYED FOR THE LAST TEN MONTHS IN...STUDYING THE ART OF FLEECING MY NEIGHBORS.

HAMILTON WAS FAR FROM THE ONLY ONE WITH BILLS TO PAY.

CONGRESS SCOUNDRELS! SETTLE YOUR ACCOUNTS!

WE DON'T ACCEPT YOUR FURLOUGHS!

WE *SHALL* PROCURE OUR PAY!

...OUR PAY!!

...AND JUSTICE!

AMERICA'S UNLIKELY VICTORY--WINNING INDEPENDENCE FROM ONE OF HISTORY'S MOST POWERFUL (AND STILL ASCENDANT) EMPIRES--STRUCK MANY AS PROVIDENTIAL, THE HANDIWORK OF RIGHTEOUS DIVINE WILL.

WASHINGTON EMERGED ALMOST WITH THE STATUS OF A DEMIGOD.

WHEN WE CONSIDER THE MAGNITUDE OF THE PRIZE WE CONTENDED FOR, THE DOUBTFUL NATURE OF THE CONTEST, AND THE FAVORABLE MANNER IN WHICH IT HAS TERMINATED...

...WE SHALL FIND THE GREATEST POSSIBLE REASON FOR GRATITUDE AND REJOICING.

THE UNITED STATES [HAS COME] INTO EXISTENCE AS A NATION...

...AND IF THEIR CITIZENS SHOULD NOT BE COMPLETELY FREE AND HAPPY, THE FAULT WILL BE ENTIRELY THEIR OWN.

BUT THE EUPHORIA THAT REIGNED IMMEDIATELY AFTER THE WAR QUITE QUICKLY BEGAN TO GIVE WAY TO DISORDER.

NEW LONDON, CONNECTICUT-- AMONG THE "FIRELANDS" BURNED BY BENEDICT ARNOLD IN 1781.

THOUGH HE HAD VOUCHED NO INTEREST IN PUBLIC LIFE, HAMILTON WAS GRATIFIED WHEN NEW YORK APPOINTED HIM TO CONGRESS IN 1782.

BUT SO FEEBLY EMPOWERED BY THE STATE GOVERNMENTS UNDER THE ARTICLES OF CONFEDERATION, CONGRESS COULD DO LITTLE TO AID NEW YORK--OR THE NATION AS A WHOLE.

IN HIS FRUSTRATIONS OVER ALL THAT WAS HOBBLING AMERICA, HAMILTON FOUND A LIKE MIND IN JAMES MADISON.

THE CEREBRAL, INTENSELY STUDIOUS ENVOY FROM VIRGINIA--TOO FRAIL TO HAVE HAD MUCH MILITARY SERVICE--WARILY EYED ALL THE WORK AHEAD.

AMERICA'S LEADERS HAD NEVER JUSTLY COMPENSATED THE ARMY.

AS HAMILTON SERVED IN CONGRESS, THERE WERE FOREBODING SIGNS THAT MENACING CONSEQUENCES MIGHT FOLLOW.

OFFICERS UNDER HORATIO GATES WERE ENCAMPED AT NEWBURGH, NEW YORK. TORMENTED BY THE PROSPECT OF BEING CHEATED OF PAY, THEY SENT CONGRESS VEILED THREATS THAT THEY MIGHT ABANDON THE COUNTRY...

...OR POSSIBLY EVEN **ATTACK** AND IMPOSE MARTIAL LAW.

HAMILTON AND OTHER MANAGERS OF NATIONAL FINANCE SECRETLY WELCOMED THIS CRISIS.

THE PERIL OF A **MILITARY COUP** MIGHT FORCE THE PEOPLE TO GRANT CONGRESS THE MAGNIFIED TAXING POWER THAT THE STATES KEPT CLAWING BACK.

THE NECESSITY AND DISCONTENTS OF THE ARMY PRESENTED THEMSELVES AS A POWERFUL ENGINE.

HAMILTON FANNED THE FLAMES OF PARANOIA. BUT HE DIDN'T WANT GATES LEADING A VENGEFUL CHARGE OF PUSHED-TO-THE-EDGE SOLDIERS...

...HE WANTED WASHINGTON.

TAKE THE DIRECTION OF [THE ARMY]. GUIDE THE TORRENT, AND BRING **ORDER**...

...PERHAPS EVEN **GOOD**, OUT OF CONFUSION.

WASHINGTON, HOWEVER, REBUKED HIM.

THE ARMY IS A DANGEROUS INSTRUMENT TO PLAY WITH.

THE POWDER KEG WAS FINALLY KEPT FROM DETONATING BY A SPECIAL, PERSONAL APPEAL MADE IN NEWBURGH FROM WASHINGTON HIMSELF.

ON NOVEMBER 25, 1783, THE LAST REDCOATS EVACUATED NEW YORK CITY. GEORGE WASHINGTON AND HIS COUNTRYMEN MARCHED BACK IN.

AN ENORMOUS 1776 FIRE HAD REDUCED A THIRD OF THE BUILDINGS TO ASHES. BUT WITH AMERICAN HANDS REBUILDING, THERE WAS A ONCE-IN-A-LIFETIME CHANCE FOR YOUNG LAWYERS TO ESTABLISH THEMSELVES.

HAMILTON MOVED HIS FAMILY DOWNSTATE AND BEGAN LIVING AND PRACTICING LAW AT 57 WALL STREET.

PAPA! *PAPA!*

SEE BOATS! *SEE BOATS!*

AND AARON BURR DID THE SAME AT 10 LITTLE QUEEN (NOW CEDAR) STREET.

IF THE TWO MEN HAD ONLY GLANCINGLY ENCOUNTERED EACH OTHER PRIOR TO THIS, NOW THEY WERE COLLEAGUES IN ALMOST DAILY CONTACT.

HAMILTON WAS MORE THAN READY TO SHRUG OFF ONCE AND FOR ALL THE RAGS, DISCOMFORTS, AND INDIGNITIES OF POVERTY AND CAMP LIFE.

HE WOULD FOREVER AFTER AIM TO BE A REFINED AND SUMPTUOUS *GENTLEMAN ABOUT TOWN.*

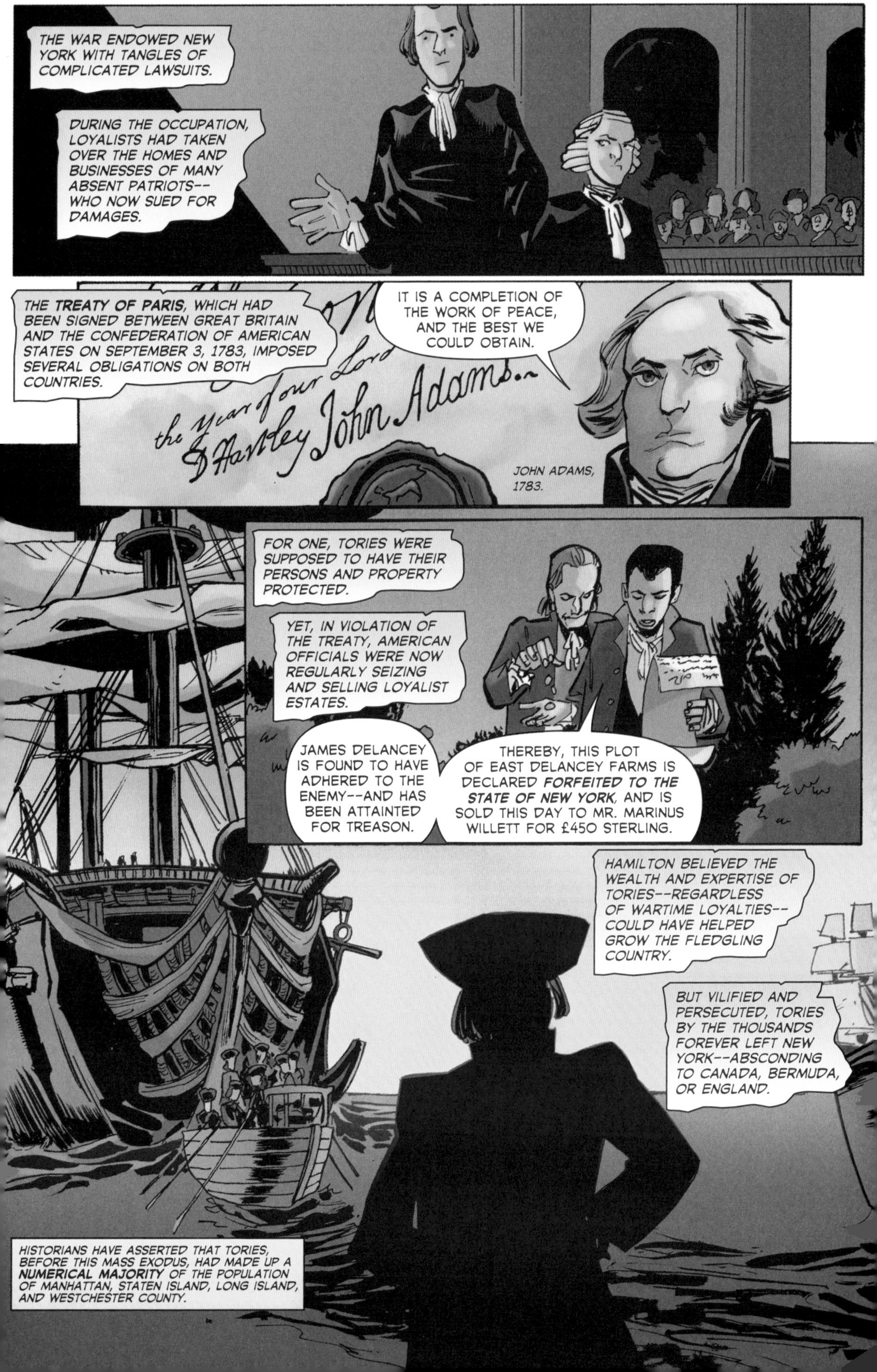
THE WAR ENDOWED NEW YORK WITH TANGLES OF COMPLICATED LAWSUITS.
DURING THE OCCUPATION, LOYALISTS HAD TAKEN OVER THE HOMES AND BUSINESSES OF MANY ABSENT PATRIOTS--WHO NOW SUED FOR DAMAGES.
THE **TREATY OF PARIS**, WHICH HAD BEEN SIGNED BETWEEN GREAT BRITAIN AND THE CONFEDERATION OF AMERICAN STATES ON SEPTEMBER 3, 1783, IMPOSED SEVERAL OBLIGATIONS ON BOTH COUNTRIES.
IT IS A COMPLETION OF THE WORK OF PEACE, AND THE BEST WE COULD OBTAIN.
JOHN ADAMS, 1783.
FOR ONE, TORIES WERE SUPPOSED TO HAVE THEIR PERSONS AND PROPERTY PROTECTED.
YET, IN VIOLATION OF THE TREATY, AMERICAN OFFICIALS WERE NOW REGULARLY SEIZING AND SELLING LOYALIST ESTATES.
JAMES DELANCEY IS FOUND TO HAVE ADHERED TO THE ENEMY--AND HAS BEEN ATTAINTED FOR TREASON.
THEREBY, THIS PLOT OF EAST DELANCEY FARMS IS DECLARED ***FORFEITED TO THE STATE OF NEW YORK***, AND IS SOLD THIS DAY TO MR. MARINUS WILLETT FOR £450 STERLING.
HAMILTON BELIEVED THE WEALTH AND EXPERTISE OF TORIES--REGARDLESS OF WARTIME LOYALTIES--COULD HAVE HELPED GROW THE FLEDGLING COUNTRY.
BUT VILIFIED AND PERSECUTED, TORIES BY THE THOUSANDS FOREVER LEFT NEW YORK--ABSCONDING TO CANADA, BERMUDA, OR ENGLAND.
HISTORIANS HAVE ASSERTED THAT TORIES, BEFORE THIS MASS EXODUS, HAD MADE UP A **NUMERICAL MAJORITY** OF THE POPULATION OF MANHATTAN, STATEN ISLAND, LONG ISLAND, AND WESTCHESTER COUNTY.

THE **RIGHT TO PROPERTY** WAS AMONG THE FIRST PRINCIPLES OF THE AMERICAN REVOLUTION. AND SO, TO HAMILTON, DEPRIVING SOMEONE-- **ANYONE**--OF WHAT THEY **LEGALLY OWNED** PROFANELY UNDERMINED THE CAUSE'S MORAL AUTHORITY.

ON TOP OF THAT, TO HIS MIND, THE STATE OF NEW YORK WAS NOT ONLY VIOLATING THE **TREATY OF PARIS**, BUT VIOLATING THE **SOVEREIGNTY OF THE UNITED STATES** AS WELL.

IF TREATIES MADE BY CONGRESS'S DULY APPOINTED DIPLOMATS HAD NO POWER TO BIND THE STATES, THEN CONGRESS HAD NO REAL AUTHORITY AT ALL.

AND IF THAT WAS THE CASE, THE NATIONS OF THE WORLD WOULD HAVE **NO REASON WHATSOEVER** TO RESPECT AMERICA--OR DEAL WITH IT ON EQUAL FOOTING.

JAMES MADISON AND SECRETARY OF FOREIGN AFFAIRS JOHN JAY SIDED WITH HAMILTON.

DOES NOT THE ACT OF CONFEDERATION PLACE THE EXCLUSIVE RIGHT OF WAR AND PEACE [AND TREATY MAKING] IN THE UNITED STATES CONGRESS?

DOES NOT THE DELEGATION OF THEM TO THE GENERAL CONFEDERACY, SO FAR ABRIDGE THE SOVEREIGNTY OF EACH PARTICULAR STATE?

STANDING FIRMLY OPPOSED TO HAMILTON WAS THE STATE'S OWN "MAN OF THE PEOPLE," GOVERNOR **GEORGE CLINTON**, AND SUPPORTERS LIKE **MARINUS WILLETT** AND **MELANCTON SMITH**. CLINTON WAS A LONG-STANDING RIVAL OF THE SCHUYLER FAMILY.

IN 1784, CLINTON HAD OVERSEEN ACTS TO LIQUIDATE LOYALIST ESTATES, DISENFRANCHISE TORIES OF THE VOTE, AND BANISH THEM FROM THE STATE. HE SAW THIS AS JUST RESTITUTION FOR NEW YORK'S WARTIME SUFFERING.

SHARPLY DEPARTING FROM NATIONALISTS LIKE HAMILTON AND MADISON, CLINTON AND HIS FOLLOWERS WERE DECIDEDLY AGAINST ENLARGING THE AUTHORITY OF CONGRESS.

WHILE IT WAS NOT AARON BURR'S STYLE TO BE POLITICALLY DOGMATIC EITHER WAY, WHEN CLINTON OFFERED HIS SUPPORT, BURR WELCOMED IT.

IN BURR'S PRACTICE AS AN ATTORNEY, HE TENDED TO SIDE WITH THE PATRIOTS WHO BENEFITED FROM THE OFFICIAL THEFT OF LOYALIST ASSETS.

HAMILTON, ON THE OTHER HAND, MADE HIMSELF THE GO-TO LEGAL ADVOCATE FOR TORY CLIENTS.

FOR THIS, HE BEGAN TO DRAW FIRE AS A MAN DIABOLICALLY PRO-BRITISH AND ANTI-AMERICAN.

HAMILTON'S LAW PRACTICE MAY HAVE REASONABLY FLOURISHED...

...BUT IN THE MID-1780s, AN ECONOMIC CRISIS SOME CONSIDER AS DEVASTATING AS **THE GREAT DEPRESSION OF THE 1930s** WAS TAKING HOLD.

THE UNITED STATES HAD SPENT APPROXIMATELY $101 MILLION ON THE REVOLUTIONARY WAR-- ESTIMATED TO BE ABOUT $2.4 **BILLION** TODAY.

POLITICAL LEADERS COULD ONLY RAISE THAT ASTRONOMICAL AMOUNT BY BORROWING HUGE SUMS OF MONEY.

LOANS HAD COME FROM FOREIGN COUNTRIES LIKE THE NETHERLANDS, FRANCE, AND SPAIN--AND FROM WEALTHY INDIVIDUALS AT HOME AND ABROAD.

HAMILTON'S MENTOR FOR ALL THINGS FIDUCIARY DURING HIS SHORT STINT IN CONGRESS, PENNSYLVANIAN **ROBERT MORRIS,** WAS KNOWN AS THE FINANCIER OF THE REVOLUTION.*

ANOTHER WAY THE STATES HAD BORROWED MONEY WAS TO ISSUE I.O.U.S: **GOVERNMENT BONDS** THAT WOULD PAY INTEREST.

THESE WERE ISSUED TO MERCHANTS AND FARMERS INSTEAD OF GOLD OR SILVER.

SOLDIERS WHO HAD RISKED THEIR NECKS AND SACRIFICED THE BEST YEARS OF THEIR LIVES--BUT WHO HAD POCKETED NOTORIOUSLY LITTLE PAY--ALSO RECEIVED BONDS.

MY OBJECTS ARE TO REDUCE OUR PUBLIC EXPENDITURES AS NEARLY AS POSSIBLE TO WHAT THEY OUGHT TO BE...

...AND TO OBTAIN REVENUES IN OUR OWN COUNTRY TO MEET THOSE EXPENSES.

*MORRIS HAD EVEN LAID HIS PERSONAL FORTUNE ON THE LINE TO FUND WASHINGTON'S ATTACK AT TRENTON.

WITH MAJOR COMBAT OPERATIONS OVER...

...IT WAS TIME FOR THE STATES TO PAY ALL THESE LOANS BACK.

HOWEVER, THE CASH-STRAPPED STATES COULD DO LITTLE MORE THAN HIKE TAXES ON THEIR CITIZENS. MANY DID SO TO UNPRECEDENTED LEVELS--OFTEN **TRIPLE** OR **QUADRUPLE** PREWAR RATES.

OUR DEBT INDEED IS HEAVY, AND...

...WILL REQUIRE TAXES DIFFICULT TO BE PAID.

A WAR STARTED OVER TAXES HAD IRONICALLY DELIVERED A PEACE WITH A **FAR MORE CRUSHING TAX BURDEN** THAN AMERICANS HAD KNOWN BEFORE.

EDMUND PENDLETON OF VIRGINIA, 1783.

THERE WAS ALSO THE MATTER OF AMERICANS (MOSTLY SOUTHERNERS) WHO HAD TAKEN PERSONAL LOANS FROM **BRITISH** MERCHANTS AND BANKERS, **BEFORE** THE WAR.

THIS HAD BEEN A FAVORITE WAY OF FINANCING THE LUXURIOUS PLANTATION LIFE EXERCISED BY THE LIKES OF THOMAS JEFFERSON--WHO ALL HIS ADULTHOOD WAS HABITUALLY IN DEBT.

THE **TREATY OF PARIS** OBLIGATED AMERICANS TO PAY BACK THESE LOANS. BUT MANY, IN ANOTHER VIOLATION OF THE ACCORD, **RENEGED**.

VIRGINIA CERTAINLY [OWES] TWO MILLIONS STERLING TO GREAT BRITAIN. SOME HAVE CONJECTURED THE DEBT AS HIGH AS THREE MILLIONS.

MONEY BECAME SO SCARCE THAT MANY PEOPLE HAD NOTHING TO PAY THEIR STATE TAXES WITH, NEVER MIND PURCHASE THE NECESSITIES OF LIFE.

AND WITHOUT TAX REVENUE BEING COLLECTED, THE BONDS THAT SOLDIERS AND CITIZENS WERE HOLDING WERE UNREDEEMABLE. THEY COULD NOT BE EXCHANGED FOR GOLD OR SILVER.

ECONOMIC ACTIVITY LULLED.

BUT ENTERPRISING **SPECULATORS**--WITH MONEY TO BURN--SAW THE BONDS AS A BUSINESS OPPORTUNITY.

WILLING TO RISK THAT BONDS WOULD **SOMEDAY** BE REDEEMABLE, THEY OFFERED TO BUY THE BONDS, FOR CASH, AT A STEEP DISCOUNT.

STRUGGLING PEOPLE USUALLY TOOK THE OFFER. A PITTANCE OF HARD CURRENCY SEEMED MORE PRACTICAL THAN WHAT MIGHT BE A USELESS PIECE OF PAPER.

WHEN TAXES **COULD** BE COLLECTED, STATES HAD TO PAY INTEREST ON THE BONDS.

AND SO, TAX REVENUE OFTEN WENT **STRAIGHT** INTO THE POCKETS OF SPECULATORS.

FOR THE EQUIVALENT OF PENNIES ON A DOLLAR, WILY BUSINESSMEN NOW COMMANDED HERDS OF PAPER CASH COWS.

HOW DID THOSE WHO HAD SOLD THEIR BONDS FEEL? **RIPPED OFF**...

...AND EVEN **LESS** LIKELY TO PAY EITHER TAXES OR PRIVATE DEBTS.

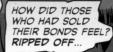

IF AMERICANS WOULD NOT PAY THEIR DEBTS, HAMILTON SAW REAL DANGER IN THE COUNTRY BEING A DISHONORABLE SCOFFLAW STATE--ONE THAT COULD ONLY BE LENT TO AT EXTREME PERIL.

"DEAR MONSIEUR. THE CREDIT OF THE UNITED STATES MUST BE **VERY LOW INDEED** IF WE MUST AGREE TO TERMS SO EXORBITANT AS THOSE YOU HAVE ENCLOSED TO ME..."

JOHN ADAMS, 1784.

AND A WEAK, DISORGANIZED AMERICA SO WILLING TO BE DELINQUENT AND INSOLENT ON THE WORLD STAGE, COULD PROVOKE **ANOTHER** WAR...

...PERHAPS WITH NO FRANCE TO AGAIN TIP THE SCALES IN ITS FAVOR.

UNLIKE THE REVOLUTION'S IDEALISTS, HAMILTON BELIEVED ONLY A FEW SELECT INDIVIDUALS-- LIKE HIMSELF--COULD MASTER THEIR INSTINCTUAL URGES, CULTIVATE THEIR FACULTIES, AND ATTAIN REAL VIRTUE. OTHER MEN? THEY WOULD ALWAYS ACT IN THEIR OWN INTERESTS. **SELFISHLY.**

YET HAMILTON THEORIZED THAT THROUGH JUDICIOUS ENGINEERING OF THE MACHINERY OF GOVERNMENT AND BUSINESS, GREED AND AMBITION COULD BE **HARNESSED**--IN ESSENCE, TRICKED INTO USE AS AN ENGINE FOR GOOD.

PHILADELPHIA HAD THE COUNTRY'S ONLY BANK. ESTABLISHING ONE IN NEW YORK, HAMILTON ARGUED, WOULD BOOST THE CITY'S AND STATE'S ECONOMIES BY:

PROMOTING INDUSTRY AND COMMERCE...

AND

...RENDER[ING] LANDED PROPERTY MORE VALUABLE.

HAMILTON THREW HIS ENERGIES INTO THIS PROJECT. HE WROTE THE INSTITUTION'S FIRST GOVERNING DOCUMENT AND SERVED AS ONE OF ITS DIRECTORS.

THE **BANK OF NEW YORK** OPENED ON JUNE 9, 1784.

THE WALTON HOUSE IN LOWER MANHATTAN, WHERE THE BANK OF NEW YORK DID BUSINESS 1784-1791.

A BANK MIGHT BRING ABOUT SOME GOOD EFFECTS LOCALLY, BUT IN MASSACHUSETTS, FARMERS BEING SUED FOR TAX DEBT *TOOK UP ARMS.* THEY BROUGHT LAWSUITS TO A HALT BY FORCIBLY CLOSING COURTHOUSES.

ADJOURN! THERE WILL BE *NO SESSION* HERE UNTIL OUR GRIEVANCES ARE ADDRESSED!

LET THE *GENTLEMEN OF BOSTON* KNOW THAT WE COUNTRY MEN WILL NOT PAY TAXES, AS THEY THINK.

SHAYS' REBELLION, 1786.

AND PIONEER WOODSMEN WERE TRYING TO SECEDE FROM NORTH CAROLINA AND CREATE THE "STATE OF FRANKLIN."

WE SHALL CONTINUE TO ACT AS INDEPENDENT, AND WOULD RATHER SUFFER DEATH AND ALL ITS VARIOUS AND FRIGHTFUL SHAPES THAN CONFORM TO ANYTHING THAT IS DISGRACEFUL.

JOHN SEVIER, "GOVERNOR" OF FRANKLIN, 1785.

IN THE *ABSENCE OF A KING* AND EMBOLDENED BY *VIOLENT REBELLION,* HAMILTON FELT SO MANY OF THE PEOPLE OF AMERICA--LISTLESS AND UNGOVERNABLE--WERE *PROVING RIGHT* HIS MOST CYNICAL BELIEFS.

HISS!

IN HIS DARKEST MOMENTS, HE COULD ONLY HAVE BEEN CHILLED BY THE ACRID, DARK-AGES WISDOM THAT HAD PROPPED UP KINGLY THRONES FOR MILLENNIA...

...THAT LIBERTY *WAS* ONLY A PRETEXT OR A SHOW OF FREEDOM. THAT LIBERTY INSTEAD *ONLY MADE MEN SLAVES* TO THE WORST ASPECTS OF THEIR OWN NATURE.

YET MOST WERE REVOLTED BY WHAT HAMILTON PRESENTED AS THE ALTERNATIVE.

A STRONG, CENTRALIZED POWER WAS IN MANY WAYS WHAT THE PEOPLE *HAD JUST REBELLED AGAINST!* ANY STRONGER FORM OF GOVERNMENT HARKENED UNCOMFORTABLY IN THE DIRECTION OF MONARCHY.

AND LINKING THE INTERESTS OF THE PEOPLE TO THE INTERESTS OF MONEY AND BUSINESS WAS POTENTIALLY INFLAMMATORY GIVEN THE PUBLIC OUTRAGE AGAINST SPECULATORS.

SHAK-A-SHAK-A-SHAK-A

TO A PEOPLE THAT HAD SUCCESSFULLY BROUGHT OFF A REVOLUTION, THAT HAD REBELLED FROM THE YOKE OF AUTHORITY, THAT HAD FRAGMENTED THEMSELVES FROM THE WHOLE OF AN EMPIRE...

...*MORE* REVOLUTION, *MORE* REBELLION, AND *MORE* FRAGMENTATION WERE THE SOLUTIONS THAT SUITED THEM.

To Make Our Independence a Blessing

...BUT THAT MANY POLITICAL PLAYERS IN THE STATES--PERHAPS MOST OF ALL HIS OWN GOVERNOR, PATRICK HENRY--WERE SURE TO OPPOSE.

MADISON CONTRIVED ANOTHER CONFERENCE. PUBLICLY, IT WAS PRESENTED AS A FORUM FOR STATES TO DISCUSS TRADE.

HAMILTON ARRANGED FOR HIMSELF TO ATTEND. HE RODE TO ANNAPOLIS, MARYLAND, IN THE FALL OF 1786.

ONCE THERE, HE PICKED UP ON MADISON'S PLAY: TO WHOLLY RECONSTRUCT AMERICAN GOVERNANCE THROUGH UNORTHODOX MEETINGS--ONES HELD OUT OF SIGHT OF STATE OFFICIALS THAT MIGHT OBSTRUCT THEM.

GIVE THESE MEETINGS AN AIR OF LEGITIMACY BY HAVING LEADING LIGHTS LIKE WASHINGTON ATTEND, AND REAL CHANGE MIGHT BE WON.

"YOUR COMMISSIONERS, WITH THE MOST RESPECTFUL DEFERENCE, BEG LEAVE TO SUGGEST THEIR UNANIMOUS CONVICTION THAT IT MAY ADVANCE THE INTERESTS OF THE UNION TO MEET AT PHILADELPHIA..."

RIDING OFF TOGETHER FROM MARYLAND, HAMILTON AND MADISON SEEMED TO BE THE COZIEST OF COHORTS-- COMPATIBLE DOWN TO THE SMALLEST DETAIL.

PHILIP SCHUYLER HELPED HAMILTON GET APPOINTED TO THE UPCOMING CONVENTION IN PHILADELPHIA TO RENDER THE ARTICLES OF CONFEDERATION MORE "ADEQUATE TO THE EXIGENCIES OF THE UNION."

ALEXANDER HAMILTON JR., BORN MAY, 1786.

ANGELICA HAMILTON, BORN SEPTEMBER, 1784.

GOVERNOR CLINTON, HOWEVER, MADE IT CLEAR HE WOULD TOLERATE ONLY SLIGHT MODIFICATIONS-- NOT A WHOLESALE REORGANIZATION OF THE UNITED STATES.

TWO OTHER NEW YORK DELEGATES--CLINTON'S MEN--WOULD SEE TO IT THAT HAMILTON REMAINED ON THE SIDELINES AT PHILADELPHIA.

THE CONVENTION, WHICH KICKED OFF IN MAY, 1787, HAD TO BE VIGILANTLY ON GUARD AGAINST ATTACKS ON ITS AUTHORITY.

ARTICLE XIII OF THE **ARTICLES OF CONFEDERATION** SPELLED OUT A PRECISE PROCEDURE FOR ALTERING GOVERNMENT-- AND THIS MEETING WAS THROWING IT OUT THE WINDOW.

WERE THE TRUE NATURE OF THE PROCEEDINGS TO GO PUBLIC, THE ATTENDANTS STOOD TO BE PERCEIVED AS **RENEGADE** AS SHAYS'S REBELS.*

ONCE INSIDE, THE VOICING OF AN UNPOPULAR OPINION OR AN ILL-CONSIDERED PROPOSAL MIGHT BE LATER USED TO SABOTAGE A MAN'S POLITICAL FUTURE, SO A "GENTLEMEN'S AGREEMENT" WAS ENFORCED TO KEEP NO WRITTEN RECORDS--AND CONDUCT THE PROCEEDINGS IN SECRECY.

*RHODE ISLAND, FOR THESE VERY REASONS, REFUSED TO SEND DELEGATES.

WASHINGTON KNEW THE HIGH STAKES. HE FRETTED FOR **MONTHS** OVER WHETHER OR NOT TO ATTEND.

SEVERAL REASONS YET EXIST COMBINED TO MAKE MY ATTENDANCE INCONVENIENT, PERHAPS IMPROPER...

BUT HE GAVE IN. AND TO MAKE FURTHER ARGUMENTS FOR THEIR OWN VALIDITY, THE ORGANIZERS ALSO GOT THE CONVIVIAL ELDER STATESMAN, BENJAMIN FRANKLIN, TO PARTICIPATE.

ONE MIGHT SAY MADISON *OUT-HAMILTONED HAMILTON* BY HOW BOLD AND PREPARED HE WAS IN PHILADELPHIA.

UNCOMFORTABLE IN THE SPOTLIGHT, THOUGH, HE OFTEN RELIED ON OTHERS TO BE HIS MOUTHPIECE.

A *NATIONAL* GOVERNMENT OUGHT TO BE ESTABLISHED CONSISTING OF A SUPREME LEGISLATURE, JUDICIARY, AND EXECUTIVE.

EDMUND RANDOLPH.

I MOVE THAT THE EXECUTIVE *CONSIST OF A SINGLE PERSON*.

!!

THIS WAS THE EXACT PROPOSAL FOR WHICH HAMILTON HAD BEAT THE DRUM FOR YEARS.

SO, WHAT CAN BE MADE OF HOW SILENT HE WAS, HOW LITTLE HE CONTRIBUTED FOR ALL THOSE FIRST WEEKS IN PHILADELPHIA?

THIS VIRGINIA PLAN OF MR. RANDOLPH DESTROYS THE SOVEREIGNTY OF THE STATES!

≥GASP!≥ A UNITARY EXECUTIVE WOULD BE THE FETUS OF MONARCHY!

WE HAVE NO MOTIVE TO TAKE THE BRITISH GOVERNMENT AS OUR PROTOTYPE!

THE PEOPLE WILL NOT BEAR SUCH INNOVATIONS!

THE STATES WILL REVOLT AT SUCH ENCROACHMENTS!

I AM AGAINST ENABLING ANY ONE MAN TO STOP THE WILL OF THE WHOLE.

SINCE WAR'S END, THE STATES HAD NOT COME TOGETHER TO IRON OUT HOW THEY MIGHT BE GOVERNED **COLLECTIVELY.**

THE QUESTIONS OF WHAT MAKES A JUST AND ENLIGHTENED POST-MONARCHY POWER STRUCTURE HAD TO BE REVISITED ON AN EPIC SCALE.

AS WITH THE ONGOING HAZARDS WITH THE **TREATY OF PARIS,** THE ISSUE OF SLAVERY WAS ONE OF THE MOST CONTENTIOUS.

SLAVERY AND GREAT WEALTH WENT HAND IN HAND. AND WEALTH WAS GENERALLY THOUGHT TO BE A CRITICAL FACTOR IN ESTABLISHING VIRTUOUS GENTLEMANSHIP.

RICHES ALLOWED A MAN TO BE ECONOMICALLY BEHOLDEN TO NO ONE AND THEREFORE LESS CORRUPT. THEY ALSO MEANT MORE TIME AND OPPORTUNITY FOR PERSONAL EDUCATION AND REFINEMENT.

THOSE WHO PAY ARE THE MASTERS OF THOSE WHO ARE PAID.

SOUTH CAROLINIANS JOHN RUTLEDGE AND PIERCE BUTLER, BALDLY DECLARING THAT...

MONEY IS POWER.

...WANTED MORE POWER AT THE NATIONAL LEVEL ESSENTIALLY BECAUSE THEIR STATE HAD A FAR MORE EXTENSIVE SLAVE ECONOMY THAN NORTHERN AND MIDDLE STATES.

MASSACHUSETTS'S ELBRIDGE GERRY COUNTERED:

IF BLACK SLAVES, WHO ARE PROPERTY IN THE SOUTH, SHOULD BE COUNTED FOR REPRESENTATION...

...THEN WHY SHOULDN'T PROPERTY IN **CATTLE AND HORSES** BE COUNTED FOR THOSE OF US FROM THE NORTH?

IN THE END, THE SOUTHERN BLOC DECIDED IT NEEDED THE UNION--AND THE UNION DECIDED IT NEEDED THE SOUTHERN BLOC.

THE CONSTITUTION WAS OUTFITTED WITH MANY CONCESSIONS TO SLAVERY, INCLUDING A FUGITIVE SLAVE CLAUSE AND THE INFAMOUS 3/5 COMPROMISE.

BY ALLOWING 3/5 OF A STATE'S SLAVE POPULATION TO COUNT TOWARD THE NUMBER OF MEMBERS OF CONGRESS AND VOTES IN THE ELECTORAL COLLEGE, VIRGINIA ESPECIALLY WAS GRANTED OUTSIZED INFLUENCE OVER THE YET-TO-BE-ORGANIZED FEDERAL GOVERNMENT.

EVEN A GOOD NUMBER OF VIRGINIANS FELT MORAL PANGS AT SEEING HUMAN BONDAGE SO WOVEN INTO THE FABRIC OF A SUPPOSEDLY FREE COUNTRY'S GOVERNMENT.

HAMILTON, ALTHOUGH AN AVOWED SLAVERY OPPONENT, NONETHELESS COULD JUSTIFY THE BEARING IT BROUGHT TO THE CONSTITUTION.

MUCH HAS BEEN SAID OF THE IMPROPRIETY OF REPRESENTING MEN, WHO HAVE NO WILL OF THEIR OWN.

BUT REPRESENTATION AND TAXATION GO TOGETHER. WOULD IT BE JUST TO COMPUTE THESE SLAVES IN THE ASSESSMENT OF TAXES AND **DISCARD** THEM FROM THE ESTIMATE IN THE APPORTIONMENT OF REPRESENTATIVES?

I THINK IT WRONG TO ADMIT IN THE CONSTITUTION THE IDEA THAT THERE COULD BE PROPERTY IN MEN.

AN ENTIRE FIVE WEEKS AFTER FIRST ARRIVAL IN PHILADELPHIA, THE PROVERBIAL DECKS OF THE CONVENTION WERE CLEARED FOR HAMILTON TO HAVE HIS SAY. **AND HE DID. FOR ABOUT SIX STRAIGHT HOURS.**

HE WAS THE ONLY SPEAKER FOR WHOM AN ENTIRE DAY OF BUSINESS WAS ALLOTTED.

HAMILTON HAD THE NERVE TO ASK WHY AMERICA SHOULDN'T CONSIDER "EXTINGUISHING" THE STATE GOVERNMENTS ENTIRELY!

IN REMARKS THAT WOULD MAR HIS REPUTATION FOREVER IN THE EYES OF MANY, HE COMMENTED THAT...

I HAVE NO SCRUPLE IN DECLARING THAT THE BRITISH GOVERNMENT IS THE BEST IN THE WORLD.

THIS STATEMENT WOULD HAVE LEFT JAMES MADISON...

...

...UTTERLY **AGHAST.**

BUT HAMILTON'S ENDORSEMENT OF THE BRITISH GOVERNMENT WAS NOT SO OUT OF LINE. IT WAS NOT, AFTER ALL, AN "ABSOLUTE" MONARCHY.

THROUGH THE HOUSE OF COMMONS, THE BRITISH GOVERNMENT (UNLIKE MANY IN THE EIGHTEENTH CENTURY) REPRESENTED THE PEOPLE-- AT LEAST TO SOME EXTENT. ONE MUST ALSO REMEMBER AMERICAN PATRIOTS' ENTHUSIASTIC TOUTING OF THEIR "RIGHTS AND LIBERTIES AS ENGLISHMEN" FROM THROUGHOUT THE REVOLUTIONARY PERIOD.

HAMILTON WENT ON TO AIR HOW HIS LOW-EXPECTATIONS VIEW OF HUMAN NATURE COULD BE PRAGMATICALLY FASHIONED INTO A STABLE REPUBLIC.

GIVE ALL POWER TO THE MANY, THEY WILL OPPRESS THE FEW. GIVE ALL POWER TO THE FEW, THEY WILL OPPRESS THE MANY.

BOTH THEREFORE OUGHT TO HAVE POWER, SO THE ONE MAY DEFEND ITSELF AGAINST THE OTHER.

HAMILTON'S CALL FOR AN EXECUTIVE "NATIONAL GOVERNOR" AND SENATORS ONLY INDIRECTLY ELECTED BY THE PEOPLE, AND ALL SERVING FOR LIFE (PENDING "GOOD BEHAVIOR"), WITH POWER TO NULLIFY ANY DISCORDANT STATE LAW, WENT ABSOLUTELY NOWHERE.

NOT A SINGLE DELEGATE SECONDED ANYTHING HE HAD TO OFFER.

BUT MAYBE THEY WEREN'T MEANT TO.

PERHAPS HAMILTON'S WHOLE PRESENTATION WAS A *NEGOTIATION TACTIC*...

...TO SWAY SMALL-GOVERNMENT ZEALOTS TO ACCEPT MADISON'S MORE MODERATE VISION OF THE CONSTITUTION. IF SO, THE GAMBIT SUCCEEDED.

NATIONALISTS WERE THE BIG WINNERS AT PHILADELPHIA. THEY HAD BUILT CONSENSUS FOR AN ENERGETIC, FAR-REACHING FEDERAL GOVERNMENT VASTLY MORE INSULATED FROM THE **VICES OF DEMOCRACY**--THAT IS, THE TENDENCY TO BEND TOO MUCH TO THE POPULAR WILL OF THE ERRATIC, SELF-INTERESTED, SHORT-SIGHTED, CORRUPTIBLE SWATH OF POPULATION WITH INADEQUATE PROPERTY OR EDUCATION.

THEY HAD CONCEIVABLY SECURED ALL THEIR DESIRED TOOLS TO UNDO THE FISCAL CRISIS.

STATES LOST THE POWER TO PRINT PAPER MONEY OR ACCEPT IT AS PAYMENT FOR DEBTS.

THE CONSTITUTION WOULD ENFORCE CONTRACTS, GIVING TAXES AND LOANS TEETH AGAIN. THIS, HAMILTON HOPED, WOULD TURN THE NATION'S HONOR AND CREDIT RATING FULLY AROUND.

THERE WAS ANOTHER CRITICAL TASK THAT HAMILTON BELIEVED THE BEEFED-UP CONGRESS WOULD NOW BE ABLE TO PERFORM...

...AND IN A LONG AFTERNOON WALK WITH MADISON, HE WOULD ALWAYS REMEMBER THEIR BEING "PERFECTLY AGREED" ABOUT...

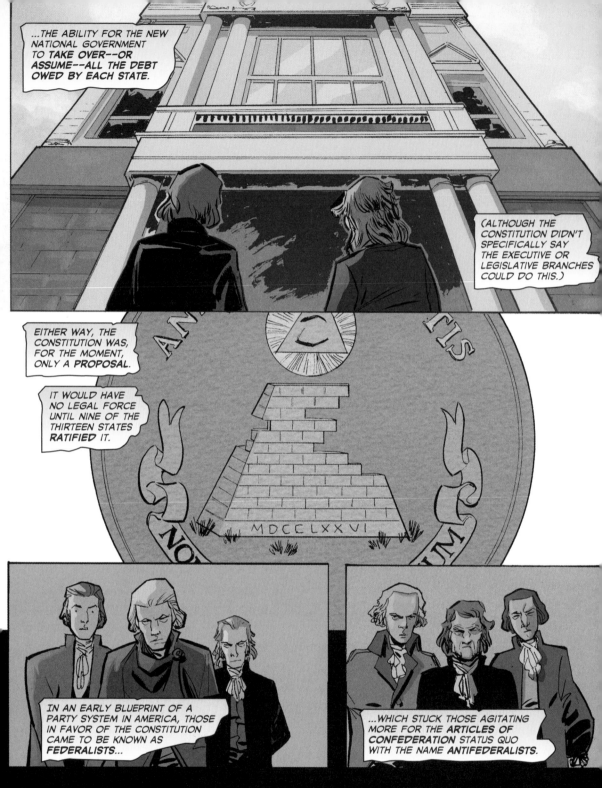

...THE ABILITY FOR THE NEW NATIONAL GOVERNMENT TO TAKE OVER--OR ASSUME--ALL THE DEBT OWED BY EACH STATE.

(ALTHOUGH THE CONSTITUTION DIDN'T SPECIFICALLY SAY THE EXECUTIVE OR LEGISLATIVE BRANCHES COULD DO THIS.)

EITHER WAY, THE CONSTITUTION WAS, FOR THE MOMENT, ONLY A **PROPOSAL**.

IT WOULD HAVE NO LEGAL FORCE UNTIL NINE OF THE THIRTEEN STATES **RATIFIED** IT.

IN AN EARLY BLUEPRINT OF A PARTY SYSTEM IN AMERICA, THOSE IN FAVOR OF THE CONSTITUTION CAME TO BE KNOWN AS **FEDERALISTS**...

...WHICH STUCK THOSE AGITATING MORE FOR THE **ARTICLES OF CONFEDERATION** STATUS QUO WITH THE NAME **ANTIFEDERALISTS**.

THE QUESTION WOULD BE SETTLED IN SPECIAL CONVENTIONS HELD IN EACH STATE, WHERE POPULARLY ELECTED DELEGATES WOULD VOTE IT UP OR DOWN.

AND IN LINE WITH HAMILTON'S PHILADELPHIA COLLEAGUES, WHO IN PROTEST WALKED AWAY FROM THE CONSTITUTIONAL CONVENTION NEVER TO RETURN, **NEW YORK WAS SET TO BE AN ALMOST IMPASSABLE ROADBLOCK TO RATIFICATION.**

IF HE COULDN'T GET NEW YORK STATE TO ADOPT THE CONSTITUTION, ALL HAMILTON'S STRUGGLES MIGHT BE FOR NOTHING.

WE SHALL LEAVE NOTHING UNDONE TO CULTIVATE A FAVORABLE DISPOSITION IN THE CITIZENS AT LARGE.

HAMILTON PLAYED TO HIS CORE STRENGTHS: THE POWER OF THE WRITTEN WORD...

...AND UNRELENTING EFFORT.

WITH AID FROM MADISON*, HE WROTE ANONYMOUS ESSAYS TO EXPLAIN AND ADVOCATE FOR THE CONSTITUTION.

APPEARING IN THREE NEW YORK CITY NEWSPAPERS, THE STAYING POWER OF THE FEDERALIST PAPERS IS ALL THE MORE REMARKABLE GIVEN THAT THEY WERE ESSENTIALLY FIRST DRAFTS.

*JOHN JAY ALSO CONTRIBUTED A HANDFUL, THOUGH ILLNESS LEFT HIM UNABLE TO CONTINUE.

THE STATE'S RATIFICATION CONVENTION HAS BEEN STYLED A "HOMERIC BATTLE." YET HAMILTON SO DOMINATED THE FLOOR, HE SUCCEEDED IN TURNING THE VOTE OF ANTIFEDERALIST MELANCTON SMITH, CLOSE AARON BURR ALLY.

GOOD CONSTITUTIONS ARE FORMED UPON A COMPARISON OF THE LIBERTY OF THE INDIVIDUAL WITH THE STRENGTH OF THE GOVERNMENT.

IF THE TONE OF EITHER BE TOO HIGH, THE OTHER WILL BE WEAKENED TOO MUCH.

AT THE TAIL END OF DEBATE, NEW HAMPSHIRE--THE FINAL STATE NEEDED TO PUT THE CONSTITUTION IN OPERATION--OPTED IN.

THE ADDED MOMENTUM OF VIRGINIA'S RATIFICATION MULTIPLIED HAMILTON'S GAINS. SIGNIFICANTLY OWING TO HAMILTON, NEW YORK JOINED THE UNION ON JULY 26, 1788.

Rearing the Superstructure of American Greatness

BUT **ARCHITECTS**, WHETHER THEY DESIGN HOUSES OR NATIONS, EXIST IN A CEREBRAL AND ABSTRACT REALM. THEIR CREATIONS ONLY HAVE TO WORK ON PAPER. BUILDERS MUST DEAL WITH REAL-WORLD COMPLICATIONS AND UNFORESEEN **CONSEQUENCES**.

THE VERY FIRST GOVERNMENT UNDER THE CONSTITUTION LEARNED EXACTLY THAT. THEY PLAYED THE SOMETIMES THANKLESS ROLE OF BUILDERS AS THEY SET UP SHOP IN NEW YORK CITY, THE FIRST CAPITAL, IN THE FALL OF 1789.

SENATE PRESIDENT PRO TEMPORE: JOHN LANGDON

SECRETARY OF THE TREASURY: ALEXANDER HAMILTON

SECRETARY OF WAR: HENRY KNOX

VICE PRESIDENT: JOHN ADAMS

SECRETARY OF STATE: THOMAS JEFFERSON

PRESIDENT: GEORGE WASHINGTON

SPEAKER OF THE HOUSE: FREDERICK MUHLENBERG

ATTORNEY GENERAL: EDMUND RANDOLPH

WHETHER GENUINELY AVERSE TO A RETURN TO PUBLIC LIFE OR CLOYINGLY DEDICATED TO THE ROLE OF ALOOF GENTLEMAN, WASHINGTON ASSENTED TO THE PRESIDENCY ONLY AFTER MUCH COAXING AND CAJOLING BY HAMILTON.

JOHN ADAMS HAD BEEN AWAY IN EUROPE FOR YEARS. ABSENCE HAD MADE AMERICAN HEARTS GROW FOND OF HIM. ACCOMPLISHMENTS HAD VAULTED ADAMS TO THE VICE PRESIDENCY. BUT NOW MANY WERE GETTING A REFRESHER COURSE IN HIS PUGNACITY.

A TICKET-BALANCING, REGIONALISTIC NOD TO NEW ENGLAND, MANY SUPPOSED ADAMS WOULD BE HUMBLE AND PRACTICAL--LIKE MASSACHUSETTS YANKEES WERE SUPPOSED TO BE.

THOUGH THE COUNTRY WAS TENSE OVER THE DIRECTION OF ITS FUTURE, ALL AGREED THAT WASHINGTON MOST EMBODIED THE VALUES AND HOPES OF THE REVOLUTION.

BUT AS A FOREIGN DIPLOMAT IN THE OLD WORLD, ADAMS HAD LEARNED A HARD LESSON: THAT FOR AMERICA TO BE TAKEN SERIOUSLY IN A GLOBAL CONTEXT, IT MUST PROJECT A CERTAIN GRANDIOSITY.

HAMILTON, WHO HAD NEVER BEEN TO EUROPE, THOUGHT ADAMS **LUDICROUS** WITH HIS GILDED COACH AND POMPOUS TITLES HE WANTED APPLIED TO THE PRESIDENT.

"HIS **ELECTED** MAJESTY?"

"HIS **REPUBLICAN** HIGHNESS?"

HAMILTON, STILL IN HIS EARLY THIRTIES, STOOD OUT BY HIS PRONOUNCED YOUTH. HE SHIMMERED WITH VIGOR, IDEAS, AND INTELLECTUAL WATTAGE. **BUT HIS EXPERIENCE BARELY QUALIFIED HIM** TO LEAD THE TREASURY--LET ALONE SAVE AMERICA FROM FINANCIAL CRISIS.

YET WHAT HAMILTON **HAD** WAS WASHINGTON'S CONFIDENCE, AND WHAT HE **KNEW** FROM YEARS OF COHABITATION WAS HOW THE GENERAL TICKED. THAT MADE HAMILTON EXTRAORDINARILY WELL POSITIONED TO BOTH GIVE AND TAKE IN THE ADMINISTRATION...

...ESPECIALLY SINCE ANOTHER ESSENTIAL DEPARTMENT HEAD HAD YET TO REPORT FOR DUTY.

IT WOULD BE ALMOST HALF A YEAR BEFORE THOMAS JEFFERSON WOULD ARRIVE IN PERSON TO TAKE THE HELM AS SECRETARY OF STATE.

HE AND HAMILTON HAD NEVER MET, BUT NO MORE THAN A DEGREE SEPARATED THEM.

WHILE AMERICAN MINISTER TO PARIS, JEFFERSON ENGAGED IN AN EXTENDED FLIRTATION WITH HAMILTON'S MARRIED SISTER-IN-LAW, ANGELICA CHURCH...

...WITH WHOM HAMILTON HAD ALSO SHARED THE THRUST AND PARRY OF A MUTUAL--POSSIBLY EVEN **ROMANTIC**-- ADMIRATION.

JEFFERSON'S ABSENCE LEFT FOREIGN POLICY TURF UNGUARDED. HAMILTON TOOK THE LEAD ESTABLISHING THE KIND OF TRADE HE THOUGHT BEST FOR THE UNITED STATES...

...A CONTROVERSIAL MOVE, TO SAY THE LEAST.

SINCE THE WAR, BRITISH NAVAL POWER HAD SHUT DOWN LUCRATIVE AMERICAN TRADE TO HAMILTON'S NATIVE WEST INDIES.

AND SINCE AMERICANS HAD NO STOMACH FOR TAXES...

...THE ONLY POSSIBLE REVENUE HAMILTON REALLY SAW TO FUND HIS AMBITIOUS SCHEMES WERE TARIFFS (IMPORT TAXES) FROM **BRISK TRADE WITH BRITAIN**...

...WHICH HAD THE CHEAPEST AND BEST-MADE MANUFACTURES IN THE WORLD.

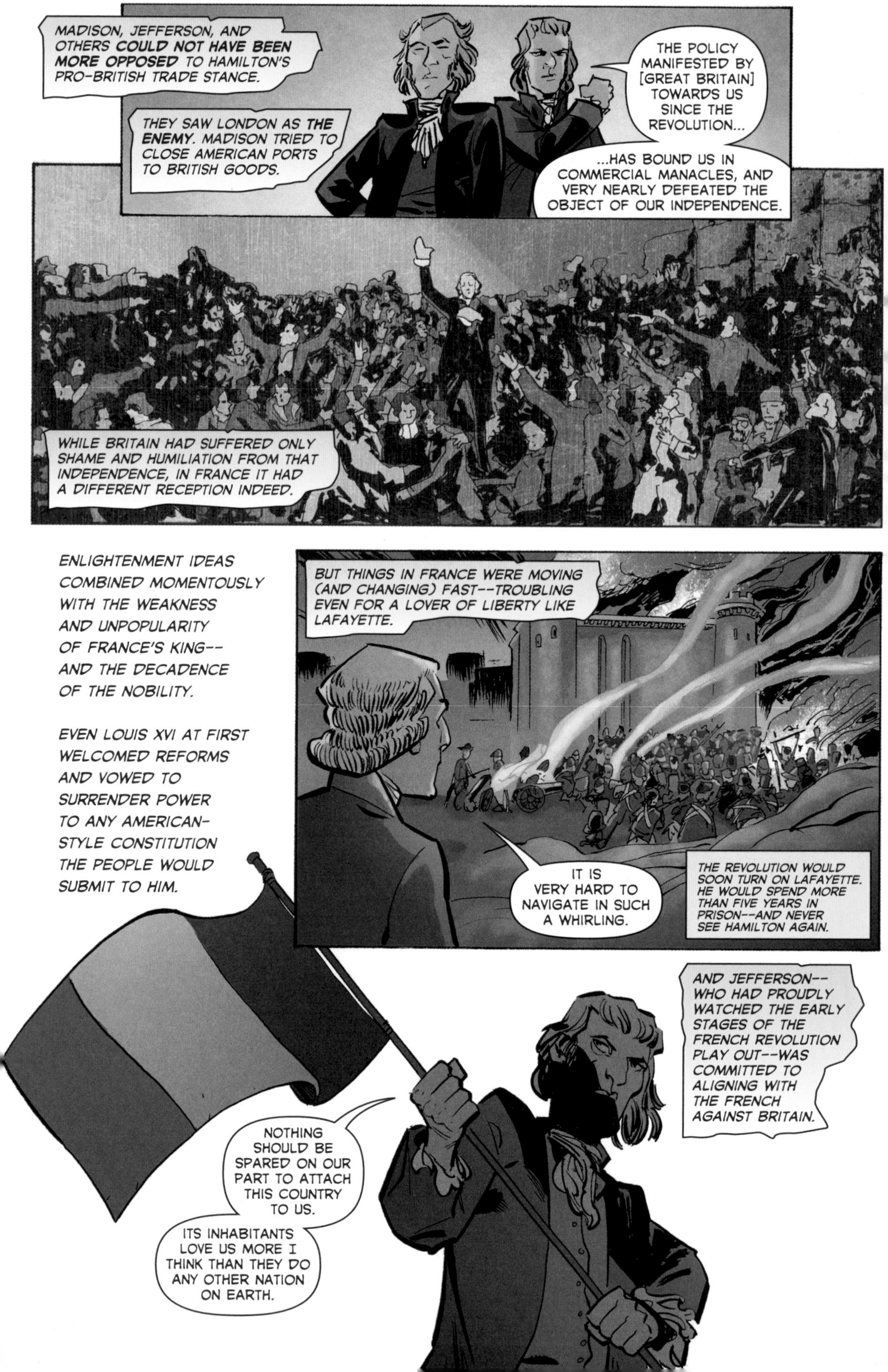
MADISON, JEFFERSON, AND OTHERS COULD NOT HAVE BEEN MORE OPPOSED TO HAMILTON'S PRO-BRITISH TRADE STANCE.
THEY SAW LONDON AS THE ENEMY. MADISON TRIED TO CLOSE AMERICAN PORTS TO BRITISH GOODS.
THE POLICY MANIFESTED BY [GREAT BRITAIN] TOWARDS US SINCE THE REVOLUTION...
...HAS BOUND US IN COMMERCIAL MANACLES, AND VERY NEARLY DEFEATED THE OBJECT OF OUR INDEPENDENCE.
WHILE BRITAIN HAD SUFFERED ONLY SHAME AND HUMILIATION FROM THAT INDEPENDENCE, IN FRANCE IT HAD A DIFFERENT RECEPTION INDEED.
ENLIGHTENMENT IDEAS COMBINED MOMENTOUSLY WITH THE WEAKNESS AND UNPOPULARITY OF FRANCE'S KING--AND THE DECADENCE OF THE NOBILITY.
EVEN LOUIS XVI AT FIRST WELCOMED REFORMS AND VOWED TO SURRENDER POWER TO ANY AMERICAN-STYLE CONSTITUTION THE PEOPLE WOULD SUBMIT TO HIM.
BUT THINGS IN FRANCE WERE MOVING (AND CHANGING) FAST--TROUBLING EVEN FOR A LOVER OF LIBERTY LIKE LAFAYETTE.
IT IS VERY HARD TO NAVIGATE IN SUCH A WHIRLING.
THE REVOLUTION WOULD SOON TURN ON LAFAYETTE. HE WOULD SPEND MORE THAN FIVE YEARS IN PRISON--AND NEVER SEE HAMILTON AGAIN.
AND JEFFERSON--WHO HAD PROUDLY WATCHED THE EARLY STAGES OF THE FRENCH REVOLUTION PLAY OUT--WAS COMMITTED TO ALIGNING WITH THE FRENCH AGAINST BRITAIN.
NOTHING SHOULD BE SPARED ON OUR PART TO ATTACH THIS COUNTRY TO US.
ITS INHABITANTS LOVE US MORE I THINK THAN THEY DO ANY OTHER NATION ON EARTH.

HAMILTON'S PREFERENCE FOR BRITAIN OVER FRANCE STEAMED MADISON AND JEFFERSON. BUT EVEN MORE, HIS FINANCIAL PLANS MADE THEIR BLOOD BOIL.

IN A BOLD AND COUNTERINTUITIVE MOVE THAT SPARKED OUTRAGE IN SOME, HAMILTON ADVANCED THE IDEA OF DOING **NEXT TO NOTHING** TO REDUCE THE STAGGERING DEBT.

UNDER CONGRESSIONAL ORDERS, HAMILTON DOVE INTO THE ACCOUNT BOOKS. HIS JANUARY 1790 **REPORT ON CREDIT** CALCULATED ALMOST $80 MILLION IN COMBINED NATIONAL AND STATE DEBT.

HE WANTED TO DEAL WITH THIS UNDER THE SINGLE, UNIFIED SYSTEM HE TERMED **ASSUMPTION,** BUT THE CONSTITUTION GAVE ONLY CONGRESS THE POWER TO ACTUALLY ADOPT SUCH A MEASURE.

NATIONAL DEBT

INSTEAD OF PAYING CREDITORS BACK, HIS ASSUMPTION PLAN WOULD **REFINANCE** THE DEBT TO A LOWER INTEREST RATE-- AND THEN INAUGURATE A CAMPAIGN OF PUNCTUAL INTEREST PAYMENTS INTENDED TO GO ON FOR THE FORESEEABLE FUTURE.

CREDITORS WOULDN'T SO MUCH BE PAID BACK--THEY WOULD BE **FINANCIALLY REWARDED** FOR MAKING LOANS IN THE FIRST PLACE.

UNDER HAMILTON'S PLAN, THESE LOANS, WOULD BE LIKE MYTHICAL **GEESE THAT LAY GOLDEN EGGS.** KEEP THEM **ALIVE,** AND THEY KEEP **PRODUCING WEALTH.**

OTHERS WITH MONEY TO LEND WOULD WANT THEIR OWN GOLD-LAYING GEESE.

AMERICA'S CREDIT RATING WOULD COME TO BE AS HIGH AS BRITAIN'S. AND THE WEALTHIEST MEN BOTH AT HOME AND OVERSEAS WOULD SUPPORT THE FEDERAL GOVERNMENT. IF CONGRESS APPROVED.

BEST IN SHOW

[I HAVE] NEVER BEEN A PROSELYTE TO THE DOCTRINE THAT PUBLIC DEBTS ARE PUBLIC BENEFITS.

I CONSIDER THEM, ON THE CONTRARY, AS **EVILS** WHICH OUGHT TO BE REMOVED AS FAST AS HONOR AND JUSTICE WILL PERMIT.

HAMILTON'S IDEAS WERE IN FACT **BRITISH** IDEAS.

BRITAIN FOR DECADES HAD ACCUMULATED ENORMOUS DEBT, YET IT KEPT COMING UP WITH INNOVATIVE TAXES AND FINANCIAL SCHEMES TO PAY INTEREST TO CREDITORS AND KEEP THEM COMING BACK FOR MORE.

SIR ROBERT WALPOLE

ONE UPSHOT OF HAMILTON'S PLAN? **REVOLUTIONARY WAR BONDS WOULD BE MORE VALUABLE THAN EVER** .

SAVVY SPECULATORS IN NEW YORK CAUGHT WIND OF THIS, BUT IN A TIME WITHOUT EVEN TRAINS AND TELEGRAPHS, RURAL PEOPLE LARGELY DID NOT.

SO, ANTICIPATING CONGRESSIONAL APPROVAL, SPECULATORS SCRAMBLED INTO THE COUNTRYSIDE IN SEARCH OF AVAILABLE GOVERNMENT BONDS.

CASH FOR BONDS

MORE REVOLUTIONARY WAR VETS WERE DEFRAUDED BY FAST-TALKING SWINDLERS FROM THE CITY.

MADISON (NOW SERVING AS A CONGRESSMAN FROM VIRGINIA) DEMANDED A LAW TO GIVE AT LEAST A **SHARE** OF INTEREST PAYMENTS TO THOSE WHOSE WARTIME SACRIFICES HAD BEEN PAID FOR IN I.O.U.S.

TO MAKE THE [ORIGINAL RECEIVERS OF DEBT CERTIFICATES] THE SOLE VICTIMS IS AN IDEA AT WHICH **HUMAN NATURE RECOILS!**

HAMILTON'S SUPPORTERS RESPONDED THAT THIS WAS IMPOSSIBLE--AND MOREOVER, **UNFAIR**. NO ONE HAD BEEN **FORCED** TO SELL THEIR "GOVERNMENT PAPER," AND THE SPECULATORS HAD TAKEN RISKS, TOO.

ELIAS BOUDINOT, CONGRESSMAN FROM NEW JERSEY, 1790.

HOW IS IT POSSIBLE THAT YOU CAN EVER TRACE A CERTIFICATE, UNDER THE CIRCUMSTANCES, UP TO THE MAN WHO WAS THE ORIGINAL BONA FIDE CREDITOR?

HAMILTON'S **FEDERALIST** COAUTHOR LOST HIS BID TO GET RESTITUTION FOR ORIGINAL BOND HOLDERS.

THE AFFECTION BETWEEN MADISON AND HAMILTON ALSO WENT DOWN IN FLAMES.

MR. MADISON'S PROPOSITION RECEIVES: YEAS, 13, NAYS, 36.

JOHN BECKLEY, CLERK OF THE HOUSE OF REPRESENTATIVES, FEBRUARY 22, 1790.

IF HAMILTON SEEMED HARD-HEARTED OVER WAR VETS CHEATED OF PAY, THIS JUST FOLLOWED FROM THE RIGOROUS, COHESIVE FISCAL POLICY FOR WHICH HE FELT THE TREASURY MUST SET A PRECEDENT.

IT IS HARD TO BELIEVE SOMEONE WHO THOUGHT MONEYGRUBBING SO **CLASSLESS** WOULD INTENTIONALLY BENEFIT THE RANKS OF SPECULATORS. HAMILTON'S EXPECTATIONS FOR MEN TO BE HONEST AND RESPECTABLE WERE TOO HIGH. AND "UNPRINCIPLED GAMBLERS" NEVERTHELESS MADE "SPORT WITH THE MARKET."

REGARDLESS, THE AFFAIRS OF TWO PARTICULAR INDIVIDUALS INVOLVED IN SPECULATION WOULD COME BACK TO BITE HIM...

...ONE, HIS ASSISTANT, FRIEND, AND EXTENDED FAMILY MEMBER **WILLIAM DUER**...

...AND TWO, A ROUGHENED LOWLIFE NAMED **JAMES REYNOLDS.**

HAMILTON'S TREASURY DEPARTMENT HAD A LOT OF INTEREST PAYMENTS TO MAKE, BUT THE COUNTRY WAS NEARLY DESTITUTE--AND IMPORT TAXES ON THEIR OWN WOULDN'T BE ENOUGH.

SO HAMILTON CALLED FOR THE SLIGHTLY MORE POLITICALLY PALATABLE (AT LEAST TO **SOME** AMERICANS) **EXCISE TAX** ON DISTILLED LIQUORS LIKE WHISKEY, WHICH WOULD ALSO "DISCOURAGE" THEIR "EXCESSIVE USE."

EVEN WITH THE FATE OF THE GOVERNMENT BONDS DECIDED, HAMILTON'S CALL TO ASSUME THE STATES' DEBTS CREATED A MONTHS-LONG **FIRESTORM** OF HEATED DISPUTES IN CONGRESS.

MOST OF VIRGINIA'S ELITE PLANTATION OWNERS WERE **PERSONALLY** DEEPLY IN HOCK--AND IN WORSE SHAPE THAN THE STATE AS A WHOLE. THEY FELT THEY COULDN'T TAKE ON ANY ADDITIONAL RESPONSIBILITIES.

SOME STATES HAD NO OUTSTANDING DEBT--OR HAD PREVIOUSLY MADE SIGNIFICANT PAYMENTS. THEY BALKED AT SHOULDERING THE TAX BURDEN FOR THOSE WHO HAD NOT.

ASSUMPTION WILL DEFRAUD THE STATE OF NORTH CAROLINA OF HALF A MILLION DOLLARS!

HUGH WILLIAMSON, CONGRESSMAN FROM NORTH CAROLINA.

OTHERS ARGUED **THEIR** CONTRIBUTIONS AND SUFFERINGS DURING THE WAR HAD BEEN DISPROPORTIONATELY LARGE--AND SO TO **NOT** ASSUME THEIR DEBTS WAS A GRAVE INSULT.

THE PEOPLE OF MASSACHUSETTS WILL NEVER SUBMIT TO A REJECTION OF THIS MEASURE. AND IF IT IS REJECTED, *IT WILL ENDANGER THE UNION ITSELF!*

THEODORE SEDGWICK, CONGRESSMAN FROM MASSACHUSETTS.

HAMILTON WAS STARING IN THE FACE NOT ONLY A BITTER REVERSAL BUT ALSO THE POSSIBILITY HIS PLAN WOULD **BRING THE GOVERNMENT AND THE CONSTITUTION DOWN WITH IT.**

JEFFERSON RECORDED HAVING A SURPRISE ENCOUNTER WITH HAMILTON ON JUNE 19, 1790.

...HEADACHE...

COLONEL HAMILTON!

MR. JEFFERSON. BEFORE YOU GO IN TO SEE THE CHIEF, I-I-I...I **MUST SPEAK WITH YOU.**

SURELY YOU ARE NOT UNAPPRISED OF THE STATE OF THE **LEGISLATURE.**

I *DESPAIR* AT THE EMBARRASSMENTS THE GENERAL GOVERNMENT MIGHT FACE SHOULD ANY STATE CARRY FORWARD A THREAT OF SEPARATION.

I WILL NOT SUFFER MYSELF TO BELIEVE YOU SONS OF VIRGINIA ESTEEM ME ANY HIGHER THAN A TOBACCO BUDWORM.

YET MEMBERS OF THE SAME ADMINISTRATION SHOULD ACT IN CONCERT. *ASSUMPTION MUST BE PASSED!*

YOU COULD PREVAIL UPON YOUR FRIENDS *TO CHANGE THEIR VOTES*--AND SET THE MACHINE OF GOVERNMENT AGAIN IN MOTION!

SIR. I AM A STRANGER TO THIS ENTIRE SUBJECT, BUT...

...*DINE WITH ME TOMORROW.* REASONABLE MEN MAY ALWAYS FIND COMPROMISE.

AND SO, ON JUNE 20, 1790...

IF ONLY THE BUSINESS BEFORE US WAS AS PALATABLE AS THE FILLETS OF PARTRIDGE AND SWEETBREADS *EN PAPILLOT.*

REGARDS TO MY MAN, JAMES. HE STUDIED THE CULINARY ARTS IN PARIS.

NOW, COLONEL. YOUR PLAN WILL BE A BITTER PILL TO THE SOUTHERN STATES...

...BUT THE OTHER *GENTLEMAN PRESENT* SHALL LIKE TO PROPOSE A *CONCOMITANT MEASURE* TO SWEETEN IT A LITTLE.

WE DEMAND *THE PERMANENT RESIDENCE OF THE SEAT OF GOVERNMENT ON THE POTOMAC.*

VIRGINIA AND HER SISTERS AT THE SOUTH ARE DUE A CAPITAL UNHAMPERED BY NEW YORK'S *STOCK JOBBERS* AND PHILADELPHIA'S *SLAVE-SNATCHING QUAKERS.*

MY HOME STATE HAS ALL BUT *EMPTIED ITS PURSE* TO HOUSE THE GOVERNMENT *HERE IN NEW YORK.*

YET, SHOULD ASSUMPTION FIND THE NEEDFUL VOTES...

...I AM MOST PERSUADED THAT A *PALACE NEWLY BUILT IN THE MARYLAND WOODS* WOULD PROVE A MOST HAPPY CONCESSION.

SO, IF WE BELIEVE JEFFERSON'S ACCOUNT, THE CORNERSTONE FOR WASHINGTON, D.C., WAS LAID AT THIS DINNER.

WHILE THE DISTRICT OF COLUMBIA REMAINED IN DEVELOPMENT FOR THE NEXT DECADE, THE U.S. GOVERNMENT WOULD MOVE TO PHILADELPHIA.

IN AIDING HAMILTON TO JAM THE ASSUMPTION BILL THROUGH CONGRESS, *JEFFERSON CAME TO BELIEVE HE AND HIS FOLLOWERS GOT A RAW DEAL.* THE TREASURY PLAN HAD MADE MANY OF THE RICH--NOW HAMILTON'S BIGGEST FANS--*RICHER.*

JEFFERSON'S OUTLOOK WAS SHARED BY MOST SOUTHERN PLANTATION OWNERS. THEY TOOK A DIM VIEW OF BANKS, MERCHANTS, MANUFACTURERS, AND ALL THAT CAME WITH URBAN CENTERS AND URBAN LIFE.

THOSE WHO LABOR IN THE EARTH ARE THE CHOSEN PEOPLE OF GOD.

THE MOBS OF GREAT CITIES [ARE] TO THE SUPPORT OF *PURE GOVERNMENT* AS SORES [ARE] TO THE STRENGTH OF THE HUMAN BODY.

AMERICANS EVERYWHERE SHARED SUCH AGRARIAN VALUES, BUT FOR ELITES FROM THE CHESAPEAKE TO CHARLESTON, THERE WAS SOMETHING MORE.

THROUGHOUT COLONIAL TIMES, SOUTHERNERS FELT THEMSELVES AT THE MERCY OF DISTANT, UNDERHANDED TOBACCO BROKERS AND MARKETERS IN LONDON WHO HAD THE POWER TO SET PRICES. GEORGE WASHINGTON'S TREATMENT BY THESE FOREIGN AGENTS WAS *INSTRUMENTAL* IN TURNING HIM TO THE CAUSE OF INDEPENDENCE.

AND THE NEXT BIT OF HAMILTONIAN HANDIWORK WAS GOING TO TOUCH *A VERY RAW NERVE* IN MEN LIKE JEFFERSON.

BY DECEMBER 1790, HAMILTON HAD MOVED TO PHILADELPHIA. IN TOP FORM AND WITH IMPRESSIVE MOMENTUM, HE RAN A GAUNTLET OF CEASELESS WORK.

PHILIP SCHUYLER, SERVING NEW YORK AS A SENATOR, WAS ALSO IN TOWN. ELIZABETH HAD TAKEN THE YOUNG CHILDREN BACK TO ALBANY.

THIS WAS HAMILTON'S CHOSEN MOMENT TO PURSUE THE NEXT GREAT PILLAR OF HIS FINANCIAL PLAN--THE *INSTITUTIONAL ARCHENEMY* OF MOST SOUTHERNERS.

FOR THE SUPPORT OF PUBLIC CREDIT, A *NATIONAL BANK* PRESENTS ITSELF AS A NECESSARY AUXILIARY.

THE (FIRST) BANK OF THE UNITED STATES WOULD BE MANAGED BY PRIVATE INDIVIDUALS--AND TASKED TO HANDLE THE GOVERNMENT'S TRANSACTIONS AND BE ON CALL TO HASTILY FULFILL LARGE LOANS.

TO RAISE CAPITAL, STOCK IN THE BANK WOULD BE SOLD. THIS USHERED IN *ANOTHER WAVE* OF SPECULATION.

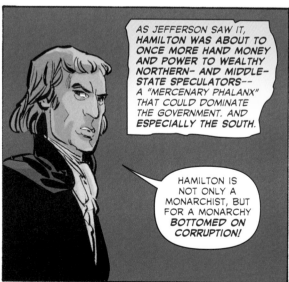

AS JEFFERSON SAW IT, HAMILTON WAS ABOUT TO ONCE MORE HAND MONEY AND POWER TO WEALTHY NORTHERN- AND MIDDLE-STATE SPECULATORS-- A "MERCENARY PHALANX" THAT COULD DOMINATE THE GOVERNMENT. AND *ESPECIALLY THE SOUTH.*

HAMILTON IS NOT ONLY A MONARCHIST, BUT FOR A MONARCHY *BOTTOMED ON CORRUPTION!*

WITH THE BANK HIS TOP PRIORITY, HAMILTON MAY HAVE BEEN SENSITIVE TO ANYTHING THAT MIGHT SEEM A BAD OMEN.

AND IN MID-JANUARY ELECTIONS, AARON BURR--GROOMED BY SCHUYLER FAMILY ENEMY GEORGE CLINTON--UNSEATED HAMILTON'S FATHER-IN-LAW IN THE SENATE.

WITH THIS AFFRONT, BURR EARNED A PERMANENT SPOT ON HAMILTON'S TO-DO LIST.

HE IS FOR OR AGAINST NOTHING, BUT AS IT SUITS HIS INTEREST OR AMBITION.

I FEEL IT A RELIGIOUS DUTY TO OPPOSE HIS CAREER.

BUT WITH SOUTHERNERS AND ANTIFEDERALISTS CRYING FOUL AT THE BANK BILL, HAMILTON PICKED HIS BATTLES ELSEWHERE.

IT IS A MONOPOLY OF THE PUBLIC MONEY FOR THE BENEFIT OF THE CORPORATION TO BE CREATED!

JAMES JACKSON, CONGRESSMAN FROM GEORGIA, 1791.

IT WAS MADISON WHO CHAMBERED AND LET FLY THE SILVER BULLET BEST EQUIPPED TO KILL HAMILTON'S PROPOSITION: THAT ONLY STATES COULD CHARTER A BANK.

IT IS NOT POSSIBLE TO DISCOVER IN THE CONSTITUTION THE POWER [FOR THE FEDERAL GOVERNMENT] TO INCORPORATE A BANK.

A POWER TO GRANT CHARTERS OF INCORPORATION HAD BEEN PROPOSED IN THE [CONSTITUTIONAL CONVENTION]...

...AND REJECTED.

NEVERTHELESS, THE NATIONAL BANK BILL PASSED WITH STRONG SUPPORT IN BOTH THE HOUSE AND THE SENATE.

THIS BROUGHT THE **BURGEONING CLASH** BETWEEN NORTH AND SOUTH, DIFFERENT ECONOMIC INTERESTS, FACTIONS IN CONGRESS, OPPOSITIONAL SCHOOLS OF CONSTITUTIONAL THOUGHT, AND **THE SUPPOSEDLY ALLIED HEAVYWEIGHTS OF THE EXECUTIVE BRANCH OF THE GOVERNMENT** CRASHING DOWN UPON...

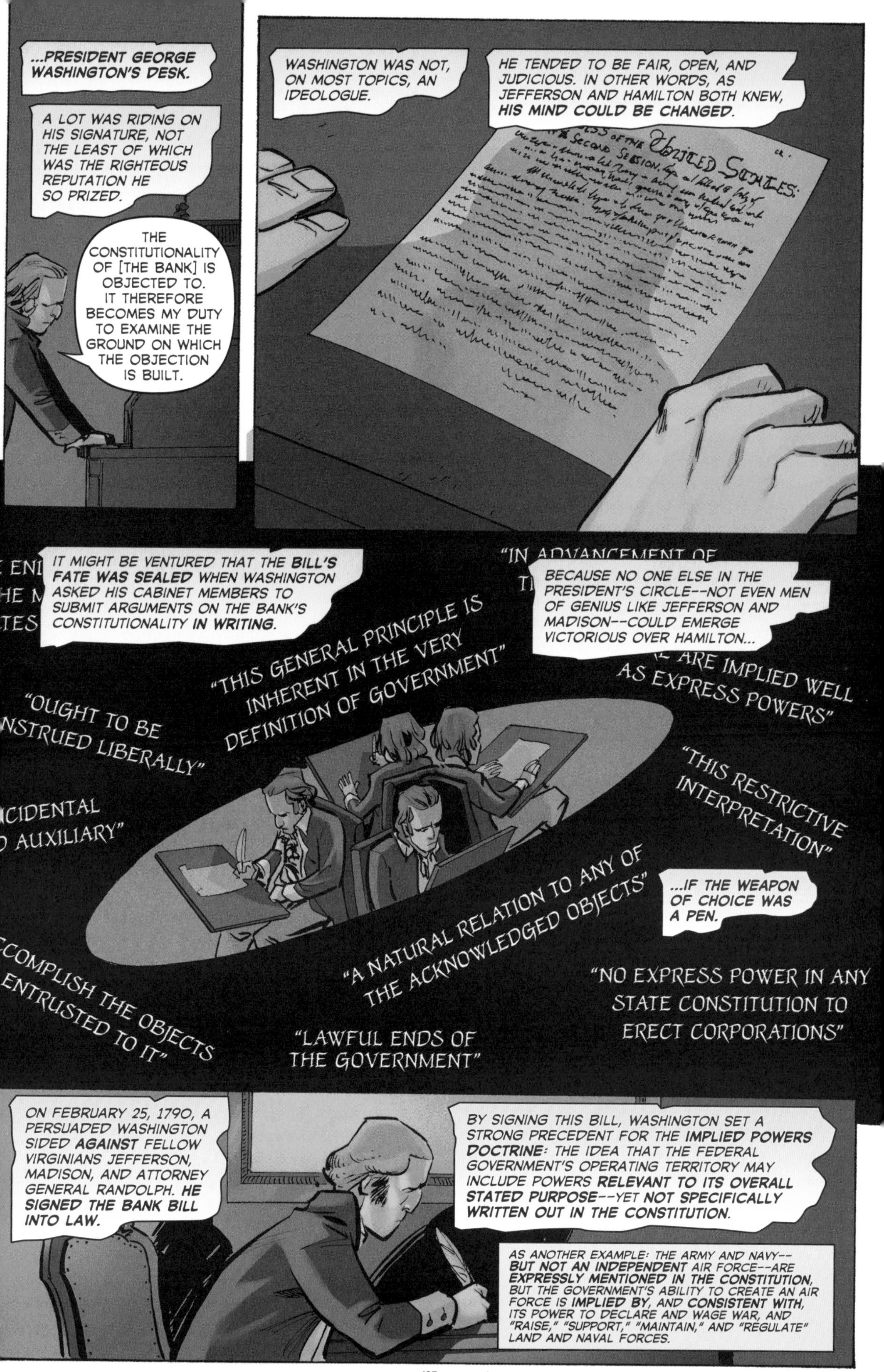

...PRESIDENT GEORGE WASHINGTON'S DESK.
A LOT WAS RIDING ON HIS SIGNATURE, NOT THE LEAST OF WHICH WAS THE RIGHTEOUS REPUTATION HE SO PRIZED.
THE CONSTITUTIONALITY OF [THE BANK] IS OBJECTED TO. IT THEREFORE BECOMES MY DUTY TO EXAMINE THE GROUND ON WHICH THE OBJECTION IS BUILT.
WASHINGTON WAS NOT, ON MOST TOPICS, AN IDEOLOGUE.
HE TENDED TO BE FAIR, OPEN, AND JUDICIOUS. IN OTHER WORDS, AS JEFFERSON AND HAMILTON BOTH KNEW, HIS MIND COULD BE CHANGED.
SECOND SESSION.
UNITED STATES:
IT MIGHT BE VENTURED THAT THE BILL'S FATE WAS SEALED WHEN WASHINGTON ASKED HIS CABINET MEMBERS TO SUBMIT ARGUMENTS ON THE BANK'S CONSTITUTIONALITY IN WRITING.
BECAUSE NO ONE ELSE IN THE PRESIDENT'S CIRCLE--NOT EVEN MEN OF GENIUS LIKE JEFFERSON AND MADISON--COULD EMERGE VICTORIOUS OVER HAMILTON...
"THIS GENERAL PRINCIPLE IS INHERENT IN THE VERY DEFINITION OF GOVERNMENT"
ARE IMPLIED WELL AS EXPRESS POWERS"
NSTRUED LIBERALLY"
"THIS RESTRICTIVE INTERPRETATION"
CIDENTAL
AUXILIARY"
"A NATURAL RELATION TO ANY OF THE ACKNOWLEDGED OBJECTS"
...IF THE WEAPON OF CHOICE WAS A PEN.
COMPLISH THE OBJECTS ENTRUSTED TO IT"
"NO EXPRESS POWER IN ANY STATE CONSTITUTION TO ERECT CORPORATIONS"
"LAWFUL ENDS OF THE GOVERNMENT"
ON FEBRUARY 25, 1790, A PERSUADED WASHINGTON SIDED AGAINST FELLOW VIRGINIANS JEFFERSON, MADISON, AND ATTORNEY GENERAL RANDOLPH. HE SIGNED THE BANK BILL INTO LAW.
BY SIGNING THIS BILL, WASHINGTON SET A STRONG PRECEDENT FOR THE IMPLIED POWERS DOCTRINE: THE IDEA THAT THE FEDERAL GOVERNMENT'S OPERATING TERRITORY MAY INCLUDE POWERS RELEVANT TO ITS OVERALL STATED PURPOSE--YET NOT SPECIFICALLY WRITTEN OUT IN THE CONSTITUTION.
AS ANOTHER EXAMPLE: THE ARMY AND NAVY--BUT NOT AN INDEPENDENT AIR FORCE--ARE EXPRESSLY MENTIONED IN THE CONSTITUTION, BUT THE GOVERNMENT'S ABILITY TO CREATE AN AIR FORCE IS IMPLIED BY, AND CONSISTENT WITH, ITS POWER TO DECLARE AND WAGE WAR, AND "RAISE," "SUPPORT," "MAINTAIN," AND "REGULATE" LAND AND NAVAL FORCES.

WITH SO MUCH OF HIS FINANCIAL PLAN IN PLACE, AND EVEN MAKING HEADWAY ON AN AMBITIOUS PROJECT TO PURPOSE-BUILD AN **AMERICAN INDUSTRIAL CITY*** NEAR THE SHIPPING AND FINANCIAL HUB OF MANHATTAN...

*THE FUTURE PATERSON, NEW JERSEY.

...IT'S NOT HARD TO SEE HOW A MAN MIGHT SLIP, TOO COMFORTABLY...

...INTO A COCKSURE, RISK-TAKING HABITUDE...

...AND GIVE IN TO TEMPTATION.

SIR. FORGIVE ME, BUT--YOU ARE COLONEL HAMILTON?

IF YOU WOULD INDULGE ME A MOMENT, AND SPEAK WITH ME...

...IN PRIVATE.

Some Concert between the Husband and the Wife

MRS. JAMES REYNOLDS, BORN MARY LEWIS BUT NOW GOING BY THE MORE LYRICAL *MARIA*, TOOK PAINS TO ESTABLISH HER RESPECTABLE FAMILY TIES.

SHE REPORTED HAVING COME TO HAMILTON BECAUSE THEY WERE BOTH NEW YORKERS.

HER WELL-PREPARED PREAMBLE SUGGESTS THAT COMING TO HAMILTON WAS NO SPUR-OF-THE-MOMENT DECISION.

MY HUSBAND ≷SNIFF≷ HAS TREATED ME EVER SO CRUELLY. HE HAS TAKEN OUR DAUGHTER AND GONE TO LIVE WITH *ANOTHER WOMAN...*

...LEAVING ME *DESTITUTE.* I WANT ONLY ≷CHOKE≷ TO RETURN HOME-- TO FAMILY AND FRIENDS--*BUT I HAVE NOT THE MEANS.*

MY DEAR MADAM.

YOUR SITUATION IS MOST UNBEARABLE AND DISTRESSING. IT WOULD GIVE MY HEART GREAT CONTENT TO PROVIDE YOU PASSAGE HOME.

THIS MOMENT HAPPENS TO BE INCONVENIENT. BUT ALLOW ME TO KNOW THE STREET AND NUMBER WHERE YOU...

...OH!

THE AFFAIR THAT BEGAN THAT EVENING IN MARIA'S BOARDINGHOUSE CONTINUED ON AND OFF FOR ALMOST A YEAR.

ONLY IN ATYPICAL CASES DOES AN INDIVIDUAL'S SEXUAL CONDUCT--GIVEN ITS *HIGHLY PERSONAL NATURE*--LEAVE DOCUMENTARY EVIDENCE FOR HISTORIANS. SO, USUALLY, WE ARE LEFT ONLY TO *SPECULATE* ABOUT WHAT MAY HAVE DRIVEN A CELEBRATED FIGURE TO MARITAL INFIDELITY.

IN HIS DAY, PURITANICAL UTTERANCES ABOUT SEX AND MARRIAGE WERE NUMEROUS AND POPULAR. SUCH WERE THE DELICACIES AND CONFUSIONS OF THE TIMES THAT THE BELIEF THAT WOMEN *WERE NOT CAPABLE OF FEELING SEXUAL URGES* STOOD ALONGSIDE THE IDEA THEY WERE ALL *SEDUCTRESSES* WHOSE BEHAVIOR MUST BE TIGHTLY CONTROLLED.

YET OUT-OF-WEDLOCK SEX WAS BY ALL EVIDENCE *COMMON*--AND KNOWN TO BE PART OF THE LIVES OF FOUNDERS BENJAMIN FRANKLIN, THOMAS JEFFERSON, AND GOUVERNEUR MORRIS (A HAMILTON FRIEND AND AUTHOR OF THE CONSTITUTION'S PREAMBLE).

HAMILTON KNEW THIS WAS A TRANSGRESSION. YET NEARLY THE ENTIRETY OF THE ENGLISH-SPEAKING WORLD AT THE TIME TOOK FOR GRANTED THAT *A WOMAN'S INFIDELITY WAS A FAR MORE SERIOUS THING THAN A MAN'S.*

A CONTEMPORARY WRITER TELLS US "MUCH LATITUDE" WAS "GIVEN TO MEN" IN CASES OF INFIDELITY BECAUSE A FATHER NEEDED TO INSURE HIS PROPERTY WAS LEFT TO *BIOLOGICAL CHILDREN ONLY.*

THE SENTIMENTALIZATION OF MARRIED WOMEN OF HIGH SOCIAL RANK--LIKE THE RELIGIOUSLY DEVOUT ELIZABETH HAMILTON (WHO, MOREOVER, WAS OFTEN IN ILL HEALTH)--MAY WELL HAVE AFFECTED A COUPLE'S SEXUAL RELATIONSHIP.

GIVEN ELIZABETH'S MANY PREGNANCIES, SHE AND HER HUSBAND WERE HARDLY STRANGERS IN BED. YET PERHAPS WE MAY ATTRIBUTE HAMILTON'S SELF-CONFESSED "ARDOR OF PASSION" FOR MARIA REYNOLDS--AND THE MYRIAD WAYS IT SET HIM UP FOR SCANDAL--TO THE PARTICULAR THRILLS OF BEING WITH SOMEONE SO *OUTSIDE* THE IDEALS OF VIRTUE AND INNOCENCE.

BEFORE THE WIDE ACCEPTANCE OF THE GERM THEORY OF DISEASE, IN AMERICAN CITIES, MOSQUITOES SPREAD VIRULENT DISEASES IN SUMMERTIME.

ALONG WITH MANY WHO TOOK SIMILAR CUES, ELIZABETH AND THE CHILDREN RETREATED TO THE SCHUYLER ESTATE.

HAMILTON'S WORK KEPT HIM IN PHILADELPHIA. FOR REASONS OF NATIONAL SECURITY, HE AND WASHINGTON WANTED AMERICA SELF-RELIANT FOR NECESSITIES LIKE GUNPOWDER, COAL, AND SAILCLOTH. SO HAMILTON WAS DRAFTING HIS **REPORT ON MANUFACTURES**.

CONTRARY TO THE **LAISSEZ-FAIRE** APPROACH OF ADAM SMITH'S GROUNDBREAKING 1776 CAPITALIST TEXT **THE WEALTH OF NATIONS**, THE REPORT URGED FOR TAX AND TRADE POLICIES THAT WOULD BOOST THESE DOMESTIC ENTERPRISES.

IT WAS NOT UNPREDICTABLE WHEN THIS CALL FOR **GOVERNMENT TAMPERING** THAT WOULD FAVOR NORTHERN STATES MADE SOUTHERNERS AND ANTIFEDERALISTS HOWL.

RECKLESSLY, ALL THE WHILE HE WAS TAKING MARIA HOME TO HIS OWN BEDROOM, AND SENDING ELIZABETH EXCUSES FOR HER TO STAY IN ALBANY.

THEN ONE DAY...

MY HUSBAND HAS WRITTEN. HE SAYS HE WISHES TO RETURN TO ME.

OH? WELL...

...THAT IS PROBABLY FOR THE BEST.

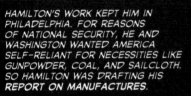

LATER, MARIA THREW HAMILTON A BIT OF A CURVE BALL. SHE CLAIMED HER HUSBAND KNEW OF TROUBLING TREASURY DEPARTMENT **IMPROPRIETIES.**

A MR. JAMES REYNOLDS TO SEE YOU, MR. SECRETARY?

WHAT'S THAT? *OH.* YES, YES.

SEND HIM IN.

BUT REYNOLDSS DIDN'T KNOW ANYTHING HAMILTON TOOK TO BE IMPORTANT.

HE DID, HOWEVER, MAKE REPEATED VISITS TO ASK FOR WORK.

WHILE HAMILTON DEMURRED...

...MARIA KEPT WRITING, PROFESSING DEEP FEELINGS FOR HAMILTON AND PLEADING TO KEEP THEIR SECRET ROMANCE GOING.

ACCORDING TO HAMILTON, THIS IS WHEN HE BEGAN TO FEEL **SUSPICIOUS.**

IT COULD NOT HAVE HELPED THAT JEFFERSON AND MADISON HAD TAKEN A TRIP ACROSS THE NORTH THAT SUMMER...

...TO FEEL OUT FUTURE POLITICAL ALLIES, LIKE AARON BURR.

ONE DAY THAT WINTER, IT ALL CAME TO A HEAD. REYNOLDS CLAIMED TO HAVE DISCOVERED HIS WIFE'S BESEECHING LETTERS...

INSTEAD OF BEING A FRIEND, YOU HAVE ACTED THE PART OF THE CRUELEST MAN IN EXISTENCE!

IF HE DOES NOT SEE OR HEAR FROM YOU TODAY, HE WILL WRITE MRS. HAMILTON!

...AND HE DEMANDED MONEY.

BEFORE THE WIDE ACCEPTANCE OF THE GERM THEORY OF DISEASE, IN AMERICAN CITIES, MOSQUITOES SPREAD VIRULENT DISEASES IN SUMMERTIME.

ALONG WITH MANY WHO TOOK SIMILAR CUES, ELIZABETH AND THE CHILDREN RETREATED TO THE SCHUYLER ESTATE.

HAMILTON'S WORK KEPT HIM IN PHILADELPHIA. FOR REASONS OF NATIONAL SECURITY, HE AND WASHINGTON WANTED AMERICA SELF-RELIANT FOR NECESSITIES LIKE GUNPOWDER, COAL, AND SAILCLOTH. SO HAMILTON WAS DRAFTING HIS **REPORT ON MANUFACTURES.**

CONTRARY TO THE **LAISSEZ-FAIRE** APPROACH OF ADAM SMITH'S GROUNDBREAKING 1776 CAPITALIST TEXT **THE WEALTH OF NATIONS,** THE REPORT URGED FOR TAX AND TRADE POLICIES THAT WOULD BOOST THESE DOMESTIC ENTERPRISES.

IT WAS NOT UNPREDICTABLE WHEN THIS CALL FOR **GOVERNMENT TAMPERING** THAT WOULD FAVOR NORTHERN STATES MADE SOUTHERNERS AND ANTIFEDERALISTS HOWL.

RECKLESSLY, ALL THE WHILE HE WAS TAKING MARIA HOME TO HIS OWN BEDROOM, AND SENDING ELIZABETH EXCUSES FOR HER TO STAY IN ALBANY.

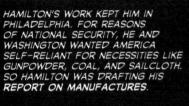

THEN ONE DAY...

MY HUSBAND HAS WRITTEN. HE SAYS HE WISHES TO RETURN TO ME.

OH? WELL...

...THAT IS PROBABLY FOR THE BEST.

LATER, MARIA THREW HAMILTON A BIT OF A CURVE BALL. SHE CLAIMED HER HUSBAND KNEW OF TROUBLING TREASURY DEPARTMENT *IMPROPRIETIES.*

A MR. JAMES REYNOLDS TO SEE YOU, MR. SECRETARY?

WHAT'S THAT? *OH.* YES, YES.

SEND HIM IN.

BUT REYNOLDSS DIDN'T KNOW ANYTHING HAMILTON TOOK TO BE IMPORTANT.

HE DID, HOWEVER, MAKE REPEATED VISITS TO ASK FOR WORK.

WHILE HAMILTON DEMURRED...

...MARIA KEPT WRITING, PROFESSING DEEP FEELINGS FOR HAMILTON AND PLEADING TO KEEP THEIR SECRET ROMANCE GOING.

ACCORDING TO HAMILTON, THIS IS WHEN HE BEGAN TO FEEL *SUSPICIOUS.*

IT COULD NOT HAVE HELPED THAT JEFFERSON AND MADISON HAD TAKEN A TRIP ACROSS THE NORTH THAT SUMMER...

...TO FEEL OUT FUTURE POLITICAL ALLIES, LIKE AARON BURR.

ONE DAY THAT WINTER, IT ALL CAME TO A HEAD. REYNOLDS CLAIMED TO HAVE DISCOVERED HIS WIFE'S BESEECHING LETTERS...

INSTEAD OF BEING A FRIEND, YOU HAVE ACTED THE PART OF THE CRUELEST MAN IN EXISTENCE!

IF HE DOES NOT SEE OR HEAR FROM YOU TODAY, HE WILL WRITE MRS. HAMILTON!

...AND HE DEMANDED MONEY.

HAMILTON SOON PAID JAMES REYNOLDS THE $1,000 HE DEMANDED (ABOUT $24,000 TODAY).

FOLLOWING A STRING OF LATER, SMALL PAYMENTS, REYNOLDS LET THE AFFAIR CONTINUE.

INCREASINGLY SURE THAT JAMES AND MARIA HAD **COLLUDED** FROM THE BEGINNING TO **BLACKMAIL** HIM, HAMILTON CALLED IT QUITS WITH BOTH.

AND HIS HEMORRHAGING OF MONEY TO EXTORTIONISTS WAS **NOTHING** COMPARED TO THE **FINANCIAL CONVULSIONS** AT THE NATIONAL LEVEL.

AMERICA'S FIRST STOCK MARKET CRASH, **THE PANIC OF 1792,** LEFT HAMILTON SCRAMBLING TO CONTAIN IT.

IT WAS THE FALLOUT OF FINANCIAL SCHEMES IN NEW YORK BY HIS FRIEND, WILLIAM DUER. THIS TO MANY MADE HAMILTON **GUILTY BY ASSOCIATION.**

JEFFERSON HAD RECRUITED WRITER **PHILIP FRENEAU** TO BE HIS PROXY; TO BE A **NEWSPAPER ATTACK DOG** AGAINST HAMILTON AND THE FEDERALISTS.

THOSE ATTACKS NOW BECAME VICIOUS.

EVERY PLAN THAT [THE SECRETARY OF THE TREASURY] HAS PROPOSED IS NOT WHAT THE CONSTITUTION DICTATES BUT WHAT **HE** THINKS IS THE BEST MODE OF DOING THE PUBLIC BUSINESS.

IS **HE** SUPERIOR TO THE SOVEREIGNTY OF **THE UNION?**

The Machinations of Factious and Intriguing Men

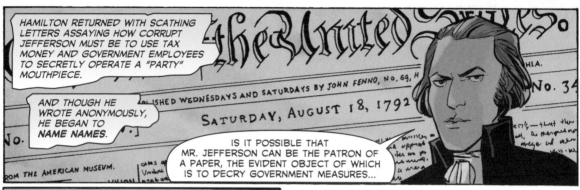

HAMILTON RETURNED WITH SCATHING LETTERS ASSAYING HOW CORRUPT JEFFERSON MUST BE TO USE TAX MONEY AND GOVERNMENT EMPLOYEES TO SECRETLY OPERATE A "PARTY" MOUTHPIECE.

AND THOUGH HE WROTE ANONYMOUSLY, HE BEGAN TO NAME NAMES.

IS IT POSSIBLE THAT MR. JEFFERSON CAN BE THE PATRON OF A PAPER, THE EVIDENT OBJECT OF WHICH IS TO DECRY GOVERNMENT MEASURES...

The United States
PUBLISHED WEDNESDAYS AND SATURDAYS BY JOHN FENNO, No. 69, H
SATURDAY, AUGUST 18, 1792
FROM THE AMERICAN MUSEUM.
No. 34

...SANCTIONED BY THE CHIEF MAGISTRATE OF THE UNION?

AND WASN'T ATTACKING THE ADMINISTRATION THE SAME AS ATTACKING THE PRESIDENT--EXALTED SYMBOL OF THE REVOLUTION--AND ALL THINGS AMERICAN?

MEANWHILE, THAT SAME CHIEF MAGISTRATE WAS GROWING EVER WEARIER OF THE TENSION AND INFIGHTING BETWEEN HIS TRUSTED MINISTERS.

WASHINGTON YEARNED FOR RETIREMENT, AND THE PEACE OF HIS PLANTATION. HE HAD HOPED HIS PRESIDENCY WOULD BE A DIGNIFIED, COMPETENT, STABLE BEGINNING TO THE REPUBLIC. BUT...

I WAS DUPED BY THE SECRETARY OF THE TREASURY AND MADE A TOOL FOR FORWARDING HIS SCHEMES, NOT THEN SUFFICIENTLY UNDERSTOOD BY ME!

HIS SYSTEM FLOWED FROM PRINCIPLES ADVERSE TO LIBERTY, AND WAS CALCULATED TO UNDERMINE AND DEMOLISH THE REPUBLIC!

I WILL NOT SUFFER THE SLANDERS OF A MAN WHOSE HISTORY, FROM THE MOMENT AT WHICH HISTORY CAN STOOP TO NOTICE HIM, IS A TISSUE OF MACHINATIONS AGAINST THE LIBERTY OF THE COUNTRY!

THERE WAS NO SMALL AMOUNT OF BLAME TO GO AROUND. BUT WHEN QUESTIONED, JEFFERSON LIED TO THE PRESIDENT, DENYING ANY INVOLVEMENT IN THE MUCKRAKING "NEWSPAPER WARS."

HAMILTON SAYS THE CONSTITUTION IS A SHILLY-SHALLY THING OF MERE MILK AND WATER, WHICH WILL NOT LAST AND IS ONLY GOOD AS A STEP TO SOMETHING BETTER!

WASHINGTON PROBABLY DIDN'T THINK THE FEUDING COULD GET WORSE.

HE WAS WRONG.

JEFFERSON WAS NOT THE ONLY ONE "TALKING OUT OF SCHOOL" ABOUT THE SECRETARY OF THE TREASURY.

WHAT DO YOU HAVE TO SAY *NOW*, YOU CONTEMPTIBLE BIT OF ROT?

HOUFF!

FOOL! YOU JAIL US UNDER A FATAL DELUSION!

YOU ARE JUST ANOTHER PLAYTHING OF THE *SHAMMING BAMBOOZLERS* HAMILTON AND DUER!

EH... HOW'S THAT?

THE LATEST UNDERHANDED MONEYMAKING SCHEME OF JAMES REYNOLDS (AND FRIEND *JACOB CLINGMAN*)--TRYING TO CLAIM THE PENSION OF A WAR VETERAN WHO WASN'T ACTUALLY DEAD--BACKFIRED.

CLINGMAN, ATTEMPTING TO WRIGGLE OUT OF TROUBLE, TOLD SPEAKER OF THE HOUSE MUHLENBERG OF HAMILTON'S SUSPICIOUS CASH PAYMENTS TO REYNOLDS.

REYNOLDS SEEMS TO HAVE LET CLINGMAN BELIEVE THAT INSTEAD OF ACTING AS HAMILTON'S PIMP, HE WAS HIS PARTNER IN *WHITE-COLLAR FINANCIAL CRIME.*

IN OTHER WORDS, TO OUTSIDERS, IT LOOKED LIKE HAMILTON WAS *ON THE TAKE.*

BEFORE TAKING OUR CASE TO THE PRESIDENT, WE FEEL HONOR BOUND TO DISCUSS THESE TRANSACTIONS WITH YOU.

RECALL IT, GENTLEMEN: *"RUMOR IS A PIPE BLOWN BY SURMISES, JEALOUSIES, AND CONJECTURES."*

DO ME THE FAVOR OF MEETING AT MY HOME THIS EVE. ALL MYSTERIES SHALL BE REVEALED.

JAMES MONROE.

THAT *YOU,* MR. SENATOR, WOULD ENDORSE SUCH CALUMNIES AS THE CHARGE THAT *I* WOULD USURP THE PUBLIC REVENUE!

BLAZES! VENABLE AND MUHLENBERG ARE *MILKSOPS.* BUT *WE! WE WERE IN THE ARMY!*

...AND SO YOU HAVE IT. RIGHT HERE IN THESE VERY LETTERS! THE WIFE'S EROTICAL SOLICITATIONS! THE HUSBAND'S ENTREATIES TO RENEW MY VISITS TO HER! RECEIPTS MATCHING THE SUMS OF HIS "LOANS!"

TH-TH-THIS IS ALL *MOST SUFFICIENT,* COLONEL HAMILTON! WE BEG YOUR PARDON!

THAT NIGHT...

FOR MEN OF HIGH STANDING, THE AFFAIRS OF *PRIVATE* VERSUS *PUBLIC* LIFE WERE PLACED BEHIND A FIREWALL. GENTLEMEN JUST DIDN'T "GO THERE."

OR THEY *PRETENDED* NOT TO. FOR GOSSIP STILL HAD A WAY OF SPREADING...

HAMILTON WAS ABLE TO WALK AWAY FEELING A CERTAIN VINDICATION.

NO MATTER WHAT HE DID IN HIS OFF HOURS, HIS RECORD AS AN OFFICER OF HIGH TRUST IN THE UNITED STATES REMAINED UNBLEMISHED...

AND HE DECIDED IT MIGHT BE EXPEDIENT TO **SECRETLY** KEEP COPIES OF THE REYNOLDS DOCUMENTS.

...OR SO HE THOUGHT.

BECAUSE MONROE STILL SUSPECTED HAMILTON OF USING HIS TREASURY POSITION FOR SHADY FINANCIAL DEALS.

MONROE WOULD SOON BE MINISTER TO FRANCE. BUT WASHINGTON WOULD DISAPPROVE OF HIS WORK-- AND ABRUPTLY, EMBARRASSINGLY, CALL HIM HOME.

MONROE, INDIGNANT, WOULD HAVE REASON TO WANT THE FEDERALISTS HARMED.

AUX ARMES, CITOYENS, FORMEZ VOS BATAILLONS, MARCHONS, MARCHONS! QU'UN SANG IMPUR ABREUVE NOS SILLONS!

AMERICANS LEARNED IN MARCH 1793, THAT HARM OF A MOST PERMANENT KIND HAD COME TO FRANCE'S LOUIS XVI.

HE HAD BEEN EXECUTED FOR TREASON. BYSTANDERS HAD MADE TROPHIES OF HIS BLOOD. AND THE KING WAS JUST ONE OF THOUSANDS ALREADY GUILLOTINED.

THE EXECUTIONS WERE GLORIOUS SUCCESSES TO THE "DEMOCRATIC-REPUBLICAN SOCIETIES" THAT HAD POPPED UP AS ORGANIZED RESISTANCE TO THE FEDERALISTS.

NORTH AND SOUTH, A **PRO-FRANCE MANIA** RAGED--EQUATING THE REVOLUTION THERE WITH AMERICA IN 1776.

TO JULY 14, 1789! AND THE RIGHTS OF MAN!

THESE MEN DESPISED THE NOTORIOUSLY PRO-BRITISH HAMILTON. AND THE FEELING WAS MUTUAL.

SECRET CLUBS ARE FORMED.

THERE [ARE] MEN IN THIS COUNTRY IRRECONCILABLY ADVERSE TO THE GOVERNMENT OF THE UNITED STATES; WHOSE EXERTIONS TEND TO DISTURB THE TRANQUILITY, ORDER, AND PROSPERITY.

JEFFERSON, THOUGH NOT UNTROUBLED BY THE VIOLENCE, EXULTED IN THE REVOLUTION--AND REBUKED HAMILTON.

THE DENUNCIATION OF THE DEMOCRATIC SOCIETIES IS ONE OF THE EXTRAORDINARY ACTS OF BOLDNESS OF WHICH WE HAVE SEEN SO MANY FROM THE FACTION OF **MONOCRATS**.

FRANCE THEN DECLARED WAR ON GREAT BRITAIN--AND SEVERAL OTHER NEIGHBORS AS WELL.

IN MILITARY CAMPAIGNS THAT YEAR, A YOUNG ARTILLERY OFFICER WHO HAD COME TO THE MAINLAND FROM A SMALL ISLAND DISTINGUISHED HIMSELF IN BATTLE. HIS NAME WAS **NAPOLEON BONAPARTE**.

SIEGE OF BRITISH-CAPTURED FORTS IN TOULON, FRANCE, DECEMBER 1793

HOW SHOULD THE PRESIDENT RESPOND? IT CAME DOWN TO ANOTHER GRUDGE MATCH BETWEEN HAMILTON AND JEFFERSON.

THE TENSION PUSHED WASHINGTON NEARLY TO THE BREAKING POINT.

BY GOD! I WOULD RATHER BE *IN MY GRAVE* THAN IN THE PRESENT SITUATION!

AS WITH THE BANK BILL, HAMILTON, BY PEN AND PAPER, CONVINCED WASHINGTON TO **PROCLAIM NEUTRALITY.**

AMERICA WOULD COME TO THE AID OF NEITHER BRITAIN NOR FRANCE.

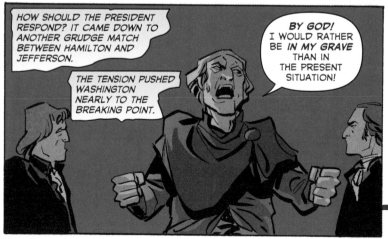

Means of Intimidation

THE UNDER-FIRE JEFFERSON HAD THREATENED TO RESIGN BEFORE. AS 1793 DREW TO A CLOSE, HE FINALLY RETIRED TO MONTICELLO.

WHATEVER JEFFERSON INTENDED IN THE MOMENT, IT WOULD NOT BE A PERMANENT RETREAT.

YET ANOTHER HAMILTON POLICY, LONG SIMMERING IN DISSENSION, BEGAN TO BOIL OVER.

THE EXCISE TAX ON WHISKEY IS SUBVERSIVE OF THE PEACE, LIBERTY, AND RIGHTS OF THE CITIZEN!

AMONG THE ADVERSARIES OF THE TAX WAS ANOTHER WARTIME IMMIGRANT TO THE UNITED STATES--A MAN SCHOOLED IN ENLIGHTENMENT IDEAS AND OFTEN MALTREATED FOR HIS FOREIGN ORIGINS.

WE ARE DISTILLERS THROUGH NECESSITY, NOT CHOICE.

SWISS-BORN **ALBERT GALLATIN**, HOWEVER, EMERGED POLITICALLY ON THE SIDE OF JEFFERSON AND MADISON--A PARTY BEING STYLED AS THE **DEMOCRATIC-REPUBLICANS**.

SEPARATED FROM THE EASTERN COAST BY MOUNTAINS...

...THIS DUTY [IS] MORE UNEQUAL AND OPPRESSIVE TO US.

IN EARLY 1794, IN THE PENNSYLVANIA FRONTIER DISTRICT GALLATIN REPRESENTED IN CONGRESS, VENGEFUL FARMERS ATTACKED ONE OF HAMILTON'S TAX COLLECTORS.

AAAHH!

FOR HAMILTON, THIS VIOLATION OF THE CONSTITUTION AND FEDERAL LAW WAS AN EXISTENTIAL THREAT TO THE UNION.

THE CRISIS HAS ARRIVED. IT MUST BE DETERMINED WHETHER THE GOVERNMENT CAN MAINTAIN ITSELF.

AN IMMEDIATE RESORT TO MILITARY FORCE IS NECESSARY TO COMPEL OBEDIENCE TO THE LAWS.

COMMANDING TROOPS HAD NOT BEEN FORESEEN AS WITHIN THE JOB DESCRIPTION OF THE SECRETARY OF THE TREASURY.

BUT WITH HAMILTON EAGER TO FLEX HIS SOLDIER'S MUSCLES AGAIN, WASHINGTON LET HIM ACT AS SECRETARY OF WAR.

DON'T KNOW IF IT'LL BE JAIL OR HANGING, BUT YOU'RE COMING WITH US.

WHAMM!

SHRIEK! MY HUSBAND!

THIS WOULD BE REMEMBERED IN THE MONONGAHELA COUNTRY FOR GENERATIONS AS "THE DISMAL NIGHT."

WHY HAD HAMILTON BEEN SO ZEALOUS TO CRUSH THE **WHISKEY REBELLION?**

IT WAS ABOUT MORE THAN COLLECTING TAXES TO FUND THE GOVERNMENT OR TO SUSTAIN ITS CREDIBILITY OVERSEAS.

TO HAMILTON, IT WAS A CHANCE TO PURGE THE COUNTRY OF ITS KNEE-JERK URGE TO USE REVOLUTION, REBELLION, AND FRAGMENTATION AS A SOLUTION TO EVERY PROBLEM.

SOME RIDICULED HAMILTON FOR HYSTERICAL OVERREACTION.

AND INDEED--HE **HAD** CALCULATED ALMOST GUARANTEED SUCCESS. THE NEXT CONSTITUTIONAL CRISIS OR REBELLION MIGHT NOT OFFER SUCH ODDS.

AN INSURRECTION WAS ANNOUNCED AND PROCLAIMED AND ARMED AGAINST, BUT COULD NEVER BE FOUND.

THOMAS JEFFERSON.

ALTHOUGH THE LIKES OF JAMES MONROE WERE SURE HAMILTON WAS GROWING RICH IN OFFICE, IN FACT HE MADE SO LITTLE HE WAS GOING BROKE.

THE COUNTRY, ON THE OTHER HAND, WAS ON FIRM FINANCIAL FOOTING.

SO, HAMILTON DECIDED TO RESIGN--AND RETURN TO LAW PRACTICE IN NEW YORK.

I HAVE FIXED UPON THE LAST OF JANUARY NEXT AS THE DAY FOR THE RESIGNATION OF MY OFFICE.

BY TURNS, ALL OF WASHINGTON'S TOP CABINET POSITIONS RESHUFFLED--LEAVING A LINEUP DOMINATED BY FEDERALISTS. ALL FRIENDS OF HAMILTON'S.

SECRETARY OF THE TREASURY: OLIVER WOLCOTT JR., 1795-1800

SECRETARY OF STATE: TIMOTHY PICKERING, 1795-1800

SECRETARY OF WAR: JAMES MCHENRY, 1796-1800

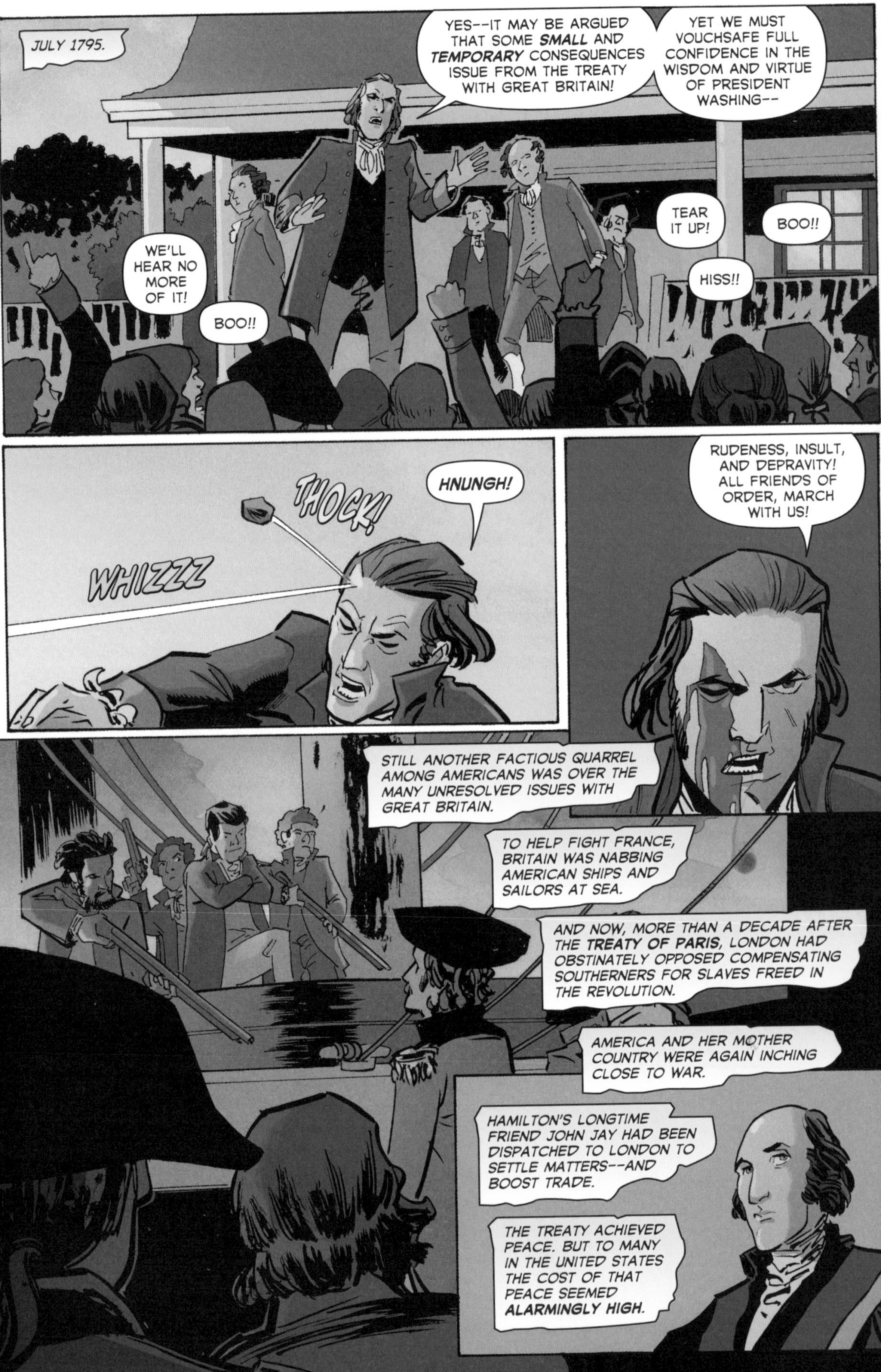
JULY 1795.
YES--IT MAY BE ARGUED THAT SOME SMALL AND TEMPORARY CONSEQUENCES ISSUE FROM THE TREATY WITH GREAT BRITAIN!
YET WE MUST VOUCHSAFE FULL CONFIDENCE IN THE WISDOM AND VIRTUE OF PRESIDENT WASHING--
WE'LL HEAR NO MORE OF IT!
BOO!!
TEAR IT UP!
HISS!!
BOO!!
WHIZZZ
THOCK!
HNUNGH!
RUDENESS, INSULT, AND DEPRAVITY! ALL FRIENDS OF ORDER, MARCH WITH US!
STILL ANOTHER FACTIOUS QUARREL AMONG AMERICANS WAS OVER THE MANY UNRESOLVED ISSUES WITH GREAT BRITAIN.
TO HELP FIGHT FRANCE, BRITAIN WAS NABBING AMERICAN SHIPS AND SAILORS AT SEA.
AND NOW, MORE THAN A DECADE AFTER THE TREATY OF PARIS, LONDON HAD OBSTINATELY OPPOSED COMPENSATING SOUTHERNERS FOR SLAVES FREED IN THE REVOLUTION.
AMERICA AND HER MOTHER COUNTRY WERE AGAIN INCHING CLOSE TO WAR.
HAMILTON'S LONGTIME FRIEND JOHN JAY HAD BEEN DISPATCHED TO LONDON TO SETTLE MATTERS--AND BOOST TRADE.
THE TREATY ACHIEVED PEACE. BUT TO MANY IN THE UNITED STATES THE COST OF THAT PEACE SEEMED ALARMINGLY HIGH.

THE SO-CALLED **JAY TREATY**, WHICH HAMILTON HELPED DEFEND IN HIS TRIED-AND-TRUE MODE AS PAMPHLETEER, WAS STUPENDOUSLY UNPOPULAR.

REJECT THE PRINCIPLE OF COMPROMISE, AND THE FEUDS OF NATIONS MUST BECOME MUCH MORE DEADLY THAN THEY HAVE HERETOFORE BEEN.

JAY

IN THE SENATE, BURR GAINED POPULARITY WITH JEFFERSON'S DEMOCRATIC-REPUBLICAN PARTY BY MAULING THE JAY TREATY--AND HOW LONG WASHINGTON D.C. HAD KEPT ITS HUMILIATIONS SECRET.

IF THE PEOPLE HAVE THE RIGHT AND CAPACITY TO GOVERN THEMSELVES, THEY ARE CERTAINLY ENTITLED TO A KNOWLEDGE OF THEIR OWN AFFAIRS!

TREATY
of
AMITY, COMMERCE,
AND
NAVIGATION
BETWEEN
His Britannic Majesty
AND
The United States of America,
CONDITIONALLY RATIF...
BY THE SENATE OF TH...
AT P...

WASHINGTON HAD TO EXPEND IMMENSE POLITICAL CAPITAL TO GET CONGRESS TO SIGN OFF ON THE TREATY.

HIS CHERISHED PUBLIC PRESTIGE WAS MAULED IN WAYS THAT IN EARLIER TIMES WOULD HAVE BEEN CONSIDERED SACRILEGIOUS.

I KNOW OF NO CRIME OR MISDEMEANOR AGAINST THE CONSTITUTION GREATER OR HIGHER THAN THAT WHICH YOU HAVE SEVERALLY COMMITTED.

THOSE SHOULD BE REMOVED FROM OFFICE WHO ABUSE POWER...[INCLUDING] THE MAN THEY ONCE STYLED THE FATHER OF HIS COUNTRY.

LET NO FLATTERER PERSUADE YOU TO REST ONE HOUR LONGER AT THE HELM OF STATE!

TYRANNY WILL NOT ESTABLISH ITS BASTILLE IN THIS COUNTRY!

WASHINGTON HAD HAD ENOUGH. MEN IN HIS FAMILY WERE KNOWN NOT TO BE LONG-LIVED.

IT WAS TIME TO PASS THE TORCH. HE WOULD NOT RUN FOR REELECTION IN 1796.

The Circumstances Disclosed

THE TUMULTUOUS RECENT YEARS HAD DISTANCED WASHINGTON FROM FELLOW VIRGINIANS-- ESPECIALLY MADISON.

HE INSTEAD TAPPED HAMILTON TO WRITE HIS FAREWELL ADDRESS.

BEYOND ALL THE GRATITUDE TO AND CELEBRATION OF THE AMERICAN PEOPLE, WASHINGTON WARNED AGAINST THE "CUNNING, AMBITIOUS, AND UNPRINCIPLED MEN" WHO WOULD ENDEAVOR TO UNDO THE UNION BY DIVIDING IT GEOGRAPHICALLY OR IDEOLOGICALLY.

IN THE 1796 ELECTION, HAMILTON'S AIM WAS TO KEEP THE FEDERALIST PARTY IN POWER. ONLY THAT WOULD PRESERVE HIS FINANCIAL SYSTEM.

YET HE HAD LITTLE ENTHUSIASM FOR HEIR APPARENT, JOHN ADAMS.

I HAVE AN AVERSION TO THE MULTIPLICATION OF BANKS. WE SHALL SOON BE PERPLEXED AND DISTRESSED, IN CONSEQUENCE OF THEM.

BEHIND THE OPPOSING PARTY'S LINES, MADISON WORKED TO PULL JEFFERSON OUT OF RETIREMENT.

BUT THE DEMOCRATIC- REPUBLICANS WOULD NEED A **VICE PRESIDENT,** TOO--PREFERABLY, TO GIVE THEMSELVES A NATIONAL PROFILE, SOMEONE **NOT FROM THE SOUTH.**

A CERTAIN SOMEONE WAS NOT SHY ABOUT LETTING ELECTORS KNOW HE FIT THE BILL.

IF NO GREAT SCHISM HAPPENS IN VIRGINIA, I THINK IT MORALLY CERTAIN THAT MR. JEFFERSON AND COLONEL BURR WILL BE ELECTED.

ANY SUPPORT BURR INITIALLY HAD IN THE SOUTH, HOWEVER, MELTED AWAY. HE PLACED FOURTH IN A FIELD OF THIRTEEN.

BEFORE THE CONSTITUTION WAS AMENDED IN 1804 TO SMOOTH OVER THIS FLAW, PRESIDENTIAL ELECTORS CAST TWO VOTES EACH FOR THE TOP EXECUTIVE OFFICE.

THE CANDIDATE RECEIVING THE MOST VOTES BECAME PRESIDENT. THE CANDIDATE WITH THE **SECOND HIGHEST NUMBER OF VOTES** BECAME VICE PRESIDENT.

vote by Ballot for two Persons.

THEY DID NOT RUN TOGETHER ON THE SAME TICKET. IT DID NOT MATTER IF ONE WINNING CANDIDATE'S PARTY MATCHED THAT OF THE OTHER.

THE 1796 ELECTION'S FINAL RESULTS MADE HAMILTON FEEL RATHER AGNOSTIC.

MR. ADAMS IS PRESIDENT, MR. JEFFERSON VICE PRESIDENT.

SKEPTICS LIKE ME QUIETLY LOOK FORWARD TO THE [ADMINISTRATION]-- WILLING TO HOPE BUT NOT PREPARED TO BELIEVE.

HAMILTON HAD REASON TO BE HOPEFUL: ADAMS DECIDED TO KEEP THE SAME CABINET MEMBERS AS WASHINGTON.

THESE MEN WERE HAMILTON LOYALISTS-- AND COULD BE COUNTED ON TO BE HIS INSTRUMENTS OF INFLUENCE. HIS EYES AND EARS.

EARLY IN THE ADAMS PRESIDENCY, FEDERALISTS OUSTED THE CLERK OF THE HOUSE OF REPRESENTATIVES. THIS WAS VIRGINIAN **JOHN BECKLEY**--A TIRELESS AND UNQUESTIONING FOOT SOLDIER AND GOSSIPMONGER FOR THE DEMOCRATIC-REPUBLICANS.

BECKLEY WAS THE MAN WHO HAD MADE COPIES OF THE REYNOLDS DOCUMENTS FOR JAMES MONROE FIVE YEARS EARLIER.

BECKLEY IS THE PRIME SUSPECT FOR **LEAKING THEM** TO MUCKRAKING WRITER JAMES T. CALLENDER.

NEITHER BECKLEY NOR CALLENDER WERE "GENTLEMEN." THEY COULD GO WHERE OTHERS WOULD NOT.

IN CALLENDER'S RESULTING PAMPHLET, THE DISCLOSURE OF HAMILTON'S ADULTERY WAS ONLY A SIDE DISH. THE MAIN COURSES DAMNING HAMILTON WERE ALLEGATIONS OF EMBEZZLEMENT AND FRAUD.

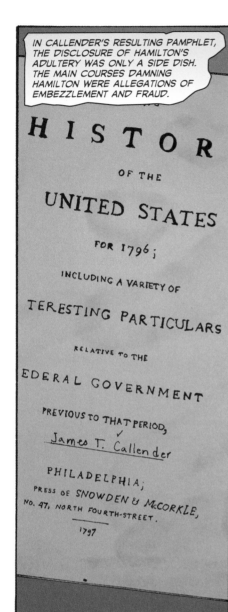

HISTORY

OF THE

UNITED STATES

FOR 1796;

INCLUDING A VARIETY OF

INTERESTING PARTICULARS

RELATIVE TO THE

FEDERAL GOVERNMENT

PREVIOUS TO THAT PERIOD,

James T. Callender ✓

PHILADELPHIA;

PRESS OF SNOWDEN & McCORKLE,
No. 47, NORTH FOURTH-STREET.

1797

fider himfelf bound.

16th. Laft night we waited on colonel Hamilton, when he informed us of a _particular connection with Mrs. Reynolds_: the period of its commencement, and circumftances attending it; his vifiting her at Infkeep's; the frequent fupplies of money to her and her hufband, on that account; his durefs by them from the fear of a difclofure, and _his anxiety to be relieved from it and them_. To fupport this, he fhewed a great number of letters from Reynolds and herfelf, commencing early in 1791. He acknowledged _all the letters in a difguifed band, in our poffeffion_, to be his. We left him under an impreffion, our fufpicions were removed. He acknowledged our conduct to—

PHILIP!

HELP THE SERVANTS WITH YOUR MOTHER AND THE SMALL ONES. I HAVE BUSINESS.

O-OF COURSE, PAPA.

DEAR--?

IGNORANT OF JOHN BECKLEY'S PROBABLE ROLE IN THE DRAMA, HAMILTON HAD OTHER IDEAS ABOUT WHO WAS OUT TO GET HIM.

ENOUGH, MONROE!!

I HAVE EVERY REASON TO BELIEVE THIS CALLENDER PROCURED THE PROOF OF MY DEALINGS WITH THE REYNOLDSES FROM *YOU!*

I BEG YOUR PARDON, SIR! YOU ARE IN A *MAN'S HOME!*

I HAVE NOT *TOUCHED* THOSE LETTERS SINCE MY RETURN FROM FRANCE. THEY REMAIN SEALED--AND IN THE CARE OF A VIRGINIA FRIEND!

"A VIRGINIA FRIEND" YOU SAY! SIR, YOU ARE GREATLY WANTING IN THE ARTS OF BEGUILEMENT.

THIS AS YOUR REPRESENTATION IS *TOTALLY FALSE!*

YOU SAY I REPRESENTED *FALSELY?* YOU ARE A SCOUNDREL!

I WILL MEET YOU LIKE A GENTLEMAN.

I AM READY. *GET YOUR PISTOLS.*

OVERHEATED WORDS ASIDE, IT WAS NOT "UP TO CODE" FOR GENTLEMEN TO DUEL ON THE SPOT. THERE WERE FORMALITIES TO BE DISPENSED WITH.

MONROE MADE AN INTERESTING CHOICE FOR AN INTERMEDIARY: AARON BURR.

BURR'S MODERN, MERCENARY REPUTATION ASIDE, HE BROUGHT EVENHANDEDNESS AND CONSCIENCE TO THE AFFAIR.

IF YOU REALLY BELIEVE, AS I DO, THAT HAMILTON IS INNOCENT OF THE CHARGE OF [FINANCIAL] SPECULATION...

...IT WILL BE AN ACT OF MAGNANIMITY AND JUSTICE TO SAY SO.

IT IS ALL BUT A CERTAINTY THAT DEEP IN HIS PSYCHE, HAMILTON--AGGRIEVED BY HIS LESS FORTUNATE BIRTH AND CHILDHOOD--FELT INSECURE ABOUT HIS SOCIAL STATUS. EMOTIONS OFTEN GOT THE BETTER OF HIM, AS WELL.

BOTH HIS INSECURITY AND HIS THIN SKIN COULD COMBINE TO MAKE HIM REACT WITH AN OVEREXCESSIVE ATTACHMENT TO SUPERFICIALITIES.

BURR, ON THE OTHER HAND, FELT HIS PEDIGREE SO UNIMPEACHABLE THAT THE ACCEPTED RULES OF ARISTOCRATIC COMPORTMENT WERE HIS TO PLAY WITH-- TO FOLLOW, BEND, OR BREAK AS HE SAW FIT.

IN A TIME WHEN HIGH OFFICE WAS SUPPOSED TO "SEEK THE MAN" (NOT THE OTHER WAY AROUND), BURR OPENLY POLITICKED. THIS CAUSED TONGUES TO WAG. BUT BURR FIGURED HE COULD GET AWAY WITH IT.

GIVEN THIS MORE ALOOF APPROACH, BURR DOWNPLAYED THE "NEED" FOR MONROE TO DUEL.

AND SO, HAMILTON AND THE MAN DESTINED TO BECOME THE FIFTH U.S. PRESIDENT NEVER DREW WEAPONS ON EACH OTHER.

YET THE WEST INDIAN TRANSPLANT'S STRIDENCY, NEARSIGHTEDNESS, AND LITERALISTIC INTERPRETATION OF HOW A "GENTLEMAN" SHOULD BEHAVE...

The charge against me is a connection with one James Reynolds for purposes of improper pecuniary speculation. My real crime is an amorous connection with his wife, for a considerable time with his privity and connivance, if not originally brought on by a combination between the husband and wife with the design to extort money from me.

...WAS ABOUT TO LEAD HIM EVEN MORE ASTRAY.

A FEW MONTHS AFTER NEWS OF HIS AFFAIR BROKE WIDELY, HAMILTON PUBLISHED SOMETHING OF HIS OWN.

IN WHAT'S KNOWN AS THE **REYNOLDS PAMPHLET**, HE NOT ONLY ADMITTED HIS AFFAIR, BUT **SPILLED MANY OF ITS MOST SORDID DETAILS AS WELL.**

HE HAD INTENDED TO DEMONSTRATE THIS: IF HE WAS WILLING TO BE SO SCRUPULOUSLY HONEST ABOUT INFIDELITY, AND CONDEMN AND IMMOLATE HIMSELF TO HIS FAMILY...

...THEN HE MUST ALSO BE TELLING THE TRUTH ABOUT BEING INNOCENT OF MALFEASANCE.

BUT HE WENT TOO FAR. A **GENTLEMAN IS NEVER INDISCREET.** AND HAMILTON, IN TODAY'S PARLANCE, SHARED TOO MUCH.

THE TACTIC BLEW UP IN HIS FACE IN THE EYES OF THE LESSER CLASSES, AS WELL.

HAMILTON HAD BEEN MALIGNED FOR BEING AN ELITIST--FOR PROMOTING THE IDEA THAT SOME MEN ARE BETTER THAN OTHERS AND, BECAUSE OF THAT, DESERVE DEFERENTIAL TREATMENT...

...LIKE BEING JUDGED SOLELY BY THEIR PUBLIC RECORD, THEIR PERSONAL AND PRIVATE CONDUCT SET ASIDE.

BUT THE FRENCH REVOLUTION AND ITS ECHOES IN THE DEMOCRATIC-REPUBLICAN PARTY WERE INTERESTED ONLY IN TEARING DOWN ALL PILLARS OF ARISTOCRATIC PRETENSION AND PRIVILEGE.

"THE PEOPLE" WERE NOT BUYING WHAT HAMILTON HAD TO SELL.

IF THEY WERE EVER RECORDED, ELIZABETH HAMILTON'S REACTIONS TO THESE REVELATIONS--**WHICH CAME WHEN THEIR LATEST CHILD, WILLIAM, WAS JUST THREE WEEKS OLD**--HAVE NEVER SURFACED.

ELIZABETH NEVER CEASED DEFENDING HER HUSBAND TO CRITICS. THE FACT THAT SHE AND HER HUSBAND WENT ON TO HAVE MORE CHILDREN SUGGESTS THAT THEIR ROMANTIC CONNECTION SURVIVED.

WHATEVER THE REPERCUSSIONS IN HER HEART OF HEARTS, IT IS PROBABLY WRONGHEADED TO VIEW THE AFFAIR WITH A MODERN LENS.

Great Souls Care Little about Small Matters

BETWEEN **THE REYNOLDS PAMPHLET** AND THE EGALITARIAN SPIRIT TAKING HOLD, HAMILTON'S POLITICAL CAREER WAS OVER.

HE DID NOT, HOWEVER, KNOW THAT YET.

DESIRING A RETURN TO PROMINENCE FOR HIMSELF AND HIS PARTY, HAMILTON MIGHT VERY WELL HAVE BEEN INWARDLY REPRISING AN OLD REFRAIN...

...I WISH THERE WAS A WAR.

ONCE MORE, IT LOOKED LIKE FATE MIGHT FURNISH HIM WITH JUST THAT.

IN THE LATE 1790s FRANCE WAS INCENSED WITH THE UNITED STATES.

CITING THE PRO-BRITISH **JAY TREATY** AND AMERICA'S WEAK DEMAND FOR ITS EXPORTS, BY JUNE 1798, FRANCE HAD EXPELLED ITS AMERICAN AMBASSADOR AND CAPTURED HUNDREDS OF U.S. MERCHANT SHIPS AT SEA.

FRENCH OFFICIALS THEN DEMANDED A BRIBE TO EVEN **SPEAK TO** A NEW SLATE OF COMMISSIONERS JOHN ADAMS HAD SENT. THIS WAS MORE THAN ANY HONORABLE NATION COULD TAKE.

P-TOWW! P-TOWW!

ALTHOUGH WE MAY VIEW WAR AS PARTICULARLY INJURIOUS TO THE INTERESTS OF OUR COUNTRY, PROVIDENCE MAY INTEND IT FOR OUR GOOD...

...AND WE MUST SUBMIT.

WAR TENSION WAS SO HIGH THAT ADAMS CALLED WASHINGTON OUT OF RETIREMENT TO COMMAND AND BUILD UP A NEW ARMY.

UNDER EXTREME DURESS, ADAMS SUBMITTED TO WASHINGTON'S DEMAND THAT HAMILTON BE ELEVATED TO **MAJOR GENERAL**--ESSENTIALLY PUTTING HIM CHARGE.

THE PROMOTION SO ELEVATED HAMILTON'S MOOD THAT HE EVEN WELCOMED COLLABORATION WITH BURR ON MILITARY PREPAREDNESS.

BURR'S TERM IN THE SENATE EXPIRED IN 1797, AND HE HAD LOST A RUN FOR THE NEW YORK GOVERNOR'S SEAT. NOW HE WAS FACING MONEY PROBLEMS--AND HAD TO CONCENTRATE ON BUSINESS.

BURR DRAFTED HAMILTON TO SUPPORT A CORPORATE PROJECT TO REPLACE MANHATTAN'S PESTILENTIAL WELLS WITH FRESH WATER.

CRAFTILY, AT THE LAST MINUTE, BURR ALTERED THE CHARTER OF **THE MANHATTAN COMPANY** TO FUNCTION NOT SO MUCH AS A WATER PROVIDER BUT, ESSENTIALLY, **AS A BANK.**

DEMOCRATIC-REPUBLICANS WERE SUPPOSED TO LOATHE BANKS.

BUT THOMAS JEFFERSON'S SALT-OF-THE-EARTH, AGRARIAN IDEALS COULD ONLY WIN SO MUCH SUPPORT IN NEW YORK. BURR EMBODIED A MIDDLE GROUND.

BY FOUNDING THE MANHATTAN COMPANY*, THEN, HE BROKE THE FEDERALIST MONOPOLY ON BANKS.

MERCHANTS AND BUSINESSMEN WHO DISDAINED FEDERALIST TAXES, EXCLUSIONARY AIRS, AND HANDS-ON MANAGEMENT STYLES NOW HAD A HOME OF THEIR OWN.

*THE BANK BECAME CHASE MANHATTAN. IT SURVIVES IN CURRENT FORM AS JPMORGAN CHASE & CO.

HAMILTON HAD BEEN **TRICKED**.

I HAVE BEEN PRESENT WHEN [BURR] HAS CONTENDED AGAINST BANKING SYSTEMS WITH EARNESTNESS.

YET HE HAS LATELY ESTABLISHED A BANK, *A PERFECT MONSTER* IN ITS PRINCIPLES, BUT A VERY CONVENIENT INSTRUMENT OF PROFIT AND INFLUENCE.

BURR WASN'T THE ONLY ONE TAKING MATTERS INTO HIS OWN HANDS.

JOHN ADAMS FINALLY CAME TO REALIZE THAT HIS ENTIRE CABINET WAS MADE UP OF AGENTS OF HAMILTON.

YOU CANNOT, SIR, REMAIN LONGER IN OFFICE!

HAMILTON IS AN INTRIGANT! A MAN DEVOID OF EVERY MORAL PRINCIPLE! A BASTARD! A FOREIGNER!

RESOLVED TO BE HIS OWN MAN, ADAMS MADE A HAIRPIN POLICY TURN AND PURSUED PEACE WITH FRANCE.

WAR HYSTERIA ABATED. HAMILTON'S ARMY **SLOWLY DIED ON THE VINE**-- MAKING HIS FINAL BID FOR MILITARY GLORY ROT WITH IT.

ANOTHER BLOW TO HAMILTON'S SUPPORT CAME ON DECEMBER 14, 1799. WITH THE FEDERAL CITY BEARING HIS NAME BEING READIED TO DEBUT, *GEORGE WASHINGTON DIED.*

WHAT STARTED AS A COLD HAD SWIFTLY SWOLLEN INTO A DEADLY INFECTION.

HAMILTON HELPED PREPARE THE MILITARY HONORS THAT WOULD BE SHOWN AT THE FUNERAL OF HIS "BELOVED COMMANDER IN CHIEF."

MY IMAGINATION IS GLOOMY, MY HEART SAD.

THE TWENTY-TWO-YEAR RELATIONSHIP HAD NOT ALWAYS BEEN SMOOTH. BUT HAMILTON HAD BEEN CONSTANT AND FAITHFUL, AND EVEN HE HAD MELLOWED A BIT WITH AGE.

THE ALIGNMENT OF WASHINGTON AND HAMILTON'S SHARED POLITICAL VALUES HAD SEEN THE TWO THROUGH TIMES OF CRISIS.

IN LIGHT OF ALL THIS, WASHINGTON HAD EASED INTO DEEPER AND DEEPER AFFECTION FOR THE YOUNGER MAN.

THOMAS JEFFERSON DID NOT ATTEND WASHINGTON'S FUNERAL.

AARON BURR SAW IN WASHINGTON'S PASSING AN UNPRECEDENTED OPPORTUNITY TO DEFEAT THE FEDERALISTS.

WITH THE ELECTION OF 1800 COMING...

...BURR HAD A PLAY TO INGRATIATE HIMSELF TO THE "OLD DOMINION" ELITES WHO HAD FAILED TO VOTE FOR HIM FOR VICE PRESIDENT IN 1796.

HE WOULD DELIVER A NEW YORK LEGISLATURE CERTAIN TO BACK JEFFERSON IN THE AUTUMN.

VIRGINIA

AT THE TIME, IN NEW YORK STATE, PRESIDENTIAL ELECTORS WERE CHOSEN *ONLY* BY THOSE ELECTED TO THE STATE ASSEMBLY.

HAMILTON WAS SHELL-SHOCKED. ANYONE COULD SEE THAT JEFFERSON WOULD REWARD BURR BY MAKING HIM VICE PRESIDENT.

YOU HAVE BEEN INFORMED OF THE LOSS OF OUR ELECTION IN THIS CITY.

THERE WILL BE AN ANTIFEDERAL MAJORITY, AND A VERY HIGH PROBABILITY THAT THIS WILL BRING *JEFFERSON* INTO THE CHIEF MAGISTRACY!

INCREDIBLY, HAMILTON HADN'T LEARNED HIS LESSON.

AS PASSIONATELY AVERSE TO ANOTHER FOUR YEARS OF JOHN ADAMS AS HE WAS TO A JEFFERSON WIN, HAMILTON COULDN'T RESTRAIN HIMSELF FROM MONKEYING IN THE ELECTION.

HE BEGAN COMPOSING A VICIOUS PAMPHLET TO DRAG THROUGH THE MUD THE MAN WHO HAD STOLEN HIS ARMY FROM HIM.

THERE IS STRONG REASON TO BELIEVE THAT, WHILE THE PAMPHLET WAS BEING PRINTED, BURR AND HAMILTON ENEMY JOHN BECKLEY GOT HOLD OF IT, AND LEAKED PORTIONS TO THE PRESS.

HAMILTON SUPPOSEDLY MEANT ONLY FOR A FEW OF HIS CONFIDANTS TO READ IT. ONCE EVERYONE KNEW ABOUT IT, HE DECIDED TO COME CLEAN AND PUBLISH IT IN ITS ENTIRETY.

A PRIMARY CAUSE OF THE STATE OF THINGS WHICH LED TO THIS EVENT, IS TO BE TRACED TO THE *UNGOVERNABLE TEMPER* OF MR. ADAMS!

IT IS A FACT THAT HE IS OFTEN LIABLE TO PAROXYSMS OF ANGER, WHICH DEPRIVE HIM OF SELF COMMAND, AND PRODUCE VERY OUTRAGEOUS BEHAVIOR TO THOSE WHO APPROACH HIM!

HE HAS CERTAIN FIXED POINTS OF CHARACTER WHICH TEND NATURALLY TO THE DETRIMENT OF ANY CAUSE OF WHICH HE IS THE CHIEF!

IF HAMILTON HAD LIVED BY THE PEN...

...NOW HE WAS DYING BY IT.

IT IS DIFFICULT TO TELL HOW MUCH HAMILTON'S BUNGLE AFFECTED THE SITTING PRESIDENT'S CHANCES IN THE ELECTION OF 1800. HAMILTON'S INFLUENCE HAD, AFTER ALL, PRECIPITOUSLY WANED.

SUCH HEEDLESS AND ERRATIC BEHAVIOR MADE A STRONG CASE--THAT HAMILTON COULDN'T BE TRUSTED TO LEAD *ANYTHING*.

THIS PAMPHLET I REGRET MORE ON THE ACCOUNT OF ITS AUTHOR, BECAUSE I AM CONFIDENT, IT WILL DO *HIM* MORE HARM THAN *ME*.

HIS CAREER OF AMBITION IS PASSED, AND NEITHER HONOR OR EMPIRE WILL EVER BE HIS.

THE RESULTS OF THE ELECTION OF 1800 WERE EXTRAORDINARY.

ADAMS LOST, HAVING COME IN THIRD. THIS LEFT THE CONTEST BETWEEN JEFFERSON AND BURR--TYING WITH SEVENTY-THREE VOTES EACH.

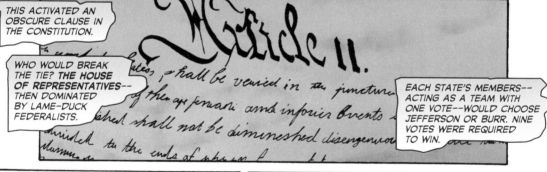

THIS ACTIVATED AN OBSCURE CLAUSE IN THE CONSTITUTION.

WHO WOULD BREAK THE TIE? **THE HOUSE OF REPRESENTATIVES**-- THEN DOMINATED BY LAME-DUCK FEDERALISTS.

EACH STATE'S MEMBERS-- ACTING AS A TEAM WITH ONE VOTE--WOULD CHOOSE JEFFERSON OR BURR. NINE VOTES WERE REQUIRED TO WIN.

EARLIER, BURR HAD VOUCHED HE WOULD NEVER DEIGN TO STAND ON THE SAME GROUND AS THE LOFTY JEFFERSON.

AS TO MYSELF, I WILL CHEERFULLY ABANDON THE OFFICE OF V.P. IF IT SHALL BE THOUGHT THAT I CAN BE MORE USEFUL IN ANY ACTIVE STATION.

YET NOW, WITH THE BIG BRASS RING SO CLOSE, BURR DECIDED NOT TO FOLD. HE GAMBLED ON SEEING HOW THE VOTES TURNED OUT.

AS WEEKS PASSED WITHOUT A FINALIZING BALLOT, THE POWERFUL MEN OF AMERICA WERE IN A STATE OF EXCRUCIATING TENSION.

THE DILEMMA WAS PERSONAL FOR HAMILTON.

HERE HE WAS, WATCHING HIS FEDERALIST PARTY DISMISSED FROM POWER, AND ITS LAST ACT WOULD BE MAKING ONE OF HIS TWO GREATEST ENEMIES THE PRESIDENT!

BURR WAS KNOWN TO BE PLIABLE ON PRINCIPLE--ESPECIALLY IN PURSUIT OF POWER. MANY FEDERALISTS SOUGHT TO MAKE A DEAL WITH HIM.

BUT HAMILTON SPLIT WITH HIS PARTY. HE BELIEVED JEFFERSON COULD BE PERSUADED TO PRESERVE THE JAY TREATY AND NATIONAL BANK--AND BE LESS DANGEROUS TO THE COUNTRY'S FUTURE.

HAMILTON IDENTIFIED DELAWARE'S SINGLE CONGRESSMAN, BURR SUPPORTER **JAMES BAYARD**, AS PLAYING A PIVOTAL ROLE IN THE VOTE. HE DIALED IN ON HIM FOR PERSUASION.

THE FEDERALISTS WILL BECOME A DISORGANIZED AND CONTEMPTIBLE PARTY.

BAYARD, ON FEBRUARY 17, 1801, DECIDED TO WITHHOLD HIS LAST VOTE.

IF THE FEDERALISTS SUBSTITUTE BURR, [HE] WILL BECOME *IN FACT* THE MAN OF OUR PARTY! AND IF HE ACTS ILL, WE MUST SHARE IN THE BLAME AND DISGRACE.

AFTER A WEEK OF TEDIOUS BALLOTING, BAYARD AT LAST **THREW THE ELECTION TO JEFFERSON**-- LEAVING BURR THE VICE PRESIDENCY.

GUIDED BY THE WISDOM AND PATRIOTISM OF THOSE TO WHOM IT BELONGS TO EXPRESS THE LEGISLATIVE WILL OF THE NATION, I WILL GIVE TO THAT A FAITHFUL EXECUTION.

NEW ENGLAND FEDERALISTS **REVILED** JEFFERSON. WITH HIS ELECTION, THEY SAW THE AMERICAN EXPERIMENT ABOUT TO END IN DISASTER.

GREAT GOD OF COMPASSION AND JUSTICE! SHIELD MY COUNTRY FROM DESTRUCTION!

The Cup of Sorrow

"JUST AS TO THE BERRIES OF A TREE AND THE FRUITS OF THE EARTH THERE COMES IN THE FULLNESS OF TIME A PERIOD OF DECAY AND FALL," WROTE THE ROMAN ORATOR AND PHILOSOPHER CICERO--A FAVORITE OF HAMILTON'S.

"A WISE MAN WILL NOT MAKE A GRIEVANCE OF THIS."

OVER THE NEXT SEVERAL YEARS, HAMILTON ALLOWED HIS AMBITION TO SLOWLY BECOME MORE PROPORTIONAL TO HIS CIRCUMSTANCES.

THE FRENCH REVOLUTIONARIES SO ADMIRED BY JEFFERSON HAD ADVOCATED ATHEISM.

HAMILTON FLIRTED WITH FOUNDING A "CHRISTIAN CONSTITUTIONAL SOCIETY" TO COMBAT THE ASCENDANT JEFFERSON PARTY.

Holy Bible

IN ANOTHER ATTEMPT TO KEEP THE FLAME OF FEDERALISM BURNING, HE STARTED HIS OWN NEWSPAPER--THE **NEW YORK EVENING POST.**

IT IS THE PRESS WHICH HAS CORRUPTED OUR POLITICAL MORALS--AND IT IS TO THE PRESS WE MUST LOOK FOR REGENERATION.

IT IS ABOMINABLE TO BE PUBLICLY INSULTED BY A SET OF *DAMNED RASCALS!*

IN JUST ITS EIGHTH ISSUE, HAMILTON'S PAPER PRINTED A STORY THAT WAS ANYTHING BUT REGENERATING.

TEENAGE PHILIP HAMILTON HAD BAITED A TWENTY-SEVEN-YEAR-OLD LAWYER--A JEFFERSONIAN KNOWN TO HAVE SPOKEN OUT AGAINST HIS FATHER THAT PAST SUMMER--INTO A PUBLIC SCENE.

THE DUELING CODE HAD BEEN INVOKED. HAMILTON KNEW OF THE IMPENDING CONFRONTATION, BUT KNEW PHILIP, LIKE HIS FATHER, ADHERED TO THE SAME CULT OF HONOR.

NOT GOING THROUGH WITH THE DUEL WOULD COMPROMISE PHILIP'S FUTURE-- AND ALEXANDER'S LEGACY.

FATHER COUNSELED SON TO **SHOOT IN THE AIR**--WHICH WOULD RENDER HIS OPPONENT A DECIDEDLY UNGENTLEMANLY **MURDEROUS ROGUE** IF HE PROCEEDED TO SHOOT TO KILL.

AGAIN, IT MUST BE REMEMBERED THAT DUELISTS SELDOM DIED. EVEN FINE PISTOLS OF THE DAY HAD SMOOTHBORE AS OPPOSED TO RIFLED MUZZLES. THEY WERE NOT TERRIBLY ACCURATE.

NEW YORK EVENING POST
TUESDAY, NOVEMBER 24, 1801

DIED,

This morning, in the 20th year of his age, PHILIP HAMILTON, eldest son of G[...] Hamilton—murdered in a duel.—

As the public will be anxious to k[...] leading particulars of this deplorabl[e...] have collected the following, which relied u[...] as correct.

On [...] and y[...] young HA[...]

Mr. GEORGE [...]

YET AFTER A SLOW, AWKWARD START TO THEIR DUEL ON NOVEMBER 23, 1801, PHILIP'S OPPONENT FIRED AND HIT THE NINETEEN-YEAR-OLD.

PHILIP DIED AT HOME THE NEXT DAY. THE FAMILY WAS STRICKEN WITH GRIEF. HAMILTON'S NEWSPAPER REVILED THE "HORRID CUSTOM" AND CALLED FOR TOUGHER GOVERNMENT ACTION AGAINST IT.

HAMILTON'S ELDEST DAUGHTER, ANGELICA'S "MIND BECAME PERMANENTLY IMPAIRED" WITH GRIEF.

THE FAMILY SOUGHT REFUGE BY BUILDING *THE GRANGE*--A COUNTRY HOUSE IN MODERN HARLEM.

IT WAS TRICKY FOR HAMILTON TO AFFORD. BUT THERE, ANGELICA HAMILTON COULD FIND COMFORT IN NATURE AND THE BIRDS SHE LOVED TO WATCH.

IT'S AN OPEN QUESTION WHETHER HAMILTON'S "CHRISTIAN CONSTITUTIONAL SOCIETY" WAS MORE THAN A CYNICAL PLOY TO BAIT OUTRAGE.

MUCH LESS DOUBTFUL IS HAMILTON'S REEMERGENCE AS A MAN WITH A DAILY PRACTICE OF PRAYER.

(HOWEVER, HE NEVER DID JOIN A SPECIFIC CHURCH.)

IT PROBABLY FELT SATISFYING TO HAMILTON TO WATCH JEFFERSON BE THE NEXT TO PERSPIRE AND PREVARICATE UNDER THE HEAT LAMP OF JAMES T. CALLENDER.

CALLENDER HAD BEEN EXPECTING A REWARD FOR HIS PART IN RUINING HAMILTON. HE GOT NONE. CALLENDER THEN OUTED THE PRESIDENT AS THE MAN WHO PAID HIM TO PUBLISH THE REYNOLDS DOCUMENTS.

CALLENDER ALSO LOOSED UPON THE COUNTRY A FRESH SEX SCANDAL, WITH ALLEGATIONS THAT THE PRESIDENT HAD FATHERED CHILDREN WITH HIS SLAVE SALLY HEMINGS*--THE HALF-SISTER OF JEFFERSON'S LATE WIFE.

*WHILE NOT ENTIRELY CONCLUSIVE, THE EVIDENCE IN SUPPORT OF THIS IS STRONG.

My Life Must Be Exposed to That Man

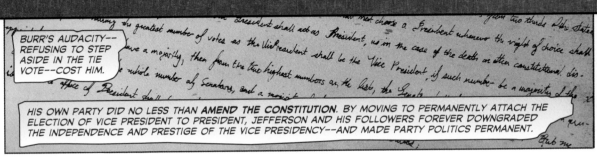

BURR'S AUDACITY-- REFUSING TO STEP ASIDE IN THE TIE VOTE--COST HIM.

HIS OWN PARTY DID NO LESS THAN **AMEND THE CONSTITUTION.** BY MOVING TO PERMANENTLY ATTACH THE ELECTION OF VICE PRESIDENT TO PRESIDENT, JEFFERSON AND HIS FOLLOWERS FOREVER DOWNGRADED THE INDEPENDENCE AND PRESTIGE OF THE VICE PRESIDENCY--AND MADE PARTY POLITICS PERMANENT.

AS THE ELECTION OF 1804 NEARED, BURR WAS ISSUED HIS WALKING PAPERS. *HE WOULD NOT SERVE AGAIN AS VICE PRESIDENT.*

SOME GESTURE IS NECESSARY TO DEPRIVE MY ENEMIES OF USING YOUR NAME TO DESTROY ME.

I BESEECH YOU--DECLARE TO THE WORLD SOME MARK OF CONFIDENCE IN ME AS I RETIRE FROM THIS POSITION.

JEFFERSON DID NOT LIFT A FINGER TO HELP BURR'S CAREER ESCAPE FREEFALL.

THE JEFFERSON PRESIDENCY WAS DEEMED EQUALLY RUINOUS BY PROMINENT NORTHEASTERNERS.

A *CONSPIRATORIAL RING* (MAINLY OF U.S. SENATORS) KINDLED A PLOT *FOR NEW ENGLAND TO SECEDE FROM THE UNITED STATES.*

THE EASTERN STATES MUST AND WILL DISSOLVE THE UNION, AND FORM A SEPARATE GOVERNMENT OF THEIR OWN; AND THE SOONER THEY DO THIS THE BETTER.

REPORTED COMMENT OF *JAMES HILLHOUSE,* SENATOR FROM CONNECTICUT, 1804.

THEY DID NOT FEEL, HOWEVER, THAT THEY COULD STAND ALONE WITHOUT NEW YORK.

THEN IT HIT THEM: *PERHAPS AARON BURR WAS THE MISSING LYNCHPIN OF THEIR PLAN.*

WITH HIS PEDIGREE, CHARISMA, AMBITION, AND LATE-BREAKING *MALICE TOWARD JEFFERSON,* WHO BETTER TO BECOME GOVERNOR OF NEW YORK? *AND LEAD THE STRIKE FOR DISUNION?*

HE HAS THE SPIRIT OF AMBITION AND REVENGE TO GRATIFY!

HAMILTON GOT WIND OF THE CONSPIRACY. IT COULD ONLY HAVE BEEN INFURIATING: *FEDERALISTS* WERE NOT SUPPOSED TO BE THE STANDARD BEARERS OF REVOLUTION, REBELLION, AND FRAGMENTATION.

THE UNION WAS *THE VERY THING* HAMILTON HAD WORKED ALL HIS LIFE TO ERECT. SECESSION WAS THE *PARAMOUNT DANGER* WASHINGTON HAD WARNED AGAINST!

HAMILTON DREW A LINE IN THE SAND. HE WOULD HAVE TO STOP BURR.

TO DENY BURR THE GOVERNOR'S SEAT, HAMILTON SLANDERED HIS NAME AROUND ALBANY.

BURR IS A *DANGEROUS MAN,* AND ONE WHO *OUGHT NOT TO BE TRUSTED.*

HE ALSO UNLOOSED AN ADDITIONAL "DESPICABLE OPINION" OF THE CANDIDATE.

ON APRIL 25, 1804, *BURR LOST THE ELECTION.*

THIS LEFT HIM A LAME-DUCK VICE PRESIDENT, DISOWNED BY HIS NATION AND HIS STATE--WITH NO CLEAR FALLBACK POSITION WHATSOEVER.

IF THERE WAS ANY PATH AHEAD FOR BURR, IT COULD ONLY GO IN ONE DIRECTION...

...THROUGH THE WALL THAT ENEMIES HAD BUILT TO CONTAIN HIM.

MOREOVER, IF THE COOL, STEADY, AND DETACHED MANNER FOR WHICH HE WAS FAMED WAS AT A LOW EBB, AND IF DISCOURAGEMENT HAD GOTTEN TO HIM AND MADE HIM *UNCHARACTERISTICALLY SENSITIVE AND CONFRONTATIONAL--* HISTORY HAS RECORDED PLENTY OF REASONS WHY.

BURR WANTED TO TAKE HAMILTON DOWN. **BUT HE NEEDED A PRETEXT.**

THEN, EARLY IN SUMMER, DAMNING WORDS FROM A ROUTINE POLITICAL DINNER FOUND THEIR WAY TO THE JILTED CANDIDATE.

"...A STILL MORE DESPICABLE OPINION"?

BURR PICKED UP HIS PEN.

HE WROTE HAMILTON A BY-THE-BOOKS OPENING MOVE OF AN AFFAIR OF HONOR.

YOU MIGHT PERCEIVE, SIR, THE NECESSITY OF A PROMPT AND UNQUALIFIED ACKNOWLEDGMENT OR DENIAL OF [YOUR SLANDEROUS REMARKS].

ONCE BEGUN, IT WAS A SLIPPERY SLOPE.

HAMILTON'S FRIEND, VIRGINIA-BORN CONTINENTAL ARMY VETERAN AND FEDERAL JUDGE **NATHANIEL PENDLETON**

LIKE BURR, HAMILTON HAD JARRINGLY AND PAINFULLY PLUMMETED FROM HIGH ALTITUDE. ARGUABLY, THEY HAD BOTH BECOME HAS-BEENS.

THE IMMEDIATE THREAT OF A SECESSION MOVEMENT HAD PASSED, BUT HAMILTON KNEW THE UNION MIGHT NEVER BE OUT OF DANGER. TO SAFEGUARD IT, **TO RESTORE FEDERALISM, PERHAPS TO PUT HIMSELF BACK AT THE HIGHEST RUNGS OF NATIONAL LEADERSHIP**-- THOSE WERE HAMILTON'S HEART'S DESIRES.

ANY CHANCE FOR POLITICAL REEMERGENCE HAMILTON MIGHT EVER HAVE HINGED ON THE PRESERVATION OF HIS HONOR AND GENTLEMANHOOD.

YES, HE HAD LOST A BELOVED SON TO DUELING. YES, HE WOULD HAVE TO WRANGLE WITH RELIGION'S CONSIDERING DUELING A SIN.

BUT HE COULD NOT REFUSE THE DUEL. TO DO SO WOULD BE TO REPUDIATE THE CODE HE LIVED BY.

HAMILTON REPORTED THAT HE PLANNED TO DEAL WITH THE RELIGIOUS SCRUPLE WITH THE SAME ADVICE HE HAD ISSUED HIS SON PHILIP.

HIS FIRST SHOT WOULD BE NOT AT BURR, BUT INTO THE AIR.

IF ADDITIONAL GUNPLAY WAS REQUIRED, HE REASONED, AFTER THAT HE WOULD BE LEGITIMATELY DEFENDING HIS OWN LIFE.

KNOWING THE NIGHT MIGHT BE HIS LAST, HAMILTON, IN HIS TOWN HOUSE, FINALIZED HIS WILL AND BUSINESS AFFAIRS.

HE LEFT AN EXPLANATION OF HIS MOTIVES FOR UNDERTAKING THE DUEL, AND A LETTER TO HIS WIFE...

...WHO WAS AWAY AT THE GRANGE. SHE HAD NO IDEA WHAT WAS ABOUT TO OCCUR.

EARLY ON JULY 11, 1804, HAMILTON, PENDLETON, AND A DOCTOR ROWED ACROSS THE HUDSON TO NEW JERSEY...

...WHERE THERE WAS NO EXPLICIT LAW AGAINST DUELING.

THEY THEN ASCENDED PART OF THE WAY UP A CLIFF TO A LEDGE SCREENED IN WITH TREES--THE EXACT SPOT AT WHICH PHILIP HAMILTON HAD RECEIVED HIS MORTAL WOUND.

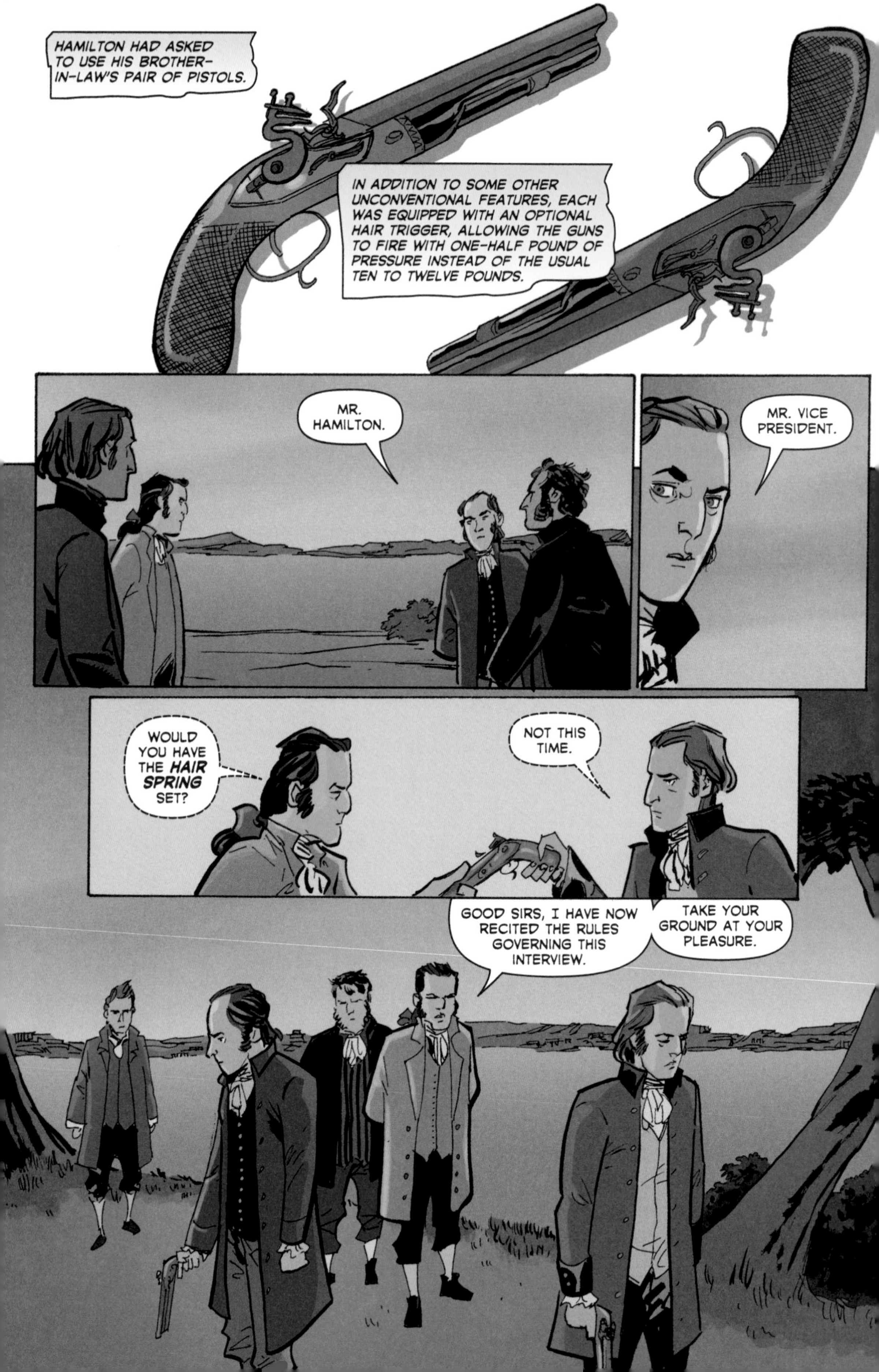
HAMILTON HAD ASKED TO USE HIS BROTHER-IN-LAW'S PAIR OF PISTOLS.
IN ADDITION TO SOME OTHER UNCONVENTIONAL FEATURES, EACH WAS EQUIPPED WITH AN OPTIONAL HAIR TRIGGER, ALLOWING THE GUNS TO FIRE WITH ONE-HALF POUND OF PRESSURE INSTEAD OF THE USUAL TEN TO TWELVE POUNDS.
MR. HAMILTON.
MR. VICE PRESIDENT.
WOULD YOU HAVE THE ***HAIR SPRING*** SET?
NOT THIS TIME.
GOOD SIRS, I HAVE NOW RECITED THE RULES GOVERNING THIS INTERVIEW.
TAKE YOUR GROUND AT YOUR PLEASURE.

IF YOU PLEASE! STOP!

IN CERTAIN STATES OF THE LIGHT, ONE REQUIRES GLASSES.

...

THIS WILL DO. NOW YOU MAY PROCEED.

GENTLEMEN, ARE WE READY?

YES.

YES.

THE GIVEN TESTIMONY OF THE DUELISTS'
SECONDS IS CONTRADICTORY.

HAMILTON'S SECOND INSISTED THAT BURR HAD FIRED FIRST,
AND THAT THE RETURN SHOT WAS NOTHING MORE THAN
THE REFLEX OF MUSCLES CONTRACTING IN DISTRESS.

BURR'S SECOND, ON THE OTHER HAND, INSISTED THAT
HAMILTON'S PROJECTILE—WHICH STRUCK A TREE AT
MORE THAN TWICE THE VICE PRESIDENT'S HEIGHT—WAS
THE EARLIEST TO FLY FROM ITS MUZZLE.

HAMILTON, WHO HAD RETAINED A CERTAIN AMOUNT OF MEDICAL KNOWLEDGE FROM HIS ABORTED PLANS TO BECOME A SURGEON, REPORTED TO THE ATTENDING PHYSICIAN:

THIS IS A MORTAL WOUND, DOCTOR.

THE BALL FROM THE PISTOL BURR HAD USED HAD GONE THROUGH HIS LIVER TO LODGE IN HIS SPINE.

ALEXANDER HAMILTON, UNCONSCIOUS BUT DESTINED TO BREATHE ANOTHER THIRTY-ODD HOURS...

...WAS ROWED BACK ACROSS TO HIS TOWN HOUSE.

ELIZABETH REACTED WITH "FRANTIC GRIEF" AS SHE WATCHED HER HUSBAND, AGED FORTY-NINE, DIE.

REMEMBER, MY ELIZA, YOU ARE A CHRISTIAN...

A MAN VILIFIED FOR SUPPOSEDLY DEBASING HIGH OFFICE FOR PERSONAL GAIN HADIN REALITY BEEN HEEDLESS OF INCOME. HE **DIED IN DEBT**.

A COLLECTION HAD TO BE TAKEN UP TO BANKROLL HIS FUNERAL.

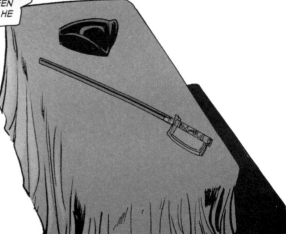

THE UNITED STATES' EXAMPLE OF A FORM OF GOVERNMENT RENOUNCING MONARCHY HAS LASTED FOR NEARLY TWO AND A HALF CENTURIES.

AS A YOUTH, ALEXANDER HAMILTON HAD RISKED HIS LIFE TO BRING ABOUT REVOLUTION.

ALL THE VIGORS OF THE YEARS CULMINATING IN HIS DEATH HAD BEEN SPENT STRIVING TO **PREVENT** IT.

LIKE THE NATION BUILDERS AND LAWGIVERS HE TOOK AS MODELS, HAMILTON NOW STRADDLES HISTORY AND MYTH.

OF ALL HIS ACCOMPLISHMENTS, EARNING "THE ESTEEM OF THE DISCERNING" WOULD HAVE SATISFIED HIM MOST.

THOMAS JEFFERSON AND **HIS** SECRETARY OF THE TREASURY, ALBERT GALLATIN, FOUND IN THE GOVERNMENT'S BOOKS ZERO DAMNING EVIDENCE OF FOUL PLAY BY HAMILTON.

JEFFERSON, VOCALLY AVERSE TO DEBT, TO ENGLAND, AND TO COMPLEX FINANCIAL SCHEMES, NOT ONLY KEPT THE BANK OF THE UNITED STATES, BUT ALSO, WITH THE HELP OF BRITISH FINANCIERS, FLOATED GOVERNMENT BONDS TO FINANCE HIS LOUISIANA PURCHASE (WHICH HE ENACTED IN THE ABSENCE OF CONSTITUTIONAL AUTHORITY).

THE TAX AND FISCAL POLICIES OF JEFFERSON, GALLATIN, AND MADISON PLACED THE ARMY AND NAVY IN SUCH NEGLECT THAT THE BRITISH EASILY INVADED U.S. TERRITORY AND BURNED WASHINGTON, D.C., IN 1814.

AARON BURR LIT OUT BEYOND THE REACH OF THE NEW YORK AUTHORITIES, WHO--SINCE HAMILTON ACTUALLY DIED IN THEIR JURISDICTION--INDICTED HIM FOR MURDER.

AFTER QUIETLY SERVING OUT THE REMAINDER OF HIS VICE PRESIDENTIAL TERM, BURR ALIGHTED ON A QUIXOTIC MISSION TO RESEIZE POLITICAL GREATNESS BY EITHER ENGINEERING A SECESSION OF THE WESTERN STATES OR RAISING A PRIVATE ARMY TO KICK SPAIN OUT OF FLORIDA AND THE SOUTHEAST. DURING JEFFERSON'S SECOND TERM HE WAS TRIED FOR TREASON. SHORTLY AFTER HIS ACQUITTAL HE WENT TO LIVE IN EUROPE.

ELIZABETH HAMILTON LIVED UNTIL THE AGE OF NINETY-SEVEN.

SHE WORE MOURNING BLACK FOR THE REST OF HER LIFE.

INDEX

Adams, John, 10, 24, 52, 96, 105, 116, 144–45, 150–52, 154, 155
Arnold, Benedict, 6, 59, 71, 88–89, 92, 98
Articles of Confederation, 73, 98, 108–9, 114

Bayard, James, 156
Beckley, John, 121, 145, 146, 154
Beekman, David, 36
Boudinot, Elias, 120
Braddock, Edward, 56
Burr, Aaron, Jr., 6, 44, 59, 62, 75, 81, 90, 100, 102, 115, 126, 132, 143, 144, 148, 151–56, 160–68
Burr, Aaron, Sr., 36, 45
Butler, Pierce, 111

Callender, James, 21, 145–47, 159
Church, Angelica, 84, 117
Church, John Baker, 84
Clingman, Jacob, 135
Clinton, George, 102, 109, 126
Clinton, Henry, 82
Cockburn, George, 7
Constitution, 111, 113–15, 130, 144, 155, 160
Conway, Thomas, 72
Cooper, Miles, 47, 55–56
Cornwallis, Charles, 85, 92–93, 95
Cruger, Nicholas, 36

Deane, Silas, 68
Declaration of Independence, 61, 73
Dickinson, John, 23
Duane, James, 87
Duer, William, 121, 133, 135

Faucette, Rachel, 25–31
Federalist Papers, 115
Filmer, Robert, 3
Fleming, Edward, 55
Franklin, Benjamin, 35, 68, 73, 109, 130
Freeman, Joanne B., 80
Freneau, Philip, 133

Gage, Thomas, 54
Gallatin, Albert, 139, 168
Gates, Horatio, 71–72, 99
George III (King of Great Britain), 55, 60, 61
Gerry, Elbridge, 111
The Grange, 159, 163
Gravier, Charles, 68
Grayson, William, 66

Hamilton, Alexander
 accomplishments of, 12, 168
 affair with Maria Reynolds, 129–33, 135–37, 145–49
 ambition of, 10, 12, 157
 birth of, 28

courtship and marriage to Elizabeth Schuyler, 83–85, 90
death of, 167
duel with Aaron Burr, 162–67
early years of, 11–12, 14, 16–17, 28–40
education of, 44–47
fiscal policy and, 105, 119–28, 133, 139
as gentleman, 76–81, 148–49, 162
as lawyer, 97, 100–103, 141
opposition to, 10, 21, 118–19, 133–38, 149–53
parents of, 25–31
political beliefs of, 105–6, 110–14
as revolutionary, 21–22, 50–55, 57–58, 60–67, 69–72, 74–76, 86–96
slavery and, 82, 111
as statesman, 98–99, 108, 110–27, 138–41, 144–45, 150–57
Hamilton, Alexander, Jr., 108
Hamilton, Angelica, 108, 159
Hamilton, Elizabeth (Schuyler), 44, 83–85, 90, 93, 97, 125, 130–31, 149, 167, 168
Hamilton, James, Jr., 28, 31, 32–33
Hamilton, James, Sr., 27–30
Hamilton, Philip, 97, 146, 157, 158, 163
Hamilton, William, 149
Hemings, Sally, 159
Henry, Patrick, 42, 108
Hillhouse, James, 160
Howe, William, 60

Jay, John, 52, 102, 115, 142
Jay Treaty, 142–43, 150, 156
Jefferson, Thomas, 9–10, 21, 92, 96, 104, 116–18, 122–25, 127, 130, 132–35, 138–39, 144–45, 152–57, 159–60, 168

Knox, Henry, 116
Knox, Hugh, 36–39, 44, 45
Kortright, Cornelius, 36
Kortright, Lawrence, 43

Lafayette, Marquis de, 9–10, 68–69, 92–96, 118
Langdon, John, 116
Lasher, John, 57
Laurens, Henry, 96
Laurens, John, 72, 76–81, 82, 96
Lavien, John Michael, 25–27, 28, 31
Lavien, Peter, 25, 31
Lee, Charles, 72, 74–81
Lee, Richard Henry, 52
Livingston, Catherine, 69
Livingston, William, 44
Louis XVI (King of France), 118, 137
Lytton, Peter, 32

Madison, James, 98, 102, 107–8, 110, 113, 115, 118, 120–21, 126, 127, 132, 144, 168
Mason, George, 73

Mayhew, Jonathan, 46
McDougall, Alexander, 51
McHenry, James, 141
Monroe, James, 75, 136–37, 145, 147–48
Morris, Gouverneur, 21, 130
Morris, Robert, 103
Muhlenberg, Frederick, 116, 135, 136
Mulligan, Hercules, 43

Napoleon Bonaparte, 138
Nicholson, James, 21
North, Lord, 49, 96

Otis, James, 42

Paine, Thomas, 61, 66
Paris, Treaty of, 101, 102, 104, 111, 142
Pendleton, Edmund, 103
Pendleton, Nathaniel, 162, 163
Pickering, Timothy, 141
Pitt, William, the Younger, 96
Prevost, Theodosia, 90
Putnam, Israel, 62

Randolph, Edmund, 66, 110, 116, 127
Reed, Joseph, 66
Reynolds, James, 121, 129, 132–33, 135
Reynolds, Maria, 129–33, 135–37, 145–49
Rush, Benjamin, 48
Rutledge, John, 111

Schuyler, Elizabeth. *See* Hamilton, Elizabeth (Schuyler)
Schuyler, Philip, 84, 108, 125, 126
Seabury, Samuel, 53
Sears, Isaac, 47, 48
Sedgwick, Theodore, 122
Shippen, Margaret "Peggy," 88–90
Smith, Adam, 131
Smith, Melancton, 102, 115
Somerset, Charles Noel, 42
Stevens, Edward, 33, 34, 40
Stevens, Thomas, 33

Tilghman, Tench, 66
Troup, Robert, 50, 55
Tryon, William, 41

Van Courtlandt, Philip, 58

Walpole, Robert, 120
Washington, George, 5, 27, 35, 52, 56–60, 62–67, 69–72, 74–76, 78, 82–83, 86, 88–89, 92–94, 96, 98–100, 103, 107, 109, 116–17, 124, 127, 131, 134, 137, 138, 141–44, 151, 153
Whiskey Rebellion, 139–41
Willett, Marinus, 101, 102
Williamson, Hugh, 122
Wolcott, Oliver, Jr., 141

169

Check out hamiltongraphicnovel.com for detailed chapter notes, additional material, news, recommendations for further reading, and more.

Published in the United States by Ten Speed Press,
an imprint of the Crown Publishing Group, a division
of Penguin Random House LLC, New York.
www.crownpublishing.com
www.tenspeed.com

Ten Speed Press and the Ten Speed Press colophon are
registered trademarks of Penguin Random House LLC.

Library of Congress Cataloging-in-Publication Data
Names: Hennessey, Jonathan, 1971- author. | Greenwood, Justin
(Comic book artist), illustrator.
Title: Alexander Hamilton : the graphic history of an American founding
  father / Jonathan Hennessey ; illustrated by Justin Greenwood.
Description: California : Ten Speed Press, 2017.
Identifiers: LCCN 2017013467 |
Subjects: LCSH: Hamilton, Alexander, 1757-1804—Comic books, strips, etc. |
  Statesmen—United States—Biography—Comic books, strips, etc. |
  Graphic novels. | BISAC: COMICS & GRAPHIC NOVELS / Nonfiction. |
  BIOGRAPHY & AUTOBIOGRAPHY / Historical. | HISTORY /
  United States / General.
Classification: LCC E302.6.H2 H456 2017 | DDC 973.4092 [B]—dc23
LC record available at https://lccn.loc.gov/2017013467

Hardcover ISBN: 978-0-399-57999-8
Trade Paperback ISBN: 978-0-399-58000-0
eBook ISBN: 978-0-399-58001-7

Printed in the United States of America

Design by Chloe Rawlins

10 9 8 7 6 5 4 3 2 1

First Edition